Praise for the "Kids Love" Gu'

On-Air Personality Comments (Te

"The great thing about these books is tha
lives these adventures" – **(WKR**

"Very helpful to lots of families when the kids say, I'm bored...and I don't want to go to same places again!" – **(WISH-TV**, Indianapolis)

"Dividing the state into many sections, the book has something for everyone...everywhere." – **(WLVT-TV**, Pennsylvania)

"These authors know first-hand that it's important to find hands-on activities that engage your children..." **(WBNS-TV**, Columbus)

"You spent more than 1000 hours doing this research for us, that's really great – we just have to pick up the book and it's done..."
(WTVR-TV, Richmond)

"A family that's a great source for travel ideas..."
(WBRA-TV, Roanoke)

"What a great idea...this book needed to be done a long time ago!"
(WKYT-TV, Lexington)

"A fabulous idea...places to travel that your kids will enjoy"
(WOOD-TV, Grand Rapids)

"The Zavatskys call it a dream come true, running their own business while keeping the family together. Their goal, encourage other parents to create special family travel memories." - **(WLVT-TV,** Pennsylvania)

"It's a wonderful book, and as someone who has been to a lot of these places...you hit it right on the money!" – **(WKRC-TV**, Cincinnati)

Praise for the "Kids Love" Guidebook Travel Series
Customer Comments (actual letters on file)

"I wanted to tell you how helpful all your books have been to my family of 6. I rarely find books that cater to families with kids. I have your Indiana, Ohio, Kentucky, Michigan, and Pennsylvania books. I don't want to miss any of the new books that come out. Keep up the great ideas. The books are fantastic. I have shown them to tons of my friends. They love them, too." – H.M.

"I bought the Ohio and Indiana books yesterday and what a blessing these are for us!!! We love taking our grandsons on Grammie & Papaw trips thru the year and these books are making it soooo much easier to plan. The info is complete and full of ideas. Even the layout of the book is easy to follow...I just wanted to thank you for all your work in developing these books for us..." – G.K

"I have purchased your book. My grandchildren and I have gone to many of the places listed in your book. They mark them off as we visit them. We are looking forward to seeing many more. It is their favorite thing to look at book when they come over and find new places to explore. Thank you for publishing this book!" - B.A.

"At a retail price of under $15.00, any of the books would be well worth buying even for a one-time only vacation trip. Until now, when the opportunity arose for a day or weekend trip with the kids I was often at a loss to pick a destination that I could be sure was convenient, educational, child-friendly, and above all, fun. Now I have a new problem: How in the world will we ever be able to see and do all the great ideas listed in this book? I'd better get started planning our next trip right away. At least I won't have to worry about where we're going or what to do when we get there!" – VA Homeschool Newsletter

"My family and I used this book this summer to explore Ohio! We lived here nearly our entire life and yet over half the book we never knew existed. These people really know what kids love! Highly recommended for all parents, grandparents, etc.." – Barnes and Noble website reviewer

KIDS ♥ LOVE FLORIDA

A Family Travel Guide to Exploring "Kid-Tested" Places in Florida...Year Round!

George & Michele Zavatsky

Dedicated to the Families
of Florida

For the latest major updates corresponding to the pages in this book visit our website:

www.KidsLoveTravel.com

Although the authors have exhaustively researched all sources to ensure accuracy and completeness of the information contained in this book, we assume no responsibility for errors, inaccuracies, omissions or any other inconsistency herein. Any slights against any entries or organizations are unintentional.

REMEMBER: *Museum exhibits change frequently. Check the site's website before you visit to note any changes. Also, HOURS and ADMISSIONS are subject to change at the owner's discretion. If you are tight on time or money, check the attraction's website or call before you visit.*

INTERNET PRECAUTION: *All websites mentioned in KIDS LOVE FLORIDA have been checked for appropriate content. However, due to the fast-changing nature of the Internet, we strongly urge parents to preview any recommended sites and to always supervise their children when on-line.*

ISBN-13: 978-0-9774434-1-3
ISBN-10: 0-9774434-1-8

KIDS ♥ FLORIDA™   Kids Love Publications, LLC

TABLE OF CONTENTS

(Amusements, Animals & Farms, Museums, Outdoors, State History, Tours, etc.)

State Detail Map

(With Major Routes and Cities Marked)

Chapter Area Map

(Chapters arranged alphabetically by chapter name)

CITY INDEX (Listed by City & Area)

CITY INDEX (Listed by City & Area)

Note: Listings in italics appear only in the Seasonal Chapter

Acknowledgements

We are most thankful to be blessed with our parents, Barbara (Darrall) and Adrian Callahan & George and Catherine Zavatsky who help us every way they can – researching, proofing and baby-sitting. More importantly, they are great sounding boards and offer unconditional support. So many places around Florida remind us of family vacations years ago…

We also want to express our thanks to the many Convention & Visitor Bureaus' staff for providing the attention to detail that helps to complete a project. We felt very welcome during our travels in Florida and would be proud to call it home!

Our own kids, Jenny and Daniel, were delightful and fun children during our trips across the state. What a joy it is to be their parents…we couldn't do it without them as our "kid-testers"!

We both sincerely thank each other – our partnership has created an even greater business/personal "marriage" with lots of exciting moments, laughs, and new adventures in life woven throughout. Above all, we praise the Lord for His so many blessings through the last few years.

We think Florida is a wonderful, friendly area of the country with more activities than you could imagine. Our sincere wish is that this book will help everyone "fall in love" with all of Florida.

In a Hundred Years…
It will not matter, The size of my bank account…
The kind of house that I lived in, the kind of car that I drove…
But what will matter is…
That the world may be different
Because I was important in the life of a child.
author unknown

HOW TO USE THIS BOOK

If you are excited about discovering Florida, this is the book for you and your family! We've spent over a thousand hours doing all the scouting, collecting and compiling (*and most often visiting!*) so that you could spend less time searching and more time having fun.

Here are a few hints to make your adventures run smoothly:

☐ Consider the **child's age** before deciding to take a visit.

☐ Know **directions** and parking. Call ahead (or visit the company's website) if you have questions *and* bring this book. Also, don't forget your camera! *(please honor rules regarding use).*

☐ **Estimate the duration** of the trip. Bring small surprises (favorite juice boxes) travel books, and toys.

☐ Call ahead for **reservations** or details, if necessary.

☐ Most listings are **closed major holidays** unless noted.

☐ Make a **family "treasure chest"**. Decorate a big box or use an old popcorn tin. Store memorabilia from a fun outing, journals, pictures, brochures and souvenirs. Once a year, look through the "treasure chest" and reminisce. "Kids Love Travel Memories!" is an excellent travel journal & scrapbook that your family can create. *(See the order form in back of this book).*

☐ Plan **picnics** along the way. Many state history sites and state parks are scattered throughout Florida. Allow time for a rural /scenic route to take advantage of these free picnic facilities.

☐ Some activities, especially tours, require **groups** of 10 or more. To participate, you may either ask to be part of another tour group or get a group together yourself (neighbors, friends, organizations). If you arrange a group outing, most places offer discounts.

☐ For the latest **updates** corresponding to the pages in this book, visit our website: **www.KidsLoveTravel.com.**

☐ Each chapter represents an area of the state. Each listing is further identified by city, zip code, and place/event name. Our popular **Activity Index** in the back of the book **lists places by Activity Heading** (i.e. State History, Tours, Outdoors, Museums, etc.).

MISSION STATEMENT

At first glance, you may think that this is a book that just lists hundreds of places to travel. While it is true that we've invested thousands of hours of exhaustive research (*and drove over 4000 miles in Florida*) to prepare this travel resource...just listing places to travel is <u>not</u> the mission statement of these projects.

As children, Michele and I were able to travel extensively throughout the United States. We consider these family times some of the greatest memories we cherish today. We, quite frankly, felt that most children had this opportunity to travel with their family as we did. However, as we became adults and started our own family, we found that this wasn't necessarily the case. We continually heard friends express several concerns when deciding how to spend "quality" and "quantity" family time. 1) What to do? 2) Where to do it? 3) How much will it cost? 4) How do I know that my kids will enjoy it?

Interestingly enough, as we compare our experiences with our families when we were kids, many of our fondest memories were not made at an expensive attraction, but rather when it was least expected.

It is our belief and mission statement that if you as a family will study and <u>use</u> the contained information <u>to create family memories</u>, these memories will grow a stronger, tighter family. Our ultimate mission statement is, that your children will develop a love and a passion for quality family experiences that they can pass to another generation of family travelers.

We thank you for purchasing this book, and we hope to see you on the road (*and hear your travel stories!*) God bless your journeys and happy exploring!

George, Michele, Jenny and Daniel

General State Agency & Recreational Information

Call *(or visit websites)* for the services of interest. Request to be added to their mailing lists.

- ☐ Bike Florida: (352) 376-6044 or **www.bikeflorida.org**
- ☐ Florida Bicycle Association: (407) 327-3941 or **www.floridabicycle.org**
- ☐ Florida State Parks: (850) 488-9872 or **www.floridastateparks.org**
- ☐ National Camping Information: **www.gocampingamerica.com**
- ☐ Office of Greenways and Trails: **www.floridagreenwaysandtrails.com**
- ☐ Visit Florida: (888) 7FLA-USA or **www.visitflorida.com**
- ☐ **C** - Orlando Visitor Center: (800) 551-0181 or **www.orlandoinfo.com**. Free Orlando Magicard discount card available.
- ☐ **CE** - Daytona Beach: (800) 544-0415 or **www.daytonabeach.org**
- ☐ **CE** - Indian River County (Vero Beach): **www.indianriverchamber.com**
- ☐ **CE** - Space Coast **www.space-coast.com** (Cape Canaveral, Titusville, Cocoa Beach)
- ☐ **CE** - St. Lucie County (Fort Pierce, Port St. Lucie, Hutchinson Island): (800) 344-TGIF or **www.visitstluciefla.com**
- ☐ **CW** - Tampa Bay: (800) 826-8358 or **www.VisitTampaBay.com**
- ☐ **NC** - Alachua County Visitors And Convention Bureau (Gainesville area). (866) 778-5002 or **www.visitgainesville.com**
- ☐ **NC** - Tallahassee Area CVB. (800) 628-2866 or **www.seeTallahassee.com**
- ☐ **NE** - St. Augustine, Ponte Vedra & The Beaches: **www.Getaway4Florida.com** (800) 418-7529
- ☐ **SE** - Fort Lauderdale CVB: **www.sunny.org**
- ☐ **SE** - Greater Miami And Beaches: (800) 955-3646 or **www.MiamiandBeaches.com**
- ☐ **SW** - Florida Gulf Islands **www.FloridaGulfIslands.com** (Anna Maria, Longboat Key, Bradenton)
- ☐ **SW** - Fort Myers / Sanibel: (888) 231-6933 or **www.fortmyers-sanibel.com**
- ☐ **SW** - Naples / Marco Island / Everglades **www.ParadiseCoast.com** (Paradise Coast):
- ☐ **SW** - Sarasota & Her Islands: **www.sarasotafl.org**

Check out these businesses / services in your area for tour ideas:

AIRPORTS

All children love to visit the airport! Why not take a tour and understand all the jobs it takes to run an airport? Tour the terminal, baggage claim, gates and security / currency exchange. Maybe you'll even get to board a plane.

ANIMAL SHELTERS

Great for the would-be pet owner. Not only will you see many cats and dogs available for adoption, but a guide will show you the clinic and explain the needs of a pet. Be prepared to have the children "fall in love" with one of the animals while they are there!

BANKS

Take a "behind the scenes" look at automated teller machines, bank vaults and drive-thru window chutes. You may want to take this tour and then open a savings account for your child.

CITY HALLS

Halls of Fame, City Council Chambers & Meeting Room, Mayor's Office and famous statues.

ELECTRIC COMPANY / POWER PLANTS

Modern science has created many ways to generate electricity today, but what really goes on with the "flip of a switch". Because coal can be dirty, wear old, comfortable clothes. Coal furnaces heat water, which produces steam, that propels turbines, that drives generators, that make electricity.

FIRE STATIONS

Many Open Houses in October, Fire Prevention Month. Take a look into the life of the firefighters servicing your area and try on their gear. See where they hang out, sleep and eat. Hop aboard a real-life fire engine truck and learn fire safety too.

HOSPITALS

Some Children's Hospitals offer pre-surgery and general tours.

NEWSPAPERS

You'll be amazed at all the new technology. See monster printers and robotics. See samples in the layout department and maybe try to put together your own page. After seeing a newspaper made, most companies give you a free copy (dated that day) as your souvenir. National Newspaper Week is in October.

PETCO

Various stores. Contact each store manager to see if they participate. The Fur, Feathers & Fins™ program allows children to learn about the characteristics and habitats of fish, reptiles, birds, and small animals. At your local Petco, lessons in science, math and geography come to life through this hands-on field trip. As students develop a respect for animals, they will also develop a greater sense of responsibility.

RESTAURANTS

PIZZA HUT & PAPA JOHN'S

Participating locations. Telephone the store manager. Best days are Monday, Tuesday and Wednesday mid-afternoon. Minimum of 10 people. Small charge per person. All children love pizza – especially when they can create their own! As the children tour the kitchen, they learn how to make a pizza, bake it, and then eat it. The admission charge generally includes lots of creatively made pizzas, beverage and coloring book.

KRISPY KREME DONUTS

Participating locations. Get an "inside look" and learn the techniques that make these donuts some of our favorites! Watch the dough being made in "giant" mixers, being formed into donuts and taking a "trip" through the fryer. Seeing them being iced and topped with colorful sprinkles is always a favorite with the kids. Contact your local store manager. They prefer Monday or Tuesday. Free.

SUPERMARKETS

Kids are fascinated to go behind the scenes of the same store where Mom and Dad shop. Usually you will see them grind meat, walk into large freezer rooms, watch cakes and bread bake and receive free samples along the way. Maybe you'll even get to pet a live lobster!

TV / RADIO STATIONS

Studios, newsrooms, Fox kids clubs. Why do weathermen never wear blue clothes on TV? What makes a "DJ's" voice sound so deep and smooth?

WATER TREATMENT PLANTS

A giant science experiment! You can watch seven stages of water treatment. The favorite is usually the wall of bright buttons flashing as workers monitor the different processes.

U.S. MAIN POST OFFICES

Did you know Ben Franklin was the first Postmaster General (over 200 years ago)? Most interesting is the high-speed automated mail processing equipment. Learn how to address envelopes so they will be sent quicker (there are secrets). To make your tour more interesting, have your children write a letter to themselves and address it with colorful markers. Mail it earlier that day and they will stay interested trying to locate their letter in all the high-speed machinery.

Chapter 1
Central (C) Area

MARION

Ocala /
Silver Springs

SUMTER Leesburg Sanford

Apopka

SEMINOLE

LAKE

ORANGE

Clermont **Orlando**

Kissimmee

OSCEOLA

Winter Haven Lake Wales

POLK

HARDEE Sebring

HIGHLANDS

Our Favorites...

* Airboat Rides - Kissimmee, St. Cloud
* Orange Blossom Hot-Air Ballons -
  Kissimmee
* Disney - Magic Kingdom -
  Lake Buena Vista
* Discovery Cove - Orlando
* Holyland Experience - Orlando
* Pirate's Dinner Adventure - Orlando
* Sea World - Orlando
* SkyVenture - Orlando
* Silver Springs - Silver Springs
* Cypress Gardens - Winter Haven

WEKIWA SPRINGS STATE PARK

Apopka - 1800 Wekiwa Circle (off Interstate 4 at exit 94. Take State Road 434 West to Wekiwa Springs Road. Turn right on Wekiwa Springs Rd.) 32712. Phone: (407) 884 2008. www.floridastateparks.org/wekiwasprings/ Hours: Daily 8:00am-sunset. Admission: $5.00 per vehicle. Miscellaneous: Wekiwa Springs State Park is often confused with the park commonly referred to by locals as "Rock Springs" where visitors can tube down the spring run. That park is Kelly Park, an Orange County Park, and their number is (407) 889-4179.*

ROCK SPRINGS RUN RESERVE STATE PARK: Sand pine scrub, pine flatwoods, swamps, and miles of pristine shoreline along Rock Springs Run and the Wekiwa River make this reserve a refuge of natural beauty. Visitors can enjoy bicycling, hiking, or horseback riding along 17 miles of trails. Guided trail rides & horse rentals are available. (407) 884 2008. **www.floridastateparks.org/ rockspringsrun/**.

WEKIWA SPRINGS STATE PARK: Located at the headwaters of the Wekiva River, the beautiful vistas within this park offer a glimpse of what Central Florida looked like when Timucuan Indians fished and hunted these lands. The Springs offer visitors the opportunity to relax in a natural setting, enjoy a picnic, or take a swim in the cool spring. Canoeists and kayakers can paddle along the Wekiva River and Rock Springs Run. Thirteen miles of trails provide opportunities for hiking, bicycling, and horseback riding. Options for camping include a full facility campground and primitive camping areas. Canoe and kayak rentals are available. Stop by the Nature Center to see the live animal exhibits and learn how the land provides for them. The Nature center is located next to the concession stand in the spring area. Enjoy a leisurely walk on the boardwalk nature trail next to the spring. It is approximately 1/8-mile beginning at a bridge that overlooks the spring and lagoon. This trail will take you through the swamps of a river hammock to a dry sandhill ending at the trail head of the main hiking trail.

PAYNES CREEK HISTORIC STATE PARK

Bowling Green - 888 Lake Branch Road (U.S. 17 to Bowling Green and follow the signs at Main Street east to Lake Branch Road) 33834. www.floridastateparks.org/paynescreek/ Phone: (863) 375-4717. Hours: Daily 8:00am-sunset. Visitor Center open 9:00am-5:00pm. Admission: $2.00 per vehicle.

During the 1840s, tensions between the settlers and Seminole Indians prompted authorities to establish a trading post in Florida's interior, away from settlements. Built in early 1849, the post was attacked and destroyed by renegade Indians that summer. In late 1849 Fort Chokonikla was built nearby as the first outpost in a chain of forts established to control the Seminoles. Paynes Creek and the adjoining Peace River provide opportunities for canoeing, kayaking, and fishing. A museum at the visitor center depicts the lives of Florida's Seminole Indians and pioneers during the 19th century. Nature trails are designed to introduce the visitor to various natural ecosystems. On the Fort Chokonikla trail, you will experience plants and animals associated with scrub habitats. The Peace River trail meanders along the banks of the Paynes Creek and the Peace River showcasing Ox Bow Lakes.

DADE BATTLEFIELD HISTORIC STATE PARK

Bushnell - 7200 CR 603 (off I-75 exit 314, west of US 301) 33513. Phone: (352) 793-4781. www.floridastateparks.org/dadebattlefield/ Hours: Daily 8:00am-sunset. The center is open 9:00am-5:00pm daily. Admission: $2.00 for up to 8 people per car.

Dade Battlefield offers a peaceful setting away from the hustle and bustle of the city. One can explore the natural beauty of the wildflowers along the park's nature trail or walk along the Old Fort King Road where Major Dade and his command encountered 180 Seminoles. The battle that started the Second Seminole War is commemorated in January each year under the oaks of Dade Battlefield. On December 28, 1835, Seminole Indian warriors ambushed 108 soldiers at this site-only three soldiers survived. The park protects not only a historic battlefield, but also the natural communities as they existed when the soldiers and Seminoles battled over 180 years ago. Strolling a half-mile nature trail through pine flatwoods, visitors might see gopher tortoises, woodpeckers, songbirds, hawks, and indigo snakes. The park has a playground, picnic area with covered shelters, and a recreation hall. The visitor center has information and displays about the battle and visitors can watch a twelve-minute video history, This Land, These Men.

CITRUS TOWER

Clermont - 141 North Hwy 27 (rte. 191 west, north about 10 miles on Hwy 27) 34712. www.citrustower.com Phone: (352) 394-4061. Hours: Monday-Saturday 8:00am-5:00pm. Closed Sundays, Thanksgiving and Christmas. Admission: Small admission per person to ride tower. Citrus browsing/shopping market is free.

The Citrus Tower is an age-old building that offers a panoramic view of rolling hills, spring-fed lakes and citrus trees from any of three Tower Observation Decks. The Tower offers in-season fresh citrus fruit for sale, either to take along or for gift shipments. A restaurant and gift shop are also on the grounds.

LAKE LOUISA STATE PARK

Clermont - 7305 US Hwy 27 (seven miles south of State Road 50 in Clermont on U.S. 27) 34714. Phone: (352) 394-3969. ***www.floridastateparks.org/lakelouisa/*** *Hours: Daily 8:00am-sunset. Admission: $4.00 per vehicle for up to 8 people.*

Come see one of Florida State Park's newest cabins! Lake Louisa now offers 20 new cabins, overlooking beautiful Lake Dixie. These cabins offer two bedrooms/ two baths, full kitchen and dining/livingroom area. All cabins comfortably sleep 6. A short drive from Orlando, this park is noted for its six beautiful lakes, rolling hills, and scenic landscapes. Lake Louisa is the largest in a chain of 13 lakes connected by the Palatlakaha River. Lake Louisa, Dixie Lake, and Hammond Lake, the park's most accessible lakes, provide access for fishing, canoeing, and kayaking. Hiking is permitted on the 14-miles of horse trails and an abundance of wildlife may be seen. A ½ mile nature trail is located at the Lake Louisa parking lot. The trail winds through three of the park's eleven natural communities with interpretive trail signs provided for visitors to read about the park's flora and fauna. The swimming area is open to the public from Memorial Day to Labor Day. The park has a beautiful white sandy beach as well as a full-facility campground and primitive campsites.

RAINBOW SPRINGS STATE PARK

Dunnellon - 19158 S.W. 81st Pl. Rd. (three miles north of Dunnellon on the east side of U.S. 41) 34432. Phone: (352) 465-8555 Campground: (352) 465-8550. Hours: Daily 8:00am-sunset. Admission: $1.00 per person (children under six years old are admitted for free).

Archaeological evidence indicates that people have been using this spring for nearly 10,000 years. Rainbow Springs is Florida's fourth largest spring and from the 1930s through the 1970s, was the site of a popular, privately-owned attraction. Whether it is swimming or paddling in the cool water of the springs, picnicking in the park, hiking or birding along the nature trails, or strolling through the gardens, Rainbow Springs has much to offer. While every season is unique, the February and March bloom of azaleas is a popular time to visit the park. The walkways are a mixture of brick, concrete and asphalt surfaces. While historically unique and offering great views of both river and gardens, the pathways were constructed prior to ADA guidelines and are steep and uneven in places. A native garden, which is a special attraction to butterflies and hummingbirds, lies behind the cultural gardens. While you are there, check out the new interpretive exhibit at the Headsprings visitor center. You can learn about the ecology of both the uplands and the springs that make up this beautiful park. Canoes and kayaks can be rented at both the headsprings and the campground. Tubing is not allowed in the headsprings area of the park, but tubers can launch at nearby K.P. Hole County Park. The full-facility campground is about six miles from the day use area.

LAKE GRIFFIN STATE PARK

Fruitland Park - 3089 U.S. 441-27 (three miles north of Leesburg, 30 miles south of Ocala) 34731. Phone: (352) 360-6760. www.floridastateparks.org/lakegriffin/ Hours: Daily 8:00am-sunset. Admission: $4.00 per vehicle for up to 8 people.

Located within an hour of central Florida attractions and theme parks, this park is home to one of the state's largest live oak trees. A short trail near the park entrance takes visitors to the mammoth oak tree. A canal connects the park to Lake Griffin, the eighth largest lake in Florida, where visitors can enjoy boating and canoeing, as well as fishing. Come rent a canoe or launch you boat from our ramp for a trip on the beautiful Dead River. Visitors can observe the park's wildlife while picnicking or strolling along the half-mile nature trail. Look for resurrection fern after heavy rains. A shady, full-facility campground is on site.

WARBIRD ADVENTURES

Kissimmee - 231-233 North Hoagland Boulevard (I-4, get off on Highway 192 and travel East, go approximately 8 miles to Hoagland Boulevard, Turn South) 34741. Phone: (407) 933-1942 or (800) 386-1593. www.warbirdadventures.com Hours: Daily 9:00am-5:00pm, except Sunday. Admission: Flights start at $190.00.

Take yourself back to the time of the great WWII airplane. Observe planes being restored and see some already restored B-25s, A-26, DC-3 and T6s up close. Guided tours, memorabilia, gift shop and warbird flights are available. Put yourself in the Pilot's seat (or co-pilot's) of a WWII fighter/trainer with thrilling aerobatics or just fun, scenic flights.

BOGGY CREEK AIRBOAT RIDES

Kissimmee - 3702 Big Bass Road (20-30 minutes from Disney, Osceola Parkway east to end. Continue east of Boggy Creek Road) 34744. Phone: (407) 344-9550. www.bcairboats.com Admission: $21.95 adult, $15.95 child (3-12). 2 and under are FREE. Boat rental $65.00 per day. Miscellaneous: We do suggest you bring your sunscreen and sun glasses. You will also want to bring your camera or video camera, too. They provide hearing protection and life jackets for everyone who goes on tour. The boats and captains are US Coast Guard approved.

This adventure into the wetlands of Central Florida (headlands of the everglades) offers you a close-up view of towering Cypress trees, walls of tall grass, and wildlife. On each ride you'll have the opportunity to experience crane, osprey, snakes, turtles and Florida alligators. You will also enjoy the excitement of whisking across the surface of the water at speeds up to 45 MPH. We liked that

they spent most of the time taking you through tall grass RIGHT UP TO the gators! Just the right amount of time and light thrill…

Nature Safari Tours (40 minutes) - their newest nature safari is on a "one of a kind" custom built monstrous land vehicle. The packhorse is an open-air transporter with buggy seating for about 18 passengers. Nature lovers love the chance to view

Look closely...there's an alligator hiding in the center of this picture...waiting for dinner...

eagles, turkeys, deer, cows and wild hogs roaming free through a cattle ranch into the wilderness.

Or, maybe try bass fishing on record-breaking Lake Toho. You can purchase your fishing license, bait and equipment right at the Fish Camp Store. They have fifteen-foot fiberglass boats that you can rent which are complete with motors, one tank of gas and safety equipment. They also have professional fishing guides available if you are interested in finding all of the hot spots. Before you leave, try a snack of frog legs or gator (even hot dogs and hamburgers) at the snack bar.

GREEN MEADOWS PETTING FARM

*Kissimmee - 1368 South Poinciana Boulevard 34746. www.greenmeadowsfarm.com
Phone: (407) 846-0770.   Hours: Tours by appointment.   Admission: varies, contact
website Miscellaneous: Picnic areas are available.*

This petting farm features a two-hour guided tour of 300 farm animals. Visitors are encouraged to have a first-hand experience by petting the animals, taking train and hay rides, milking a cow and riding a pony. A guided tour includes fun in the pigpen, a chance to milk a cow, and chick cuddling. In October, visit the Pumpkin Patch.

MEDIEVAL TIMES DINNER & TOURNAMENT

Kissimmee - *4510 W. Irlo Bronson Memorial Hwy (Hwy 192) (Hwy 192, 6 miles east of I-4, exit 64A, between guide markers 14 & 15) 34746. Phone: (407) 396-2900 or (888) WE JOUST.* ***www.medievaltimes.com*** *Hours: Generally showtimes Weekdays 7:30pm, Weekends 6:30pm and 8:30pm. Your party needs to arrive about 45 minutes prior to show time (doors open 90 minutes prior) and the dinner and show lasts approximately 2 hours. Admission: $49.95 adult, $33.95 child (3-11). Online discounts are available at Walmart Orlando Ticket Center (next door). Miscellaneous: Medieval Life working village employs skilled artisans who practice crafts of ages gone by. Carpenters, blacksmiths, potters, weavers and coppersmiths work in the village and display their work. The Dungeon may be too evil for kids. A vegetarian entrée is also available upon request.*

You'll know you've arrived when the European-style castle-front appears on the horizon. This show transports guests back 900 years to a time when chivalry was honored and knights performed daring feats to entertain the lords and ladies of the court. As you are assigned seating, you'll also be assigned a knight to cheer for and a "take home" crown to wear to show your support. You will sit with others who join cheers of support for your chosen knight of the round. Serfs and wenches dressed in period costumes serve guests a feast of fresh vegetable soup, roasted chicken, spare ribs, herb basted potato, a pastry and beverages. In order to honor medieval tradition, guests eat their meals without silverware (your kids will love HAVING to eat with their hands!). As the lights dim, the story begins with the battle-

King Daniel...cheer for your team's knight!

weary King and his Knights returning to the Castle. The King calls for a grand tournament to determine the realm's new champion. As everyone is feasting, the Knights spar in tournament games and jousts. As the plot unfolds - we all hope truth, honor and love will eventually triumph over evil, and peace is restored. An unexpected event in the final minutes of the show rocks the crowd, and brings you to your feet - cheering! The beautiful Andalusian horses and remarkable displays of choreographed sword and jousting ability make this show so engaging!

OSCEOLA COUNTY HISTORICAL MUSEUM & PIONEER CENTER

Kissimmee - 750 N. Bass Road 34746. Phone: (407) 396-8644.   Hours: Open Thursday-Sunday only. Admission: $1.00-$2.00 donation.

See the 1898 "Cracker House", a 1900s general store, pioneer artifacts like a pole-barn, blacksmith shop and sugar cane mill. Traverse the eight-acre pristine nature preserve and picnic under 100-year old trees.

ARABIAN NIGHTS DINNER SHOW

Kissimmee - 6225 W. Irlo Bronson Hwy (1/2 mile east of I-4 on Hwy 192 exit 64A) 34747. Phone: (407) 239-9223 or (800) 553-6116.   www.Arabian-Nights.com Hours: 6:00pm every night except Wednesday and Saturday when the time is 8:30pm showtime. The VIP Experience starts one hour before the show time. Some matinees, too. Admission: $~55.00 adult, $~30.00 child (3-11). Tax and gratuity not included. $15.00 add-on for VIP. Discounts are available to military personnel and veterans, AAA, AARP, college students and seniors with ID. Their website often has a substantial online special, too.

...see the fun antics of the Genies

Combine the near forgotten, mysterious relationship of horse and man together with a royal wedding story. The show's cast of 60 horses, including Walter Farley's Black Stallion and a handful or two of actors, displays themed acts for the dining audience. Boys love the daring Gypsy Acrobats and action-packed Chariot Races. The 1hr. 45 minute nightly production incorporates colorful costumes and funny antics of the Genies, too. Your kids favorite part may just be the Black Stallion liberty (non-rider) act - true to the spirit of the book's mysterious power of the free horse. And the food? Individually plated three-course dinners feature salad, a choice of oven-roasted prime rib, grilled chicken breast, Black Angus chopped steak, vegetable lasagna or chicken tenders, and specialty dessert to fill you up as you're served in tiered arena table seating. Unlimited beverages are included.

ORANGE BLOSSOM BALLOONS

Kissimmee - (depart from the Restaurant of LaQuinta Inn, Lakeside. 7769 West Irlo Bronson Memorial Hwy.- Hwy 192) 34747. **http://orangeblossomballoons.com** *Phone: (407) 239-7677. Admission: $175.00 adult, $95.00 junior (10-15), FREE child (age 9 or less). One child per full paying adult.*

$20.00 per person if you just want to ride in the chase vehicle. Miscellaneous: Balloons can carry 4-9 passengers each.

How do you describe this? You see things but yet have little physical sensation. You feel a slight breeze and occasional heat from the burners, yet if you close your eyes...it seems you're floating, almost in a dream. This company offers hot air balloons rides daily at sunrise in the Disney World resort area. The three to four hour program includes a pre-flight briefing and one hour flight. Our favorite part was the take-off or landing and, "helping" the crew get the balloon open or packed up. After

A must do! Over 1000 feet high in a wicker basket - No Fear... Really!

the flight, you celebrate with a traditional champagne (or juice) ceremony, then return to the hotel for a complimentary full breakfast buffet. Each passenger is presented with a personalized first flight certificate. Trust us, we're not big fans of height, but you feel so safe due to the huge size of the balloon (compared to your basket). The expert pilots also do a wonderful job of explaining all of the things they do to make your flight so stress free. Imagine this – 3 balloons take off from a field - an hour or so later, they all land together in a field nearly 20 miles away. All without the aid of a "steering" device – just floating on directional currents. You have to check this activity off your "Dream to Do" list - so go ahead and try it!

CIRQUE DU SOLEIL, LA NOUBA

Lake Buena Vista - 1478 East Buena Vista Drive (at Downtown Disney West Side) 32830. Phone: (407) 939-7600. **www.lanoubaorlando.com** *Hours: Two shows nightly, 5 days a week. Reservations requested. Admission: varies by show date.*

This show features renowned blends of acrobatics and state-of-the-art special effects with more than 70 world-wide artists performing in a custom-made theater.

WALT DISNEY WORLD - GENERAL

Disney World is the world's largest entertainment complex!

Lake Buena Vista - 32830. Phone: (407) 824-4321. www.disneyworld.com Miscellaneous: Disney Cruise Vacations (800-811-5533 or www.disneycruise.com) set sail on a vacation created especially for every member of the family with separate areas for kids, teens and adults. Disney's Character Dining: (407) WDW-DINE - prices vary for hugs and food with Disney characters for breakfast, lunch or dinner.

Rise and Shine! The shuttle will drop you off at the Ticket and Transportation Center and from there you'll make you way by some mode of transport to get to your Kingdom or Park. You should arrive at any Disney World park as close to opening as possible (usually 9:00am). Once inside, stop at the Entrance booth and get a daily schedule and map. Now, off to the races! Here's some advice we've received and used:

1) "We always have Park Hopper passes and early on, when we ran into that situation (over-crowded) and hopped to another park, the difference was unbelievable! The other parks are practically empty by comparison". *(friend & frequent Disney-er, Chris S.)*

2) Bring a backpack (be sure to check latest park rules for carry-ins) filled with items such as: sunscreen, wipes, light towels, water bottles, snack baggies, cell phones or walkie-talkies, ID (for each child to wear), band-aids, camera, bottle of OTC allergy or headache medicine and, if you can fit it in, rain ponchos.

3) **www.TourGuideMike.com** is the place to organize your visit (if you want the most bang for buck & less stress). For around $21.95, Mike will provide online advice and a personal itinerary based on your interests, time, etc. His Automated Vacation Planner (AVP) service has photo tours of every show or ride - this is how my kids picked what they really wanted to do. Want to know the best view or best seats? Find out where to be scared or splashed - or not. What's the most comfortable view of parades and the best exits from

those parades? Get last minute details and changes on the monthly vacation club pages. And, of course, Mike's itinerary for each park - specifically programmed by time of day to best be at everything! Print the itinerary off before you go (it may be a dozen sheets like ours) and then cross off what you've accomplished. Best for families who want to do their favorites first - fast…then, slow down and pace the rest of the day. We successfully did MK in one day - done with our favorites by 3:00pm - just in time for the parade. We don't know how we could have enjoyed all of this without the insights from Tour Guide Mike. We used every mode of transportation and every secret passage or route he recommended and had time left to do everything we loved twice.

WALT DISNEY WORLD - ANIMAL KINGDOM

Lake Buena Vista -   32830. Phone: (407) 824-4321.   www.disneyworld.com Hours: Daily 9:00am-5:00pm. Admission: $67.00 adult (10+), $56.00 child (3-9) - one day/one park - purchase at gate. Magic Your Way tickets are attractive beginning at 4-day park hoppers. Miscellaneous: Plan to arrive in the morning (best time for animals) and spend 6+ hours here. Plan to go on safari first, then see Lion King shortly after that (arrive 20 minutes early for the show). Use your Discovery Book as you wonder through the various educational walking trails.

This park offers exciting adventures and unique encounters with real, exotic animals, plus one-of-a-kind guest experiences with fictional animals and giant dinos. The giant Tree of Life, the park's centerpiece of a carved trunk tree is home to unusual, rare creatures and within the 3-D film "It's Tough to be a Bug!". Careful, you might get sprayed or tickled by bugs! Travel Hanging out with Donald & friends in large, open-sided safari lorries, following bumpy trails exploring acres of forests, rivers, hills and grassland filled with free-roaming African wildlife. Or, Raft through Asia (be prepared to get soaked). Expedition Everest looms above but only the daring should go beyond the lowlands beneath. The ride's high speed adventure climbs up to the peak, then "lets go" as the track ends in a gnarled mass of twisted metal - eventually coming face-to-face with the abominable snowman. The musical drama Festival of the Lion King or Finding Nemo—The Musical, is colorful and quite a spectacle! Dinosaur is a bit scary for young ones (under 8) but well done - don't you love where they take the picture? Eeeek!

WALT DISNEY WORLD - DISNEYQUEST INDOOR INTERACTIVE THEME PARK

Lake Buena Vista - Downtown Disney West Side (I-4 exit 67) 32830. Phone: (407) 939-4636. www.disneyworld.com Hours: Daily 11:30am - 11:00pm or midnight. Admission: $36.00 adult, $30.00 child (3-9). Miscellaneous: Downtown Disney Marketplace (other side) has the outdoor Lego Imagination Center. Children use buckets of colorful bricks to get started. Guarded by friendly dinosaurs and a huge sea serpent built of Lego bricks, this play station lets kids explore their creativity at no cost to parents.

Shop, watch, dine, and play for as long as you like! This indoor park is a 5-story, indoor, interactive theme park that focuses on cutting-edge game technology. Create your own music, portrait or (not to miss) animation drawing. Guests climb aboard a real river raft, ride a roller coaster of their own design or become part of a human pinball game (all very creative and much different than any arcade games). On "Pirates" a crew of four go into a 3-D world of plundered towns, fortress islands and erupting volcanoes. (plan to ride this more than once!) Take a magic carpet ride on a journey through the streets of Agrabah. There are four distinct entertainment environments to choose from: the Explore Zone, the Score Zone, the Create Zone, and the Replay Zone. Be prepared to spend some time here to do everything and get you money's worth. Also, don't come with a headache as it gets loud on the top floors - and, every game requires action.

WALT DISNEY WORLD - EPCOT

Lake Buena Vista - 32830. Phone: (407) 824-4321. www.disneyworld.com Hours: Generally 9:00am-7:00pm. World Showcase often doesn't open until 10:00am. Admission: $67.00 adult (10+), $56.00 child (3-9) - one day/one park - purchase at gate. Magic Your Way tickets are attractive beginning at 4-day park hoppers. Miscellaneous: This is the

best Disney park to take the grandparents to, besides the memories of old at Magic Kingdom.

Epcot takes guests to 11 nations at World Showcase and fast-forwards them to tomorrow in Future World.

WORLD SHOWCASE offers a marketplace bustling with international flavor - The American Adventure, Canada,

A family favorite tradition...the French Bakery's cream puffs and pralineage...

China (look for lots of red), France (ah, the pastries!), Germany (ohmpa), Japan, Mexico, Morocco, Norway and the United Kingdom. Young guests can create their own Epcot souvenirs at the park's Kidcot Funstops. This is also where you can have your purchased passport stamped. Craftsmen teach the budding artisans how to create their own special mask or musical instrument. We've always said: a great way to "culture" you kids - arts & crafts and FOOD! Around "town" you might spot Mickey and his friends at the American Adventure, Belle and the Beast at France, Snow White in Germany (home to a mini-train and village), or Jasmine and Aladdin in Morocco. At night, IllumiNations thunderous fireworks light the sky. PLEASE don't miss the night show over the lagoon!

FUTUREWORLD focuses on discovery and scientific achievements with major attractions such as Test Track (buckle up and brace yourself for a fast ride!) or the Marine ride into the ocean, The Seas with Nemo & Friends, a whimsical and visually stunning attraction that has the stars of "Finding Nemo" swimming amid the live marine life of the huge aquarium in The Living Seas pavilion. "Honey, I Shrunk the Audience" is where everyone gets small. Visit a home of the future and thrill to the pulse-racing liftoff on Mission: SPACE.

WALT DISNEY WORLD - MAGIC KINGDOM

Lake Buena Vista -   32830. Phone: (407) 824-4321.   www.disneyworld.com Hours: Generally 9:00am to 7:00pm or later. Admission: $67.00 adult (10+), $56.00 child (3-9) - one day/one park - purchase at gate. Magic Your Way tickets are attractive beginning at 4-day park hoppers. Miscellaneous: Many suggest to begin and end your visit to Disney World at this park. We also suggest you purchase Mickey ears for each child with their names embroidered on the back (all for under $8.00) at Sir Mickey in Fantasyland (right behind Cinderella's castle). We recommend Cosmic Rays (Tomorrowland) for counter service.

Special moments happen...

Magic Kingdom features seven magical lands with attractions based on favorite Disney themes of fantasy, yesterday and tomorrow. Journey through seven "lands" where classic Disney tales and characters come to life. Young ones gravitate to Fantasyland and Toontown Fair because there's lots of "meet and greet" with characters and little rides. The older kids will want to strategize the path of mild thriller rides weaved into every land. Take the train and ride to Frontierland, where kids can ride Splash Mountain or Thunder Railroad and explore Tom Sawyer Island. As a family, immerse yourselves into a world of animation in 3-D musicals. Mickey's Philharmagic is not to be missed! Get caught in the middle of the mayhem caused by aliens in Buzz Lightyear's "laser tag" ride. The Laugh Floor Comedy Club, a new interactive adventure inspired by "Monsters, Inc", opens early 2007. Plan at least one front seat (curb side) watching the afternoon parade. Now, gather in the evening for a nighttime spectacular filling the sky. Of all the parks, this one still has the most magical feel!

WALT DISNEY WORLD - MGM STUDIOS

Lake Buena Vista -   32830. Phone: (407) 824-4321.   www.disneyworld.com Hours: Daily 9:00am-7:00pm. Admission: $67.00 adult (10+), $56.00 child (3-9) - one day/one park - purchase at gate. Magic Your Way tickets are attractive beginning at 4-day park hoppers. Miscellaneous: This park is definitely the most manageable on the feet - much less walking and people seem to like the fact that you can do most everything in 6-7 hours without rushing. We recommend the Commissary for counter food service. Did you get showered "Singing in the Rain"? Look for the umbrella on the streets of New York and

grab onto it for a pleasant surprise.

Disney-MGM Studios is a theme park with a complete motion picture and television studio (and tour). Guests are immersed in the excitement of show business - strolling down Hollywood Blvd. surrounded by classic Disney characters brought to life through the magic of animation. Exciting additions include "Playhouse Disney" or Muppet 3-D. Feel like an ant in the movie set of "Honey, I Shrunk the Kids". Stage shows include Beauty and the Beast and Little Mermaid. Our true "backsceen" favorite: The Backlot Tour - the tram tour takes guests behind the scenes of a staged movie production in Catastrophe Canyon and past vehicles, costumes and props from Hollywood films. Peek in backlot sets used for shooting movies and many television shows taped here.

WALT DISNEY WORLD - WATERPARKS

Lake Buena Vista -   32830. www.disneyworld.com Phone: (407) 824-4321. Hours: Daily 10:00am-5:00pm. Admission: $36.00 adult, $30.00 child (3-9). Miscellaneous: We personally observed the normal "Disney cast member charm" wasn't as prevalent here.

BLIZZARD BEACH: What do you do when a freak snowstorm hits Florida? Build a ski resort - well, sort of. All the snow has turned to water - 66 acres of it. The Blizzard features one of the world's tallest, fastest free-fall speed slides alongside 22 water slides, a "ski jump" tower and "icy" bobsled runs that stay comfortably warm and thrillingly fast (or slow at Cross Creek). And don't miss the exciting 'Teamboat Springs', the longest family slide in the world. It seems to go on and on and on! Designated areas for pre-teens and young children in addition to a one-acre wave pool create spaces for everyone to get wet or watch and stay dry.

TYPHOON LAGOON: Storms came and went. And when the storm of storms finally blew out to sea, it left behind a topsy-turvy tropical playground. A paradise opportunity for snorkeling, sliding and bodysurfing, the park also includes a gigantic wave pool with waves averaging four feet. Best features may be the speed slides or snorkeling amid a coral reef full of colorful fish, live sharks and coral.

FLORIDA'S NATURAL GROWERS GROVE HOUSE

Lake Wales - 20160 US Hwy 27 (Interstate 4 West to Highway 27 South) 33853. www.floridasnatural.com Phone: (800) 237-7805. Hours: Monday-Friday 10:00am-5:00pm, Saturday 10:00am-2:00pm (seasonally). Closed in the summer.

A few steps from the main road is a cracker style Visitors Center lined with welcoming rocking chairs on the front porch. Take a few minutes to walk through the gift shop. Have a glass of Florida's Natural® Brand juice, choose from several variety of flavors and visit the museum area and theater. The theater is cool and comfortable as you sit and watch Florida's Natural Brand juices develop from the tree to the glass.

HISTORIC BOK SANCTUARY

Lake Wales - 1151 Tower Boulevard (55 miles southwest of Orlando, east of Tampa) 33853. Phone: (863) 676-1408. www.boksanctuary.org Hours: Daily 8:00am-6:00pm. Center 9:00am-5:00pm. Admission: $10.00 adult, $3.00 child (5-12).

A National Historic Landmark, the Sanctuary includes gardens by Frederick Law Olmsted Jr., a 205 foot tall majestic marble and coquina belltower carillon (daily recitals); Pinewood Estate, a classic 20-room Mediterranean Revival winter estate open for tours and the Pine Ridge Nature Preserve Trail. Children love the sanctuary. At the Visitor Center, they can check out a free reading and puppet basket available in three topics: Winged Wonders, Creepy Crawlies and Animals of the Wild. Children also discover a variety of fun things to do throughout the gardens: Tile rubbing posts feature plants and animals that can create rubbings on paper that appear like magic; a vine-covered arbor tunnel to explore; a large sandbox with toys; a fort-like basket created from willow branches and palms; and a fly-by garden featuring plants that attract butterflies. Benches and interpretive signs abound as swans swim gracefully near the Reflection Pool or birds and frogs chirp.

LAKE KISSIMMEE STATE PARK

Lake Wales - 14248 Camp Mack road (off SR 60, 15 miles east of Lake Wales) 33853. Phone: (863) 696-1112. **www.floridastateparks.org/lakekissimmee/** *Hours: Daily 8:00am-sunset. Admission: Contact park for seasonal admission pricing.*

Florida's cowboy heritage comes alive with living history demonstrations of the early Florida "cow hunters" in an 1876-era cow camp, open 9:30am-4:30pm, weekends and holidays. Sit a spell and spin tales with the cowmen at the State Park's 176 Cow Camp. Sip on camp coffee "strong enough to float a bullet." Pack up a picnic lunch and bring the family to walk among the cattle descended from those the Spaniards brought in the 16th century. The park also offers 13 miles of hiking trails which showcase white-tailed deer, bobcat, bald eagles, sandhill cranes, turkeys, and other bird life. The trails take you through pine flatwoods, oak hammocks, by freshwater marshes, and out to Lake Kissimmee. You may take your pick from a ½ mile self-guided nature trail, two loop trails, and a spur trail out to the lake. There are two backcountry campsites along the trails available for those who wish to spend the night under the stars. Six miles of trails are open to equestrians. The park has full-facility campsites, as well as a primitive camping facility. The youth camping area can accommodate up to 50 people. Visitors enjoy boating, canoeing, and fishing in the picturesque lakes. The new fishing docks are in place and can be used by fishermen & boaters.

EXPLORATIONS V CHILDREN'S MUSEUM

Lakeland - 109 N. Kentucky Avenue 33801. **www.explorationsv.com** *Phone: (863) 687-3869. Hours: Monday-Saturday 9:00am-5:30pm. Admission: $2.00-$4.00 per person (ages 2 +).*

Three floors of mind-stretching, kid-powered exhibits featuring art, science, literature, math, health, life skills and cultures from around the world. Grab your passport at the Visitor's Center and journey around the world - downstairs. Escape to another time and culture and learn about family life, art and habitat of past civilizations of the Americas, Africa, Asia and Australia...all through hands-on arts and crafts. On the Our Town Floor - Try being a doctor, artist, school teacher, banker, grocery clerk or newscaster. There's a Tot Spot for the little ones, too.

OCALA NATIONAL FOREST

Ocala - 34470. www.fs.fed.us/r8/florida/recreation/index_oca.shtml Phone: (352) 236-0288 or (386) 752-2577. The Ocala is a unique and fascinating forest that offers an accommodating climate for year round recreating. The mild winters are fine for family camping while a summer canoe trip down a palm-lined stream is a cool way to spend an August day. The temperatures for the dry months of November through February range from a daily average of 50 F. to a high of 72 F. The summer season is much warmer and wetter. Water plays an important part in a variety of recreational opportunities on the forest. There are huge springs, twisting streams and lakes for fishing and water skiing. Many of the scenic lakes were formed when limestone bedrock dissolved, permitting the surface layer to slump and fill with water. The cool crystal-clear water of Juniper Springs, Alexander Springs, Salt Springs and Silver Glen Springs entices many visitors to take a cool dip. Snorkelers frequently find a thrilling underwater view of fish, swaying vegetation and cavernous springs. The Ocala portion of the FLORIDA NATIONAL SCENIC TRAIL traverses the forest north to south, winding through multiple ecosystems. Hikers can experience rolling hills in the open longleaf pine forest, vast prairies, wooden boardwalks through swamps, thick scrub oak – sand pine, and oak hammocks. The Trail meanders approximately 67 miles through the Ocala National Forest.

SILVER RIVER STATE PARK

Ocala - 1425 N E 5th Avenue (SR 35) (east of Ocala, one mile south of State Road 40 on State Road 35) 34470. Phone: (352) 236-5401.   www.floridastateparks.org/silverriver/ Hours: Museum/Center: Weekends 9:00am-5:00pm. Also open Tuesday-Friday, 10:00am-4:00pm (mid-June - late July). Park open daily 8:00am-sunset. Admission: $2.00 per person, children 6 and under are FREE. $4.00 per carload entrance fee. Cabin Fee All Year $100.00 plus tax. Camping Fee All Year $21.00 plus tax. Miscellaneous: Visitors can canoe down the crystal clear river, hike or bike along one of the nature trails, or just sit and watch for the wide variety of birds and wildlife. For overnight stays, the park has a full facility campground and 10 luxury cabins.

Visitors to the museum take a journey through Silver River's past. Everything from mammoths to movies are included in the exhibits. Upon entering the museum, you come nose to tusk with a Columbian Mammoth skeleton. This cast is one of the few full size mammoth skeletons on display in Florida. Be awe struck by the giant jaw and teeth of the Megalodon (prehistoric shark) that swam over Florida so many years ago. A young mastodon skull and an adult skull are both displayed. A variety of fossils is found throughout the museum. Artifacts from some of Florida's first human inhabitants are also found within the museum. You can see tools and weapons constructed from native materials dating as far back as 12,000 years ago. The shells of other smaller creatures living in Florida's prehistoric seas, called Foramnifera, formed the basis of the Floridan Aquifer, our modern day water source. An interactive exhibit informs visitors about some of the current issues affecting local water supply. The collection in the second half of Silver River Museum illustrates a period of time spanning over 500 years, beginning with the initial Spanish exploration. It's a fascinating display of cultural and natural history in Central Florida.

DON GARLITS MUSEUM OF DRAG RACING AND CLASSIC CARS

Ocala - 13700 SW 16th Avenue (I-75 exit 341, one block east on CR 484) 34473. Phone: (877) 271-3278 or (352) 245-8661. www.garlits.com Hours: Daily (except Christmas) from 9:00am-5:00pm. Admission: $15.00 adult, $13.00 senior (60+) and youth (13-18), $6.00 child (5-12).

Mention the name "Big Daddy" around anyone familiar with auto sports and one name comes to mind, "Don Garlits". A legend in Top Fuel Drag racing, Don has inspired generations to reach for their best in the ¼ mile. In recent years, Don even borrowed a car and still ran over 300 MPH to prove he could still do it! See the Museum of Classic Cars (Vintage Cars, Early Fords, Hot Rods, and '60s & '70s muscle cars) and the Museum of Drag Racing (many of the record-breaking "swamp rat" cars) that will inspire both young and old alike.

ORANGE COUNTY REGIONAL HISTORY CENTER

Orlando - 65 E. Central Blvd. (I-4 exit 82C. Anderson St. east to Left on Magnolia one block. Downtown) 32801. Phone: (407) 836-8500. www.thehistorycenter.org Hours: Monday-Saturday 10:00am-5:00pm, Sunday Noon-5:00pm. Admission: $7.00 adult, $6.50 senior (60+) and student, $3.50 child (3-12). Miscellaneous: Online discount couplon.

Wonder how this region has made its transition from a small town surrounded by citrus groves and cattle ranches to today's vacation haven? Housed in a restored 1927 county courthouse, the History Center offers a selection of interactive presentations and hands-on exhibits through four-floors of exploration. The Orientation Theater (decorated like a Florida back porch), gives an overview of the region's history as visitors relax in rockers while surrounded by the sights and sounds of Central Florida. In Natural Environment, you'll look at the geology of the area and have an opportunity to probe Winter Park's famous sinkhole. A recreated early 19th century Seminole Settlement provides a look at the state's most famous tribe. The replica Florida Pioneer cabin lets curious guests test a Spanish moss-filled mattress and discover the much-discussed origin of the term "Florida Cracker".

FLORIDA SYMPHONY YOUTH ORCHESTRA

Orlando - Bob Carr Performing Arts Centre (Loch Haven Park on the corner of Mills Avenue & Princeton Street. I-4 exit 85) 32803. Phone: (407) 999-7800. ***www.fsyo.org*** *Hours: Three shows one in the fall, winter and spring.*

This long-standing orchestra provides an educationally sound musical experience that motivates students to fulfill their potential and strive for excellence. FSYO is comprised of nearly 200 students in grades three through twelve from counties and schools in Central Florida.

ORLANDO MUSEUM OF ART

Orlando - 2416 North Mills Avenue (I-4 exit 85) 32803. Phone: (407) 896-4231. ***www.omart.org*** *Hours: Tuesday-Saturday 10:00am-4:00pm, Sunday Noon-4:00pm.*

The art museum boasts permanent collections of American art, African art and art of the ancient Americas as well as touring exhibitions, some relating to storybook illustrations. Check out the Family Discovery Centers.

ORLANDO REPERTORY THEATRE

Orlando - 1001 East Princeton Street (Loch Haven Park. I-4 exit 85) 32803. Phone: (407) 896-7365. ***www.orlandorep.com***

The Rep brings a six show season of professional theatre to families based on classic and contemporary children's literature. The Rep is a place where young audiences can come and experience the adventure and creativity of watching their favorite characters come to life.

ORLANDO SCIENCE CENTER

Orlando - 777 E. Princeton Street (Loch Haven Park, corner of Mills Avenue & Princeton St. I-4 exit 85)) 32803. Phone: (407) 514-2000 or (888) OSC-4FUN. **www.osc.org** *Hours: Monday-Thursday 9:00am-5:00pm, Friday-Saturday 9:00am-9:00pm, Sunday Noon-5: 00pm. Closed Monday (except major school holidays). Admission: $14.95 adult, $9.95 child (3-11) includes unlimited giant screen films, planetarium shows, exhibits, observatory visit and live programs. Admission is discounted after 4:00pm. Miscellaneous: KidsTown is a pint-sized town made just for the youngest family members. Kids can farm oranges and explore underground.*

The Orlando Science Center offers interactive learning with hands-on exhibits, live programs, films and planetarium shows, and an observatory with a giant refractor telescope. Journey into the minds of chimpanzees during the showing of Jane Goodall's Wild Chimpanzees on the gigantic eight-story high domed screen in CineDome. Spend a day in a cypress swamp and never get damp while you feed and touch alligators and turtles in NatureWorks. Experience countless discovery fun like flying a real flight simulator, digging for dino bones, playing with lasers and holograms, exploring Mars and the cosmos and investigating the complex machine that is the human body.

ORLANDO BALLET

Orlando - 1111 North Orange Avenue 32804. **www.orlandoballet.org** *Phone: (407) 426-1733. Hours: the Family Series includes performances with a different theme each fall, holiday, and spring. Admission: $30.00 Family Series subscription. $15.00 individual tickets.*

The Family Series performances are the same performances featured in the regular season except they are abbreviated versions. The performances run 45 minutes to an hour and feature an educational component and/or narration. This is great for younger children. What they see is just long and interesting enough to keep their attention (ex. The Nutcracker, Cinderella).

ORLANDO MAGIC BASKETBALL

Orlando - 8701 Maitland Summit Blvd. (home games played at the T.D.Waterhouse Center) 32810. Phone: (407) 89-MAGIC. **www.nba.com/magic/news/**

Professional NBA basketball played in the TD Waterhouse Centre. Kids: look for "Stuff, the Magic Dragon" mascot lurking around the corner. Ultimate Fan Nights include a ticket to the game, a hot dog, a soda, an Orlando Magic hat, and a post-game lay-up line coupon, all for only $28.00. Other family-oriented game nights include: Scout Night and Faith & Family Nights.

For updates & travel games visit: **www.KidsLoveTravel.com**

HOLYLAND EXPERIENCE

Orlando - 4655 Vineland Road (I-4 exit 78, corner of Conroy and Vineland Roads 32811. Phone: (407) 872-2272 or (866) 872-4659. **www.holylandexperience.com** *Hours: Monday-Saturday, 10:00am-5:00pm. Extended hours on weekends and peak seasons. Closed Thanksgiving and Christmas. Allow 4-6 hours visiting here to catch the scenes and shows. Admission: One Day Plus 7 Pass, $35.00 adult, $23.00 child (6-12). Small parking fee. Miscellaneous: The Holy Land Experience is a mix of both indoor and outdoor activities so come dressed for both. The Oasis Palms Café offers a wide variety of American and Middle Eastern food items – many of which are themed to the historical and geographical setting, including the "Thirsty Camel Cooler" and "Goliath Burger". Because some of the movies are very realistic, we'd recommend this site for ages 10+.*

This Bible Adventure Park re-creates the city of Jerusalem and its religious importance between the years 1450 B.C. and A.D. 66 through themed, costumed characters; dramatic enactments and high-tech presentations. Everything you hear, see, smell and touch brings Bible stories to life! The productions put you into the thick of the action. Hear the busy sounds of a merchant's market, see the precise rituals in

...seeing the stone that was rolled away at Jesus' tomb

the Tabernacle (watch for the "cloud of God"), touch the Centurion's garment as he begs of the Lord's healing, hear the narration about the recreated miniature Jerusalem, and feel the pain of Calvary. 500,000 pounds of concrete were used to create a detailed scale recreation of the Qumran Caves where the Dead Sea Scrolls were hidden. Children love interacting with the live animals, including a camel. Updated musical shows follow the parallel between great art, song, dance and music through ancient history. The Qaboo & Company Oasis Outpost is an area designated for kid-fun. Kids can climb a rock wall or go on a kid-sized archeological dig. The living Biblical museum on the premises is home to the Scriptorium, a collection of biblical antiquities dating back to 2200 B.C. You can tell they put a lot of effort here to be authentic. To get the best value, plan to spend 1/2 day and catch every show and presentation. You'll be more Bible-smart afterwards.

FUN SPOT ACTION PARK

Orlando - *(I-4 exit 75 -A, between Belz Outlet Mall and Wet 'N Wild just off International Drive and Kirkman Road at the base of the GIGANTIC Ferris Wheel) 32819. Phone: (407) 363-3867.   www.Fun-Spot.com Hours: Weekdays 2:00pm-11:00pm, Weekends 10:00am-Midnight. Admission: FREE to enter. Tickets for rides/tokens for games begin at $3.00. Armbands $15.00-$35.00. If you're going to ride for more than 1 hour, go for the armbands.*

Fun Spot is a five-acre action theme park consisting of 4 innovative (and patented!) Go-Kart tracks. One is really challenging - OK, Dad, go for it, but most are great for the whole family and each features different turns or hills. They also feature 13 different family thrill rides and attractions. Some are kiddie rides and some are classic amusement park rides like the Paratrooper or Scrambler. The 10,000 square-foot Video Arcade is one of the area's largest and the Oasis Café serves moderately priced food. The place is clean and friendly and offers a nice diversion from the overwhelmingly large theme parks. Everything is compactly situated where mom and dad can see half the park at one time. Because they are a Free admission park, everyone can come and play as they want…or, just watch.

TRAIN LAND INTERNATIONAL

Orlando - *8990-A International Drive (Just south of Pointe Orlando shopping mall) 32819. Phone: (407) 363-9002.   Hours: Monday-Saturday 10:00am-9:00pm, Sunday 10:00am-8:00pm. Admission: $8.00 adult, $6.00 senior (55+) and child.*

This combination train store/museum boasts one of the largest G-gauge layouts in the world — and G-gauge is four times bigger than HO. The layout is impressive, rising high overhead and twisting and turning through mountain passes, quaint small towns, industrial zones, and idyllic farm valleys. There's even a spur line to Santa-Land. The rivers have fish in them and the mountaintops are home to Bigfoot and the Abominable Snowman. Train and trolley rides, scavenger hunts and a hobby shop are on the premises, too.

PIRATES DINNER ADVENTURE

Orlando - *6400 Carrier Drive (just off International Drive) 32819. Phone: (407) 248-0590 or (800) 866-2469.   www.piratesdinneradventure.com Hours: Shows begin at 7:30pm or 8:00pm. Doors open 90 minutes prior to showtime and the Maritime Museum and appetizers are served 45 minutes beforehand. Admission: $51.95 adult, $31.95 child (3-11).   Great discount ordering online.*

Pirate's Dinner Adventure is a dinner show attraction that puts you and your family right in the middle of all of the swashbuckling action. Visiting the King's Festival in the old seaport village, voyagers feast on an assortment of hors d'oeuvres being served in honor of the King's daughter, Princess Anita. Pre-show entertainment abounds as the Gypsy King, an exotic snake dancer, the Golden Gypsy girl, street vendors, fortune tellers and face painters vie for guests' attention. The Main Show is staged on a full-sized authentic replica of an 18th Century Spanish galleon afloat in a 300,000-gallon lagoon. Many guests gasp upon entering! Daredevil pirates dangle from 50 and 70-foot tall masts, delighting the 825 voyagers – each with the best seat in the house due to the theater-in-round design. Each night, over one hundred guests are invited to participate in the show (all the kids and men in our party got to "dress up" and "act"). With a crack of lighting and a jolt of thunder, a classic story of good versus evil unfolds. Each dining section cheers on their respective-colored pirate (we had the funny Saxon the Purple) as the "actors" sing, dance and perform acrobatics - swinging and bouncing almost continuously!

Our own pirates haulin' treasure!

The meal begins with a fresh salad, followed by a main course of seasoned beef or shrimp and marinated chicken served with the Captain's favorite West Indies yellow rice teeming with Caribbean seasonings. Steamed fresh vegetables and roasted potatoes round out the meal, with a warm apple cobbler a la mode dished up for dessert. Chilled drinks, soft drinks, and vegetarian meals are available, and the little tikes in the bunch may dine on the Captain's "Kid's" meal -- if the Captain approves. After the show, party like a disco pirate at the Buccaneer Bash (included in admission). If you can only go to one dinner show with the kids in Orlando - this is the best choice. High action and loads of interactive fun!

RIPLEY'S BELIEVE IT OR NOT! ORLANDO ODDITORIUM

Orlando - 8201 International Drive 32819. Phone: (407) 345-0501 or (800) 998-4418. www.ripleysorlando.com   Admission: $12.00-$17.00. Hours: Daily, 9:00am-11:00pm.

Housed in a building that appears to be sinking, the Odditorium looks like it fell victim to one of Florida's infamous sinkholes. Explore artifacts, collections, weird art/hobbies and interactive exhibits in 16 galleries of the odd and unusual from around the world. Stories you can't imagine, people you won't believe…

SKY VENTURE

Orlando - 6805 Visitors Circle (across from Wet n Wild) 32819.   Phone: (407) 903-1150 or (800) SKYFUN1.   www.skyventureorlando.com   Hours: Weekdays 2:00pm-11:30pm, Weekends Noon-11:30pm. Entire experience takes about one hour. By reservation is suggested as they book times full up to two weeks in advance. Admission: $39.95 General, (discount coupons on website) Miscellaneous: A video of the experience of entire party in the tunnel is available for an extra fee. No parachute, no jumping and no experience is necessary...Really!

SkyVenture, indoor skydiving vertical wind tunnel (float on air), is a very unique attraction that most people may not think is kid-friendly. They actually fly children 3 years and up. Your instructor will collect you from the observation level (a free area for viewing those in the tunnel) and bring you to the second level of the tunnel. Your instructor will show you a brief video to start your training. You will learn the hand signals necessary to communicate in the tunnel as each of you practice your skydiving position. Each person will take two turns flying in the tunnel. Your instructor assists you each step of the way. Remember to relax and enjoy this amazing experience. Kids are naturals and even mom and dad learn easily, no matter how flexible you are. To commemorate this event, you'll receive a flight certificate and we recommend you pre-order purchase a flight video of your group. What a rush!

UNIVERSAL ORLANDO

Orlando - 1000 Universal Studios Plaza 32819. www.universalorlando.com   Phone: (407) 363-8000. Hours: Park opens at 9:00am daily. Closing time varies but generally 6: 00pm or later. Admission: $67.00 adult, $56.00 child per day per park. 5 park discounts or 2 day discounts available (change yearly) Online discounts available. Miscellaneous: On-site hotel guests can simply show their room key at each ride to receive preferred access (they can also have gift purchases sent directly to their room).

The single theme park now encompasses an entertainment complex, three on-site hotels and two theme parks. Out to be very different, these parks appeal to unexpected, hip older kids. The back-to-back theme parks are action oriented, high energy. Its attractions are based on pop-culture icons and blockbuster films. Its three on-site Loews Hotels, the Portofino Bay Hotel, the Hard Rock Hotel and the Royal Pacific Resort are upscale compliments to the restaurants and nite-life of Universal CityWalk.

UNIVERSAL STUDIOS: This park is known as the theme park where guests "ride the movies." Jimmy Neutron's NickToon Blast brings the famous boy genius to life - along with SpongeBob, the Rugrats and the Fairly Odd Parents. Jimmy pulls guests into the action to help him save the planet and his friends. Travelers are on a crash-course with their fate as they roar, spin, crash and careen into the action. Shrek 4-D features 12 minutes of 3D animation as guests don specially created OgreVision glasses. The audience is transported into the center of fast-paced sequences that include an aerial dogfight between fire-breathing dragons and a plunge down a 1,000 foot deadly waterfall. Surprising sensory elements in the seat produce motion, touch, air and water. Time-traveling volunteers fly into the futuristic Hill Valley and blast back to the chilling Ice Age on Back to the Future...The Ride. Watch out for JAWS around the corner. Twister...Ride It Out places guests a mere 20 feet away from the awesome fury of a incredible tornado. Earthquake: The Big One invites you to experience an 8.3 Richter scale quake from the seeming comfort of a San Francisco subway train. In KIDZONE, play with thousands

Universal friends...

of balls, gallons of water or a kid-friendly roller coaster or E.T. Adventure uplifted bicycle ride. The KidZone also unites several other existing children's attractions, including Animal Planet Live! (TV animal star show), A Day in the Park with Barney show, and other playland areas. Seasonally, this park offers a nightly lagoon show called Universal 360: A Cinesphere Spectacular. The show relies on 360-degree "cinespheres," an original music score, 300 outdoor speakers, lasers and pyrotechnic effects to place guests in the midst of their favorite films. Many of the indoor rides are very creative yet beware of motion sickness (if you're prone).

UNIVERSAL ISLANDS OF ADVENTURE: This park features some of the most thrilling and technologically advanced rides and attractions. Toon Lagoon includes Sunday funnies and Dudley Do-Right's Ripsaw Falls - the first water flume ride ever to send its riders plummeting 75 feet downward beneath the surface of the water. Seuss Landing is where whimsical characters spring to life (Cat in the Hat, Green Eggs and Ham). The High In The Sky Seuss Trolley Train Ride transports guests through the world of Seuss stories. Marvel Super Hero Island catches the excitement of super heroes and villains with such rides as the Amazing Adventures of Spider-Man and the Incredible Hulk Coaster. The Lost Continent is where myths and legends come to life in this mysterious, fog-shrouded land, which features the Dueling Dragons dual coaster and the Eighth

Voyage of Sinbad stage show. Finally, in the Discovery Center of Jurassic Park, you'll find a dinosaur nursery and Camp Jurassic play area full of lava pits, amber caves, tropical rainforest, and the soaring Pteranodon Flyers.

WET' N WILD ORLANDO

Orlando *- 6200 International Drive (I-4 exit 75A. International Drive @ Universal Blvd.) 32819. Phone: (407) 351-WILD or (800) 992-WILD.* ***www.****Wetnwildorlando.com* Hours: *Daily generally 9:30am-7:00pm or 10:00am-5:00pm depending on the season. Extended summer night hours. Admission: $35.95 (age 10+), $17.98 senior, $29.95 child (3-9). A nominal parking fee is charged. Miscellaneous: Pools are heated seasonally.*

This waterpark opened its gates in 1977 and was the first amusement park to feature numerous water activities and attractions in one location. They keep updating or enhancing rides and now they even have a live DJ that greets guests and "broadcasts" throughout the park, hosting games and distributing prizes. The park offers the best variety of multi-passenger rides (many have tubes big enough to hold the entire family). You can boogie down the retro raft adventure, Disco H²O - splashing to the hits of the 70s as you spin circles through an enclosed aqua disco (lasers, lights, music and disco balls). Take a more relaxed journey into Florida's past on the newer Lazy River or get soaked down a ruptured pipeline on The Blast. Children love the Kids' Park featuring smaller versions of the park's popular adult rides. Try the triple-dip Bubba Tub family slide. Soak up the sun by the Surf Lagoon wave pool or challenge yourself to the ultimate "free fall" on the Bomb Bay.

WONDERWORKS

Orlando *- 9067 International Drive (At Pointe Orlando) 32819. Phone: (407) 351-8800.* ***www.wonderworksonline.com*** *Admission: see website for current pricing packages.*

WonderWorks is an indoor attraction with over 100 different interactive exhibits that are sure to exercise your imagination...an amusement park for the mind. Try your luck playing basketball against sharks, surviving the 65 MPH winds from the hurricane simulator, as well as voluntarily sitting through an earthquake! Ride a virtual glider above the Grand Canyon or play a keyboard with your feet. Along with three levels of interactive fun, make sure you schedule time to see the Outta Control Magic Show. Watch the exciting shenanigans of the duo performers on stage while enjoying the unlimited hand-tossed pizza, popcorn and beverages. (Two shows each evening, 6:00pm and 8:00pm).

DISCOVERY COVE

Orlando - 6000 Discovery Cove Way (I-4 east exit 71. Bear right onto Central Florida Parkway, just past SeaWorld) 32821. Phone: (877) 4-DISCOVERY. www.discoverycove.com Hours: Daily, 9:00am-5:30pm by reservation only. Maximum of 1,000 guests per day. Night programs offered in the summer only. Admission: Depending on the season: approximately $259.00+ plus per person (age 6+) for park and dolphin swim. Approximately. $159.00 plus per person (age 3+) for non-dolphin swim and park. Special events and Trainer-for-A-Day programs have an upcharge in addition to regular admission. Groups can reserve discounted admission. Miscellaneous: One price covers everything a guest needs for a full day of fun at Discovery Cove. General admission includes the dolphin-swim experience (or opt not) and unlimited access to the Coral Reef, Ray Lagoon, Aviary, Tropical River and Resort Pool, self-parking; a freshly prepared gourmet lunch; continental breakfast; snacks throughout the day; use of all snorkeling and beach gear (marine animal friendly, even sunscreen); plus a pass for seven consecutive days of unlimited admission to SeaWorld Orlando or Busch Gardens Tampa.

Picture paradise. You and your family are playing with dolphins, snorkeling through a colorful reef filled with tropical fish and rays, hand-feeding exotic birds, and relaxing on sandy white beaches - all in the middle of a metropolitan city. Discovery Cove is an exclusive, reservations-only park that offers its guests extraordinary adventures through up-close encounters with dolphins and other exotic marine life. What makes this Cove so special?

Dolphin Lagoon - The highlight of your visit is the rare opportunity to swim and play with a beautiful bottlenose dolphin during a 30-minute interactive adventure. Orient yourself with dolphin "talk" and commands. Accompanied by a trainer, groups of 6-8 guests wade into shallow water and become acquainted with their dolphin through hugs, kisses and rubdowns. The instructors are so calm and confident - it is easy to follow their lead and "bond" or "play" with the mammal. You

...off to meet some new underwater friends!

even get to kiss your new friend! Then, taking the relationship one step further, guests interact with their dolphin in deeper water for an exciting dorsal tow ride.

.

Discovery Cove (cont.)

<u>Coral Reef</u> - Snorkelers can follow colorful schools of tropical fish in the realistic coral reef. Swim within inches of barracuda and shark safely housed behind clear acrylic walls.

<u>Ray Lagoon</u> - This quiet, protected area provides a lagoon full on southern and cownose rays - gentle animals that grow up to 4 feet in diameter. Guests can snorkel, wade and playfully interact with the rays.

<u>Tropical River</u> - This waterway meanders through most of the property. It has beaches and rocky lagoons to simulate an island, tropical forest and an underwater cave. Our kids loved snorkeling trying to find ancient ruins beneath. Swimmers going under a waterfall emerge inside the Aviary where guests can hand-feed hundreds of tiny birds and interact with other birds as tall as 4 feet.

By providing this amazing experience in a safe, managed environment, the trainers hope that each guest comes away with a heightened appreciation of the importance of conserving marine animals and their habitats. Pricey to manage on a typical family budget, but "wow" is it amazing to be there!

DIXIE STAMPEDE, DOLLY PARTON'S DINNER AND SHOW

Orlando - 8251 Vineland Avenue (across from Orlando Premium Outlets, just off I-4) 32821. Phone: (407) 238-4455 or (866) 443-4943. www.dixiestampede.com Hours: Year-round, almost daily at 6:00pm. Peak weekends and seasons also at 8:30pm. Admission: $45.00 adult, $20.00 child (3-11). Miscellaneous: Farm animal allergies? Be prepared with your medications, once the horses get "kickin'" you might notice the allergies flare up. The Carriage Room preshow entertainment is provided by Australia's Electric Cowboy and his horse, Starstruck.

The very action-packed dinner and show features dozens of horses, beautiful costumes, incredible horsemanship, and a patriotic finale…all in the massive indoor arena. All of this North vs. South competition while enjoying a fabulous four-course feast that you have to eat with your hands. While you're finishing your main course, you may be asked (kids AND parents) to participate in several races. You'll love the dancing horses and the comical actors and unusual animals that show up from time to time.

SEA WORLD ADVENTURE PARK

Orlando - 7007 SeaWorld Drive (intersection of I-4 and FL528 - the Bee Line Expressway. 10 minutes south of downtown) 32821. Phone: (407) 351-3600. www.seaworld.com Hours: Open year-round at 9:00am with extended hours during summer and holidays.

Allow a full day. Admission: $62.00 adult, $50.00 child (3-9). Discounts available for guests with disabilities, seniors, military and AAA members. Online discounts, too. Miscellaneous: You can Dine With Shamu ($18.00-$36.00 per person) or visit the Oyster's Secret pearl diving lagoon. The nightly Aloha Polynesian Luau is an authentic tropical feast with entertainment ($30-$46 per person).

The main attractions are the amazing animal encounters with killer whales, dolphins, hilarious sea lions and lurking sharks. You have to meet Shamu (Believe ballet) and Clyde and Seamore - they are truly the stars! Guests may feed and touch dolphins in a tropical lagoon with rolling waves, a sandy beach, underwater viewing and naturalistic coral reef, as well as feed stingrays, and see endangered sea turtles and manatee up-close. There are separate areas just for Shark and Penguin Encounters...even a Dolphin Nursery (home to new dolphin mothers and their

...a huge walrus climbs onto the platform and steals the show!

calves). Blue Horizons dolphin spectacular showcases amazing special effects and awesome animal and bird experiences. A young girl's vivid imagination sets the stage for a show filled with action both above and under the water performed by a cast of divers and aerialists.

Moving away from aquatics and focusing on rescued animals from shelters is Pets Ahoy! This comical show features the talents of a menagerie of dogs, cats, birds, rats (yes, rats), skunks and pot-belly pigs. The world's most popular marine life park also features some sea-themed rides, including Kraken and Journey to Atlantis (part water ride, part coaster with twists, turns and drenching!) The Wild Arctic takes guests on a motion-based flight over the frozen North Arctic campus via simulated jetcopter. Take a break and let the kids climb in Shamu's Happy Harbour play area with wet and dry landscapes. (warning: parents, be prepared to climb the whole length of the nets - if you dare!) Newer additions to Shamu's Happy Harbor play area include a family friendly roller coaster, a jellyfish-themed samba tower ride and a beach bucket-themed tea cup ride.

Before you leave, make absolutely sure you see Odyssea, the underwater "circus" - it is amazing and worth seeing more than once!

GATORLAND

Orlando - 14501 S. Orange Blossom Trail 32837. Phone: (407) 855-5496 or (800) 393-JAWS. www.gatorland.com Admission: $13.00-$20.00.

Gatorland is home to thousands of alligators and crocodiles, some of which have appeared in movies, television shows and commercials. The 55-year old (plus) park combines a petting zoo, bird sanctuary, mini-water park, eco-tour and action-packed outdoor entertainment, including daily alligator wrestlin' shows. There's wet fun for young children at Lilly's Pad play area, and a train ride through the swamp can be a little thrill. They call themselves "Orlando's Best Half Day Attraction" and the "Alligator Capital of the World."

WORD SPRING DISCOVERY CENTER

Orlando - 11221 John Wycliffe Blvd. (southeast Orange Countynear Moss Park. SR 15 south of airport. Head southeast on Moss Park Rd. at the Wycliffe sign) 32862. Phone: (407) 852-3626 or (800) WYCLIFFE. www.wycliffe.org/wordspring Hours: Weekdays 9:00am-4:00pm. Also 1st and 3rd Saturday of each month 10:00am-4:00pm. Closed on New Years, Thanksgiving and Christmas. Admission: $6.00 adult, $5.00 senior (55+), $4.00 student (grades 1-12), $20.00 family. Miscellaneous: Lunch is served at the WordSpring Café from 11:30am-1:00pm.

The museum is full of hands-on exhibits, interactive media, games and video presentations focused on the history of the Bible, the world's languages, and the ongoing work of Bible translation. Visitors are able to write their feelings about the Bible on a large "graffiti scroll" or print their name in several languages. Create rubbings of the Hebrew ten commandments as well as John 3:16 from John Wycliffe's translation of 1384. Now, pretend you're a missionary, take your picture in virtual scenes from around the world, and send an electronic postcard to friends.

FANTASY OF FLIGHT

Polk City - 1400 Broadway Boulevard Southeast 33868. Phone: (863) 984-3500. www.fantasyofflight.com Hours: Daily 9:00am-5:00pm. Admission: $26.95 adult, $24.95 senior (60+), $13.95 child (5-12).

This aviation-themed museum invites guests to explore the romance and nostalgia of flight in self-guided "immersion" experiences that trace the history of aviation. The North Hangar displays part of the world's largest private collection of vintage aircraft. Daily tours include a recreated WWII bombing mission. Flight simulators, Back-Lot tours and open cockpit bi-plane rides are available. In "They Dared to Fly," you can see the human potential of achievement and struggle in the lives of airmen. Visitors can soar to new heights over in Fantasy of Flight's Great Balloon Experience - a tethered balloon ride.

CENTRAL FLORIDA ZOOLOGICAL PARK

Sanford (Lake Monroe) - 3755 NW US Hwy 17-92 (I-4 exit 104) 32747. Phone: (407) 323-4450. www.centralfloridazoo.org Hours: Daily 9:00am-5:00pm. Admission: $8.95 adult, $6.95 senior (60+), $4.95 (3-12). Closed Thanksgiving day and Christmas day.

Enter the enchanted, tropical world of the Central Florida Zoo, a relaxing, entertaining and educational experience for the entire family. Discover a world of animals from around the world within this intimate park nestled in the heart of Florida. Stroll along shaded, winding boardwalks and paths as you see classic elephants, search for elusive cheetahs (for $5.00 more, have an Encounter), appreciate the beauty of bright-faced mandrills and listen to the song of the kookaburra. Or dare to meet some of the world's most venomous reptiles and non-venomous snakes, lizards and frogs in the Herpetarium. See new animals like the rare Puerto Rican crested toads, endangered Amur leopards, venomous king cobra and colorful hyacinth macaws. The recently transformed Butterfly Sensory Garden incorporates touch, look, listen and smell stations, contrasting human and insect senses. Bird, bug, elephant and reptile feeding or educational demonstrations are held on weekends.

HIGHLANDS HAMMOCK STATE PARK

Sebring - 5931 Hammock Road (off US 27 on SR 634 (also known as Hammock Road), four miles west of Sebring) 33872. www.floridastateparks.org/highlandshammock/ Phone: (863) 386-6094. Hours: Daily 8:00am-sunset. Admission: $4.00 per vehicle for up to 8 people. Camping and equestrian fees.

An elevated boardwalk traverses this old-growth cypress swamp. For equestrians, there is an 11-mile, day-use trail. Picnicking is another popular activity as are ranger-guided tours of the park. Tram tours are a great way to understand the diversity of nature at the park. Highlands Hammock State Park's campsites are always in demand during the busy season. You can sleep late while the Barred owls serenade and wake to the White-tailed deer feeding a few campsites away. Enjoy walking the nature trails in silence, with only the birds singing or the cicadas buzzing. Take an evening walk around the Loop Drive and marvel over the multitudes of fire flies. Enjoy the cooling effects of the afternoon thunderstorms and the chorus of frogs that follows. Don't forget to stop at the Hammock Inn for a cool cone of Wild Orange soft serve ice cream, a tasty lunch, or the Friday night Fish Fry. While visiting, consider biking the county's multiuse path for a 14-mile bike ride around beautiful Lake Jackson. Bike or drive to either of the community parks on the lake for a cool dip or swim. Or consider visiting LAKE JUNE IN WINTER SCRUB STATE PARK in Lake Placid for a look at Florida Scrublands (12 miles south of Sebring, off US 27 & CR 621).

SILVER SPRINGS

Silver Springs - 5656 E. Silver Springs Blvd. (I-75 exit 352 east of Ocala on SR 40) 34488. Phone: (352) 236-2121. ***www.silversprings.com*** *Hours: Daily 10:00am-5:00pm. Admission: $33.00 adult, $30.00 senior (55+), $24.00 child (3-10). Add $3.00 for Wild Waters Waterpark. Good discount specials online.*

Silver Springs, famous for its Glass-Bottom Boat ride, encompasses the largest artesian limestone spring in the world. Start your day with this enchanting tour of 7 major parts of the spring. The glass-bottom allows everyone to see the changes in water color and wildlife below. Look for turtle, fish, movie props and hidden

See the underwater scenery that has amazed folks for over a century - the glass bottomed boat was invented here in 1878!

caves. The Lighthouse Ride combines a carousel and gondola ride with a telescoping outer tower that quietly rises 98 feet above Silver Springs. This ride is a good way to see an overview of the park. The Fort King River Cruise showcases Silver Spring's history through scenes on the riverbanks featuring period props, sound and even some funny living history characters. Guests encounter a working archeological dig site, homestead and a typical movie set representing the classic films and television shows that have been filmed at the park (ex. Tarzan). This tour is a nice, easy educational and historic overview of the creatures and Indians that once roamed this area. Other highlights include bear, alligator and crocodile exhibits (watch feeding at 2:30pm during summer months); a children's petting zoo; Jeep Safari; Lost River Voyage; animal shows; a historical museum; and headline concerts. All in all, relaxed fun - especially the boat rides - kids love 'em!

GLADES ADVENTURES

St. Cloud - *4715 Kissimmee Park Road (take Hwy. 192 Eastbound, 3 miles past the Florida Turnpike (exit 244) to Kissimmee Park Road, Turn Right. Located at the Lake Toho R.V. Resort) 34772. Phone: (407) 891-2222.* ***www.gladesadventures.com*** *Miscellaneous: Private 2 hour nighttime alligator trips (with spotlights) are available - best in hot summers. You'll look for the dozens of eyeballs reflecting the water-eerie - yes! Skinny Al's restaurant is on the property serving a refreshing break from tourist fare: fried gator, catfish, frog legs, burgers and chicken - Florida Swamp Style! If you're nice, a waiter might play a song for ya! Daily, 10:00am-5:00pm.*

Glades Adventures lies on scenic Lake Tohopekaliga with tens of thousands of acres of wilderness, cypress and oak hammocks and Spanish moss lining winding creeks, marshes and wetlands. Look for blue heron, cattle, turtle and, of course, the American alligator. The six passenger airboats are smaller so

they can access the hard-to-reach

areas of the glades or wander off to follow wildlife as your guide discovers them. Blaze through lilly pads, tall grasses and marsh! You will learn so much. The tours are one-hour long and cover a wide area (very educational). You'll love your air boat hair. Onsite is an interactive Alligator Nursery display, where kids and brave parents have the opportunity to actually handle a live baby alligator…if you dare! *(we did).*

Jenny holding a
baby 'gator

CYPRESS GARDENS

Winter Haven - *6000 Cypress Gardens Blvd. (I-4 west to exit 55, Hwy 27 south. Turn right at SR 540/Cypress Gardens) 33884. Phone: (863) 324-2111.* ***www.cypressgardens.com*** *Hours: Open daily 10:00am. Closing hours vary. Closed Christmas and Thanksgiving. A special sunrise service will be held on Easter, with a select area of the park opening for the day. Admission: Parking $7.00. $39.95 adult, $34.95 senior (55+) and juniors (3-9). Admission includes a second day free for six days following the park visit and admission to the waterpark. Miscellaneous: Night Magic, a 3-D laser and fireworks show lights the* *skies to music. They now give a few children free ski lessons each day, too. Theme weeks abound with added shows or discounts. Well worth a visit to their website each season to see what's new.*

Discover 38 exciting rides, including four roller coasters and the world's tallest spinning rapids ride (you slide and spin uncontrollably - fun). Hurricanes took their toll on quite a bit of Florida but one wooden structure remained unscathed

Something here for all ages!

by the fury of nature and The Hurricane ride stands ready for guests to challenge. Actually, it's one of those coasters that is classic, and very enjoyable (unlike a real hurricane). With other ride's names like Swamp Thing, Okeechobee Rampage, Storm Surge and Thunderbolt, you can just strap in and hang on. The Citrus Line Railroad carries passengers along a track that encompasses both Paradise Pier and Adventure Grove plus a narrated history of the Gardens including stops at Flagler and Pope Stations. For another view of the park, ride Sky Adventure up 16 stories in the air, overlooking a revolving 360 degrees of view. Enjoy concerts, daily shows (you'll love the Pirates side-splitting parody), Wings of Wonder tropical butterfly area, and a craftmen's village, too. And, what is most remembered from years gone by: the historic gardens, beautiful belles and the world-famous water ski shows and figure skating shows. Did you know the first water ski show was performed here in 1943? Lots of bare-footin' and Aquamaids beauty. Seasonally (Spring-fall) they have a nice waterpark called Splash Island featuring wave pools, waterslides and a children's area - a nice way to cool off around tons of water.

Wow...looks like fun!

SUGGESTED LODGING AND DINING

Orlando Area -

ALL STAR VACATION HOMES. Kissimmee. (office: 7822 West Irlo Bronson Highway) (888) 249-1779 or **www.allstarvacationhomes.com**. Whoever said, "There's no place like home..."? This place has thought of everything the family   needs for a great vacation. Most homes feature bedrooms decorated specifically for children. These bedrooms (along with all bedrooms) are equipped with a TV/VCR. All properties feature a DVD player, and a video game station with games in the main family areas. Estate, Luxury and Resort Homes are equipped with private pools and jacuzzis. Resort clubhouses have a movie theatre, game room, pool, basketball/tennis/ volleyball courts...everything a kid needs to relax and feel as if they're in a fun neighborhood. When choosing your property, guests can look at the exact home by viewing photos, floor plans, virtual tours, maps, availability calendars and amenities of each home - online! We love the fact that you know exactly what you're getting...no surprises! The properties are all located within 4 miles to the entrance to Disney World. Budget-wise, for the "home-like" amenities (compared to hotel rooms or suites) and the number of bedrooms, you may only spend $109.00 to $339.00 per night for 3-7 bedroom housing. Share that with another family or two and you're all set. Being able to eat some meals at "home" saves lots of money (the grocery store is close - in the AllStar office plaza) and having the ability to take a day off from touring the parks allows for relaxed "hanging out" options (we recommend every 3-4 days). Our Grandmas felt so comfortable in the kitchen they even made their famous cabbage rolls or spaghetti w/meat sauce. Everyone who stayed with us never wanted to leave!

NICKELODEON FAMILY SUITES BY HOLIDAY INN - Orlando. 14500 Continental Gateway (I-4 exit 67 east, SR 536, I mile). **www.nickhotel.com**. (407) 387-5437 or (866) GO2-NICK. This is the first Nick-themed hotel with 1-2 or 3-bedroom KIDSUITES with kitchenettes or kitchen/whirlpool (Nick at Nite suite). The 2-bedroom suite we tried can sleep a family of up to seven (six comfortably) and featured themes from stars of Nickelodeon shows (ex. Rugrats). The kids' bedroom includes bunk beds with a kidsize pullout sleeper bed or 2 twin beds, their own TV & DVD player, in-room game system and activity table and chairs. The parents' room has its own TV and vanity/work station. The cozy Family Room features a pullout sleeper, TV, Table w/chairs, and mini-kitchen. The rest of the property is what really makes this unique! In the Mall, guests have access to a convenience store, Food Court and a prize Arcade. At the Kids' Check-In Desk, kids sign in- just like mom and dad - as well as learn about daily scheduled entertainment programs (i.e. Bingo and karaoke). Nicktoons Café and the Buffet offer dining for lunch and dinner - kids 12 and under eat free from a special kids' menu. Everyone else in Orlando has Character Breakfasts, why not Nickelodeon? During Character Breakfasts, spend time eating off the buffet with favorite friends including Dora, Tommy or Chuckie. ($12.00 adult, $8.00 child (under 12). Studio Nick presents nightly family entertainment including live stage shows and Nick-style family activities. Now, outside, you have The Lagoon or The Oasis. Both are wet/dry playground areas including: sand play, snack bar, poolside contests, and water play structures. Water towers, slides, water jets, water basketball, lap pools and whirlpools abound. So colorful and cute – but high energy!

BAHAMA BREEZE - Orlando area. Along International Drive, one near Disney, the other near Universal. (407) 248-2499 or **www.bahamabreeze.com**. *"No worries...Mon"*. If the thought of escaping to the islands sounds like a great idea, then Bahama Breeze is the next best thing to the Caribbean. The menu features made-from-scratch favorites with an island twist. Jamaican-style marinated chicken is one of the best dishes. Fresh fish and seafood, pork and beef are on the menu, too. Portions are very generous, and for more moderate appetites, many appetizers are great for sharing or, you can order "light versions". Entrees start at about $10.00 and most menu items are priced below $20.00. The colorful setting reminiscent of a Caribbean resort, and the friendly, lively service really make this a fun family favorite "escape" eatery. Kids' menu (we recommend pizza).

MCDONALD'S - ORLANDO. Bistro locations. Most are within a few miles of I-4 and Universal Studios. **www.mcfun.com**. The Oerther's, the family owners of these very a-typical McDonald's, yes, gourmet McDonald's, starting making history years ago by operating the "Highest Volume McDonald's" in the USA which also became the "World's Largest Entertainment McDonald's." They hired a Corporate Chef to execute the Gourmet Taste additions to the menu. The staff makes regular fast-food fare but also wonderful Paninis, made-to-order pizzas, gourmet salads and soups, elegant desserts and specialty coffees. Obviously, they're the talk of the whole McDonald's system! For under $6.00, you can get a Quesadilla, Buffalo Chicken Panini, Eggs Benedict Panini, Kickin Crab Soup or Crème Brulee Cheesecake - from McDonald's - dine in or drive-thru! But food like that mostly appeals to the parents so they've added a few themes to make it interesting for the kids. There's a sports, safari, motorcycle or European theme - or, most especially, the World's Largest Entertainment & Playplace (Sand Lake Road location). This Playplace actually has pool tables, video games, slides and an arcade with prizes. Too cool!

MING COURT - 9188 International Drive (adjacent to the Rosen Plaza Hotel, just north of the Convention Center), Orlando. **www.ming-court.com**. (407) 351-9988. Ever try Dim Sum? Sushi? Lotus Leaf? Or, doesn't Lemon & Walnut Shrimp sound tempting? (Michele's favorite) All are wonderfully presented here (especially the color), but that's not the best part. The best part is their Kids Menu. For $5.95, children can enjoy kid-style versions of adult entrees like Chicken Tenders, BBQ Pork or Beef, or Tempura Shrimp served with Shrimp Chips, French Fries, Veggie Lo-Mein Noodles, Super Ming Dragon Mystery Dipping Sauce plus a Very Happy Fortune Cookie. It all comes in an adorable, large oriental box with compartments for each food item. While waiting for food - read the Legend of the Ming Dragon (on menu) or go out to the gardens and feed the Koi fish (you can purchase food from vending machine). School groups can arrange a meal to correspond with their Chinese or Asian curriculum. Staff wear authentic costumes and they have the kids do a dragon parade before lunch is served. Adult lunches ranged from $7.00-$12.00 and the service is prompt.

CLASSIC HOLIDAY VILLAS/ FAMILIES FIRST VACATION HOMES. Orlando area. (800) 373-8455 or **www.ClassicHolidayVillas.com** or **www.familiesfirst.com**. Check-in address: 215 Celebration Place, Suite 100. Bring your whole family - Vacation homes at Hotel Prices...really. Prices per night range from $100.00 for a condo to $300.00+ for a presidential level home (6-7 bedrooms) at peak rental times. Discounts are available off-season. Good for families with toddlers, the furnishings are comfortable and the nick-nacks minimal. You can save money by cooking some meals each day and taking turns with other members of your party - chillin', cookin' or cleaning up. The homes are in neighborhoods with sidewalks and many have playgrounds and sport courts. We especially love the screened-in pool areas (during winter months, we highly recommend paying for heated water in pool/ jacuzzi - otherwise, it just won't be enjoyable). Most homes have several TVs, some have one in every bedroom. Close to the theme parks yet so spacious you'll want to stay put at "home."

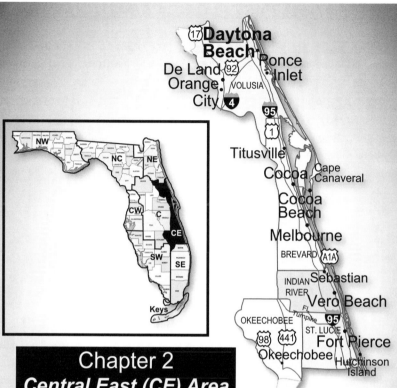

Chapter 2
Central East (CE) Area

Our Favorites...

* Chocolate Factory, Angell & Phelps, Daytona Beach
* Daytona USA & Speedway - Daytona Beach
* The Beach - Daytona Beach
* Trolley Boats - Daytona Beach
* FPL Energy Encounter - Hutchinson Island
* Blue Spring State Park - Orange City
* Ponce De Leon Inlet Lighthouse - Ponce Inlet
* Kennedy Space Center - Titusville
* McLarty Treasure Museum - Vero Beach

CENTRAL EAST FLORIDA BOAT TOURS

CENTRAL FLORIDA AIRBOAT TOURS - (407) 321-0753. $10.00-$20.00. Weekends 10:00am-sunset. **www.centralfloridaairboattours.com**. A 30-40 minute ride off Daytona Beach.

SUNNY DAZE AND STARRY NIGHT CRUISES - Docked at Aunt Catfish's Restaurant. (386) 253-1796. Drift through creeks and tributaries along the Halifax River. See pelicans, herons, egrets, manatee and dolphin. Captain Mark Sheets, a Daytona Beach native and avid environmentalist, will interpret any tour to take passengers on a dolphin chase or point out historical or ecological points of interest.

JUNGLE ADVENTURES

Christmas - 26205 East Highway SR 50 (7 miles west of Titusville, 17 miles east of Orlando) 32709. Phone: (407) 568-2885. www.jungleadventures.com Toll-free (877) 4-AGATOR. Hours: Daily 9:30am-5:30pm with 4 shows daily at 10:30am, 12:30pm, 2:30pm, and 4:20pm. Admission: $18.50 adult, $15.00 senior (60+), $9.50 child (3-11). Online coupon.

Jungle Adventures is a 20-acre park and wildlife sanctuary that has been in operation for over 30 years. Just look for "Swampy", the world's largest alligator sunning himself along side the road. Jungle Adventures is dedicated to "eco-tourism," a unique experience for close encounters with native wildlife. Each visitor has the option of enjoying the park at his or her own pace. You may spend as much time in the park as you prefer, however, the average stay is about three hours. They offer a wide variety of programs and tours dealing with Florida native history. The tours and shows each run four times a day, with no overlapping times so guests can be sure to enjoy each and every show at their leisure. Watch as huge alligators come to Feast at the Gator Feedings (their jaw power is a sight), take a relaxing ride on the Jungle Cruise, take a trip back in time through the Native American Village, hold a baby alligator in the Wildlife Show, and stroll through the park and see many animals including the endangered Florida Panther.

ASTRONAUT MEMORIAL PLANETARIUM AND OBSERVATORY

Cocoa - 1519 Clearlake Road (Brevard Community College campus) 32922. www.brevardcc.edu/planet/ Phone: (321) 433-7372. Showtimes: Wed. 2:00 and 3:00 pm, Friday - Saturday 7:00, 8:00 and 9:00pm. Call for additional times or check Web site. Admission: $7.00 adult, $6.00 senior/student, $4.00 child (under 12).

It's been called one of the world's most unique astronomical educational facilities. Features include a continuous schedule of planetarium shows, special "Iwerks" movie presentations and "Rock" Laser Shows. Spy comets crash on Jupiter, sneak a peek at the rings of Saturn and study the surface of Mars up to 450 million light years away at the planetarium with a signature 70-foot aluminum dome.

BREVARD MUSEUM OF HISTORY AND SCIENCE

Cocoa - 2201 Michigan Avenue (I-95, Exit 202 E. to Clearlake Rd. Turn W. on Michigan, proceed 1/2 mi. to museum) 32926. Phone: (321) 632-1830. **www.brevardmuseum.com** *Hours: Monday-Saturday 10:00am-4:00pm, Sunday Noon-4:00pm. Closed most major holidays. Admission: $3.50-$5.50 (ages 5+).*

The Brevard Museum of History & Science traces the area's history from the days of the wooly mammoths to space shuttles. See a simulation of an archaeological dig of the 7,000 plus year-old Windover burial site. It's a bizarre collection, including swarms of honeybees and Indian trading beads, reflecting the pioneering period of the Space Coast while 22 acres showcases three ecosystems and a butterfly garden outside. A hands-on science Discovery center complements them all.

ISLAND BOAT LINES

Cocoa Beach - 500 Cocoa Beach Causeway (Rte. 520) (on the Banana River) 32931. Phone: (321) 302-0544. **www.IslandBoatLines.com**

Three daily eco-tours on the "Miss Florida" and "Sunshine" pontoon boats depart from various locations throughout the Space Coast immersing visitors into the nature of the area while they glide alongside dolphin fins and manatee "footprints." A special trip through the Locks of Port Canaveral provides up-close excitement seeing the cruise and Navy ships, submarine base, Space Lab and US Coast Guard Station. Regardless of your choice, your family will have the opportunity to see herds of Manatees, flocks of Birds and playful Dolphins. Reservations are absolutely necessary.

CHOCOLATE FACTORY, ANGELL & PHELPS

Daytona Beach - 154 S. Beach Street 32114. **www.angellandphelps.com** *Phone: (386) 252-6531. Admission: FREE. Store Hours: Monday-Friday, 10:00am-5:30pm, Saturday 10:00am-5:00pm. Tours: Monday-Friday, 10:00am, 11:00am, 1:00pm, 2:00pm, 3:00pm & 4:00pm. Sorry, No tours on Saturdays.*

Free guided tours take visitors down a viewing hallway and behind the scenes of how chocolate candies are made from scratch and box shipped to chocolate lovers nationwide. The company was started in the 1920s (before air conditioning) by two women. Learn about their original recipes and see some original equipment.

Why do they use copper kettles for cooking? Folks especially are wowed looking at workers around the giant vats of caramel or spinning chocolate. Ever seen a chocolate waterfall?

DAYTONA CUBS BASEBALL

Daytona Beach - *32114. Phone: (386) 257-3172. www.daytonacubs.com*

The Daytona Cubs are the Chicago Cubs Class A affiliate in the Florida State League playing home games from April to September. Back in 1946, Jackie Robinson revolutionized modern baseball when he played his first training game with the Brooklyn Dodgers farm team, the Montreal Royals. In honor of this historical event, a bronze statue was erected at the entrance to the ballpark which bears his name.

DAYTONA USA & DAYTONA INTERNATIONAL SPEEDWAY

Daytona Beach - *1801 W. International Speedway Blvd. (I-95 exit 261 or I-4 exit 129) 32114. Phone: (386) 947-6800 or (386) 253-RACE.* *www.daytonausa.com Hours: Open daily 9:00am-7:00pm. Admission: $21.50 adult, $18.80 senior, $15.50 child (6-12). Speedway tours $8.50. Acceleration Alley $5.00 extra.*

...the famous banked curves

SPEEDWAY: The 2.5 mile super speedway lives up to its billing as the World Center of Racing as it is involved in some type of high-speed activity every day for more than four months of the year - from stock cars (Daytona 500 and Pepsi 500) and sports cars to motorcycles and go-carts. The new infield allows fans to stroll along the FAN ZONE with activities. The TRACK TOUR takes you along the bottom of the track. We wondered why they weren't taking us on the track. Did you know the track is banked 17 to 31 degrees - even at the start line? Imagine 4 story high asphalt walls that only hold cars on track if they're going 95 MPH or more! And, get a good look at the lake right in the middle of the track - stocked with fish. One stop on the tour is Victory Lane for photo ops.

DAYTONA USA: An interactive motorsports attraction designed to entertain and inform race fans about the history of motorsports in the Daytona Beach area. Especially fun for NASCAR fans. Included in the indoor attraction are opportunities for visitors to participate in a NASCAR Nextel Cup Series stock car pit stop; talk to favorite competitors (via video); take a walk through the history of Daytona Beach racing and play radio or television announcer by calling a race. Begin with a piece-by-piece breakdown of a NASCAR as the body, chassis and tires move apart to reveal all the precision parts - you don't just put in gas and go....The Great Moments video is worth a sit down to see stunning finishes. Racing simulator rides Acceleration Alley and Daytona Dreams laps are also "interactive fun" along with daily track tours and NASCAR 3D: The IMAX Experience presentation.

See the current winner...straight from Victory Lane!

MUSEUM OF ARTS AND SCIENCES

Daytona Beach - 352 S. Nova Road (I-95 exit 261, Rte. 92 east to Nova Rd. south) 32114. Phone: (386) 255-0285. **www.moas.org** *Hours: Monday-Saturday 9:00am-5:00pm, Sunday 11:00am-5:00pm. Admission: $12.95 adult, $10.00 senior, $6.00 child (6-17). Miscellaneous: There's a planetarium here, too.*

The site features a Center for Florida History that is home to a 13-foot tall, 130,000 year-old Giant Ground Sloth, which was found during a road excavation/ expansion project in 1974. The amazingly complete skeleton is considered one of the finest specimens of its kind in North America. You can't miss it as you're wowed turning the corner! The Family Museum has a huge collection of Teddy Bears and Coca-cola artifacts plus other fun displays. See displays on the invention of cola bottling and the first Coke to go to space. The giant teddy bears capture everyone's heart and the rail cars outside are exciting to look through. Children can make their own discoveries in the Children's Wing through interactive exhibits, games and activities in this area. Design a Picasso plate, play with the solar system, dinos, puzzles, and light. Make a new face, delay your speech or freeze your hand in the Science Corner. The Preserve Discovery Center allows visitors to follow a one mile network of boardwalk trails leading to interactive, outdoor exhibits. The museum is also renown for its multi-cultural exhibitions. The Cuban exhibit features great examples of modern Cuban art and the African Wing contains 165 objects from numerous African ethnic groups. Look for carved commemorative staffs, ritual ornaments, and 130 pieces of Ashante gold highlighting this collection of art.

SEASIDE MUSIC THEATER

Daytona Beach - *(News Journal Center) 32114. www.seasidemusictheater.org Phone: (386) 267-1520.*

The only professional music theater in the Southeastern United States which combines a pit orchestra with its productions like Beauty and the Beast or Jesus Christ Superstar. Summer and winter performances.

TINY CRUISE LINE

Daytona Beach - *425 S. Beach Street (Halifax Harbor Marina) 32114. Phone: (386) 226-2343. www.visitdaytona.com/tinycruise Admission: Waterway $10.00-17.00, Riverfront or Rivertown $7.00-$11.00.*

Dolphin, jumping fish and wading birds are close by as you quietly glide past islands and estates or delightful 1890s style fantail launch. The River is a treasure trove of timeless stories and beautiful sights, always changing, always entertaining, let them share it with you.

DAYTONA BEACH, THE BEACH

Daytona Beach - *250 N. Atlantic Avenue (Ocean Walk) 32118. Phone: (386) 257-5367.*

The beach is up to 500 feet wide at low tide and is perfect for castle building, cycling, fishing or just relaxing in the sun. While at the beach, watersports abound and rentals are everywhere. The Atlantic Ocean is perfect for swimming especially during spring and summer when temperatures range from 74-80 degrees. Visit the Boardwalk with its arcades, rides, the Clocktower and "Speeding Through Time" exhibit, and concerts at the open-air bandshell. All along Atlantic

Driving on the beach...too cool!

Avenue (www.volusia.org/parks) are public beachside parks, some with sport courts, fishing docks, spirting fountains, playgrounds and restrooms. On South Atlantic Avenue, there are many vehicle driving beach access points ($5.00 per day per vehicle). It is unbelievable to be driving on the sand, just several feet from the ocean! If you and your family can manage to tear yourselves away from the beach, walk over to OceanWalk. The area's newest shopping, dining and entertainment district, Ocean Walk Shoppes are family fun. Enjoy the 10-cinema theater complex and many new fun eateries like Bubba Gumps. Try their Hush Pups and any entrée that mentions spicy - so many flavors blended so well! Their fun environment, occasional Forrest Gump trivia and super wait staff really add to the motif. Prices are moderate for most dishes, a little higher for seafood and famous shrimp dishes but well worth the taste and portion size. Try one of their lemonades as a beverage. Across the street is Daytona Lagoon waterpark and amusement center (be careful with kids if a lot of teens are hanging out here – from our experience they may be too rowdy and rough on the rides).

TEAUILA'S HAWAII

Daytona Beach - *2301 S. Atlantic Avenue (Hawaiian Inn) (Rte 92 east to A1A south about 3 miles) 32118. Phone: (386) 255-5411 or (800) 922-3023.* **www.teauilashawaii.com** *Dinner Shows: 4-6 nights/ week. 6:30pm seating, 8:00pm show. Admission: $29.95 adult, $16.95 child (5-10). Show only $15.00.*

An authentic Hawaiian luau show features hula and fire knife dancers, a comedy act with audience participation, and an all-you-can-eat Luau Feast featuring exotic Polynesian dishes. Try tropical fruit, chowder, pepper steak, roast pork, lemon pepper chicken, mahi mahi, fried rice, stir fry veggies and desserts. They also have the area's only indoor volcano. Kids can hula and later the dads might get picked to volunteer to hula. The show is corny but lots of laughter. And, the whole show is done under black lights to really highlight the moves.

TROLLEYBOATS

Daytona Beach - *250 N. Atlantic Avenue, Kiosk #2 (Ocean Walk Shoppes) 32118.* **www.daytonatrolleyboattours.net** *Phone: (386) 238-3738.   Admission: $23.00 adult, $21.00 senior (60+), $17.00 youth (6-17) and $5.00 pre-schooler (age 3-5).*

These unique crafts seem like an ordinary trolley bus until your first mate explains that you are about to head into the River! Splash, as the pontoons fill with air and quickly convert the bus into a boat. Floating south on the waterway, your guide will tell you about aboriginal Indians and the days of the notorious hoodlums and millionaires. Cruising the Halifax River for the first 1/2 hour, you'll

Drive over a bridge...and then under a bridge on the water... Only in a "Trolleyboat"!

sight yachts, mansions and wildlife including dolphins and manatee (in season). Notice the hand-painted and installed mosaics on the bridge pylons. With wit and wisdom, they'll chronicle Cuban ties (like why the largest Cuban art collection outside of Havana is here?) and the birth of NASCAR, too. They speak of ancient treasure - there might still be some out there along the beach. As you come ashore, your guide takes you past the Riverfront Marketplace, the Chocolate Factory and the Daytona Cubs stadium in historical downtown. Finally, they drive past all the tourists right on the beach in a trolleyboat! Doesn't this sound like a hoot?

DE LEON SPRINGS STATE PARK

De Leon Springs - *(SR 92 from Daytona Beach to SR 17. Turn right to DeLeon Springs State Park) 32130. Phone: (386) 985-4212.* ***www.floridastateparks.org*** *Admission: Park charges $5.00 per car. Breakfast costs around $3.50-4.50 per person.*

The spring-run sugar mill at DeLeon Springs and its water wheel mechanism were built by Colonel Orlando Rees, the owner of the plantation in the late 1820s. There are many myths about the spring and its part in the story of Spanish explorer Ponce de Leon's search for the "fountain of youth," although there is no evidence that he visited here during his 1513 and 1521 explorations of Florida. The wheel has been reconstructed and the original chimney is still in use by the Sugar Mill Restaurant, known for its pancake breakfast and bakery. Children can make their own pancakes and add chocolate-chip, nut and fruit toppings at the park's Old Spanish Sugar Mill Grill & Griddle House. Order a batch of pancakes, french toast, or eggs, and cook them on the griddle right at your own table. Afterwards, work off your high carb breakfast swimming in the spring/swimming pool (located right outside the restaurant entrance). Outdoor fun includes a dip in the semi-warm natural spring, a canoe ride, or a nature walk through a floodplain forest.

DEBARY HALL HISTORIC SITE

Debary - *210 Sunrise Blvd. (I-4 exit 108 west on Dirksen Drive) 32713.* ***www.echotourism.com/debaryhall*** *Phone: (386) 688-3840. Hours: Tuesday-Saturday 10:00am-4:00pm, Sunday Noon-4:00pm. Admission: $1.00-$3.00 (age 5+).*

Once the retreat of the rich and famous, this public site now offers a window on the history of the St. John's River. The Visitors Center Imagidome Theater presentations recaps the history of the river and Debary's role in development. Trek along spring trails that traverse the river.

BERESFORD LADY TOUR BOAT

Deland - *1896 W. Beresford Road 32720. Phone: (386) 740-4100 or (888) 740-7523.* ***www.beresfordlady.net*** *Admission: $32.00-$37.00 adult, $25.00-$28.00 child (6-12).*

Tour the beautiful St. John's River and reminisce the old way of traveling the St. John's River or authentic Side Wheel Paddle Boat. Visit old Florida and relax to the sounds of the paddles churning. Delight in scenic views of undisturbed nature on picnic or dinner cruises.

HONTOON ISLAND STATE PARK

DeLand - 2309 River Ridge Road (located six miles west of Deland, off SR 44) 32720. Phone: (386) 736-5309. ***www.floridastateparks.org/hontoonisland/*** *Hours: Daily 8:00am-sunset. Admission: Tent and cabin fees vary.*

Hontoon Island State Park is a remote and rustic getaway along the St. John's River near Orange City in central Florida. Accessible only by boat or park operated ferry; Hontoon Island is 1,648 acres of solitude and tranquility. A single day can include a scenic hike around an island once home to an extensive village of pre-Columbian Native Americans, a kayak or canoe paddle, a picnic under the spreading Live Oaks, or some quiet time fishing from the banks of the historic St. John's River. Twelve tent sites and six rustic cabins in a shady setting are within easy walking distance of the river. A Visitor Center is open daily to tell the island's story. The park's ferry operates daily from 8:00 a.m. to one hour before sunset.

MANATEE OBSERVATION AND EDUCATION CENTER

Fort Pierce - 480 Indian River Drive, downtown (across from the Fort Pierce Utilities Power Plant) 34949. Phone: (772) 466-1600. Hours: Tuesday-Saturday 10:00am-5:00pm, Sunday 1:00-4:00pm (October-June). Admission: $1.00 donation per person.

The manatee is one of Florida's favorite residents. You can view these gentle giants and their offspring in a natural habitat protected here by the local community. Guests can also tour the butterfly garden, view a replica of a natural spring and climb an observation tower to look at the Indian River. Inside, there are aquariums, a digital lagoon tour and fish displays. Manatee were near extinct years ago. During the winter months, manatee seek out warm water in natural springs and outflows of power plants where they congregate in large numbers. With no natural enemies, loss of habitat is their biggest threat. Manatees generally only produce one calf every 3-5 years and the calf stays with the mother for its first two years (the reason you see many mother/child families). Mature manatees can grow up to 13 feet long and weigh 3500 pounds.

ST. LUCIE COUNTY MARINE CENTER

Fort Pierce - 420 Seaway Drive (east end of the PP Cobb Bridge on South Hutchinson Island in South Causeway Park) 34949. Phone: (772) 465-FISH. ***www.sms.si.edu/SMEE*** *Hours: Tuesday-Saturday 10:00am-4:00pm, Sunday Noon-4:00pm. Admission: $1-2.00.*

This center features the Smithsonian Marine Ecosystems Exhibit. Six living exhibits each feature a unique marine ecosystem: Caribbean coral reef, Oculina coral reef, sea grass, mangroves, as well as the fish and organisms found in these habitats. These exhibits are supported by aquariums ranging from 500 gallons to 3,000 gallons that showcase a microcosm of each ecosystem and animal life found in the lagoon and ocean. Can you find the hidden flatfish? What new juvenile species have joined the seagrass bed? As an erosion prevention educator, the exhibit displays the deep root system of the mangrove as well as a simulated tide cycle to demonstrate erosion prevention in action.

TREASURE COAST BEACHES

Fort Pierce - 34949. Phone: (800) 344-TGIF. www.visitstluciefla.com or www.floridas tateparks.org/fortpierceinlet/

Located in the heart of Florida's Indian River Citrus district, St. Lucie County is known as the Grapefruit Capital of the State. Comprising Fort Pierce, Port St. Lucie, and Hutchinson Island, visitors to the area find spectacular barrier islands boasting 21 miles of beautiful beaches, some of the best surf and deepwater fishing in the State, and centuries-old shipwrecks which attract divers from around the world. Beach access is about every mile (ex. AVALON STATE PARK). One can spend the morning fishing, swimming, snorkeling, or horseback riding on the beach and the afternoon at attractions in the area. Nature lovers love the many parks and recreation areas which offer a diversity of wildlife from river otters to bird watching. Shorebirds are best observed at FORT PIERCE INLET at low tide, and Jack Island, which allows only foot traffic, is best known for birding in the early morning or late evening. One of the most unique wilderness spots is Savannas State Preserve, the last freshwater lagoon system existing in the State of Florida.

UDT/SEAL (FROGMAN) MUSEUM

Fort Pierce - 3300 N Highway A1A, North Hutchinson Island 34949. Phone: (772) 595-5945. www.navysealmuseum.com Hours: Tuesday-Saturday 10:00am-4:00pm, Sunday Noon-4:00pm. Mondays (January - April only). Admission: $6.00 adult, $3.00 child. (6-12)

Located on the same beach where the first U.S. Navy Frogmen trained in 1943, this museum serves as a tribute to the Navy's underwater demolition teams of World War II and the present Navy Sea, Air and Land Teams (SEALS) displaying many artifacts from Navy combat missions. View uniforms and diving gear indoors but outdoors is the fun place for kids. Maybe a dozen military vehicles are along the long entrance walkway and yard. Look for boats or a Huey helicopter - many very stealth looking for secret missions. How long can a Frogman hold his breath? What training does it take and how special is it be one of this elite force?

FPL ENERGY ENCOUNTER

*Hutchinson Island - 6501 South Ocean Drive (A1A), Jensen Beach (on South Hutchinson Island between Ft. Pierce & Stuart at St. Lucie Nuclear Power Plant) 34983. Phone: (772) 468-4111 or (877) FPL-4FUN.   **www.FPL.com/encounter** Hours: Sunday-Friday 10:00am-4:00pm. Closed Saturdays and Major Holidays. Admission: FREE Miscellaneous: Turtle Walks every Friday night in June and July. Educational lecture at dark, followed by a night-time walk on Hutchingson Island to witness turtles lay their eggs.*

You walk in and are greeted by the pirate parrot "Hutch." Hutch invites you on an Energy Treasure Hunt (be sure to get your treasure hunt swipe card). The parrot directs you through the hands-on displays that explore the wonders of energy. How do we get electricity? In the 30 interactive displays, you take a self-guided tour of exhibits. See a model of the containment building of nuclear reactors of the St. Lucie plant and even be in command on the controls as you raise and lower the control

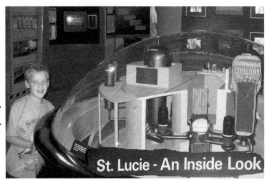

....so nuclear

rods of a simulated reactor. Kids can simulate splitting the atom, play computer games, generate electricity on a treadmill and play with a huge, enclosed Energy Roller Coaster. Watch a cute movie entitled "The Amazing Chain Reaction" which uses cartoon dominos to show how nuclear energy is formed. Visitors can also walk next door to Turtle College. View dioramas of giant turtle moms nesting and baby turtles hatching. "This place is so cool" was the comment from our kids -an excellent nuclear energy unit study - for credit - or just for fun. We all learned something new.

SAVANNAS PRESERVE STATE PARK

*Jensen Beach - 9551 Gumbo Limbo Lane 34957. **www.floridastateparks.org/savannas/** Phone: (772) 398-2779.   Hours: Daily 8:00am-sunset.   Miscellaneous: The Education Center is located in Port St. Lucie, two miles east of US 1 on Walton Road.*

Freshwater marshes or "savannas" once extended all along Florida's southeast coast. Stretching more than 10 miles from Ft. Pierce to Jensen Beach, this preserve is the largest and most intact remnant of Florida's east coast savannas. A good place for visitors to start is the Environmental Education Center where they can learn about the importance of this unique and endangered natural system. Picnic tables are available near the center. Canoeing, kayaking, and fishing in the wetlands are popular activities. Over eight miles of multi-use trails provide opportunities for hiking, bicycling, and horseback riding. When they have ample rain and the marsh is chock full of life, canoe and kayak programs, offered on Wednesdays and Sundays, will usually be sold out. When there is drought, the marsh dries up and life changes drastically for its usual residents. Visitors can finally use the 12-mile trail system without getting their feet wet. Guided walks and canoe trips are available by reservation.

BREVARD ZOO

Melbourne - 8225 N. Wickham Road (just east of exit 191 off I-95) 32940. Phone: (321) 254-WILD. www.brevardzoo.org Hours: Daily 9:30am-5:00pm - No admissions after 4:15. Admission: $9.95 adult, $8.95 senior (60+), $6.95 child (2-12). Miscellaneous: Brevard Zoo is handicapped accessible with wheelchair & stroller rentals. FREE parking, snack bar, gift shop, picnic tables.

The only zoo in the United States with on-site kayaking and an educational Zoo School, the Brevard Zoo includes a 7,000 square foot educational complex "Paws On," "Animal Encounters" and "Wild Side Zoo tours." Newer exhibits, like "Expedition Africa" place guests in the wilds of Africa during nose-to-nose meetings with exotic animals. Here, you can hand-feed giraffes, kayak through the man-made river, ride the train through a lush savanna or explore an aviary of African and Australian birds. Up close to the giraffe, you'll notice their gorgeous brown eyes with glamorous lashes, a wet nose and a long faded purple-pink tongue. Alligator and Crocodile demonstrations are at 3:30pm every Wednesday, Friday, and Sunday and can be seen from the bridge to Wild Florida. River Otter feedings are at 2:00pm every Tuesday and Saturday at the otter habitat in Wild Florida.

SEBASTIAN INLET STATE PARK

Melbourne Beach - 9700 South A1A 32951. www.floridastateparks.com Phone: (321) 984-4852. Hours: Daylight hours. Fishing Museum: Daily 10:00am-4:00pm. Admission: Park admission is $3.25 per vehicle, museum is free.

Sebastian Inlet State Park offers an adventure back into Florida history, to the days of Spanish treasure fleets. The Inlet and the surrounding waters provide excellent fishing, shrimping and clamming. Manatees may be seen off the jetty, and migrating whales appear in the ocean seasonally. In summer, sea turtles nest here. Catwalks under the Inlet bridge as well as two jetties offer easy fishing. This state park is one of the best surfing sites on Florida's Atlantic coast. Three miles of ocean beach are designated for swimming, surfing, snorkeling and scuba diving (for current conditions check: **www.glgs.org**). Adjacent to the beach picnic area is the park concession. The park marina rents canoes, kayaks and power boats. Ecotours of the Indian River, aboard a 49-passenger boat, are offered daily for a fee. Many campsites and nature trails wind through the property.

SEBASTIAN FISHING MUSEUM - commemorates three of Sebastian's early families that operated fish houses. Inside the museum, you'll find a replica of an original fish house and dock, a homemade fishing boat, nets, fishing gear and photos of fishing in the Indian River Lagoon. The site shows a 24-minute video about fish and wildlife with the Lagoon.

KISSIMMEE PRAIRIE PRESERVE STATE PARK

Okeechobee - 33104 NW 192 Ave. (25 miles northwest of Okeechobee via U.S. 441 and County Road 724) 34972. www.floridastateparks.org/kissimmeeprairie/ Phone: (863) 462-5360. Hours: Daily 8:00am-sunset.

While driving the five-mile-long road into the park, visitors can enjoy sweeping vistas of grasslands reminiscent of the Great Plains of the Midwest. The park offers excellent seasonal birding opportunities and is home to the endangered Florida grasshopper sparrow, as well as the crested caracara and sandhill crane. Over 110 miles of dirt roads allow hikers, bicyclists, and equestrians to explore prairies, wetlands, and shady hammocks. Ranger-led swamp buggy tours take visitors to remote areas of the park. For overnight stays, the park has full-facility and equestrian campgrounds.

BLUE SPRING STATE PARK

Orange City - (I-4 Orange City exit) 32763. Admission: $5.00 per carload to enter park grounds. Miscellaneous: Visitors can enjoy camping, hiking, fishing, boating, too.

Nature lovers can get an up-close-and-personal view of Florida's manatee population here. The age-old Blue Spring maintains a constant temperature of 72 degrees year-round. Every winter, endangered Florida manatees flock to the warm Blue Spring waters, and park rangers keep track of them so well they can tell children who's who. The park features elevated wooden boardwalks right up to, and around, the wildlife (including fantastic bird, alligator and turtle sightings, too). There is a great film and Q&A session about manatees; a historical log home to tour; hikes and picnicking make for a great day in the outdoors. Some bring their boats and practically glide alongside creatures big and small!

TOMOKA STATE PARK MOUNDS AND MIDDENS

Ormond Beach - 2099 North Beach Street 32174. www.floridastateparks.org/tomoka Phone: (386) 676-4050. Hours: Daily 8:00am-sundown. Museum hours are 9:30am-4:30pm. Admission: $4.00 per vehicle. Miscellaneous: just 2 miles north of the state park lies Dummett Sugar Mill Ruins, these ruins are of what is believed to be the first steam-powered sugar mill in Florida. (free admission)

This site was once the site of the Timucuan Indian Village of Nocorocco. It later became the Mount Oswald Plantation in 1766. Today, the 1,540-acre park offers camping, fishing, nature trails, picnic areas, a boat launch and canoe rentals for access to Tomoka River. The Museum features artifacts and exhibits about the largest archaeological site of burial mounds and shell middens from early Central East Florida Native American settlements. The remains of Fort McCrea (in the area of Tomoka State Park) are known as the ADDISON BLOCKHOUSE. The blockhouse, manned by South Carolina militia men, was made to guard the Carrickfergus plantation. A skirmish occurred in early 1836 and when the militia men barely survived they soon abandoned the fort. The old blockhouse can be visited, but one has to bushwhack through the woods a bit.

MARINE SCIENCE CENTER

Ponce Inlet - 100 Lighthouse Drive (south on S. Atlantic Ave / CR 4075 into Ponce Inlet. Right on Harbour Village, left on S. Peninsula, left on Lighthouse) 32127. Phone: (386) 304-5545. Hours: Tuesday-Saturday 10:00am-4:00pm, Sunday Noon-4:00pm. Admission: $1.00-$3.00 (age 5+).

Come visit the turtle hospital...

This Center opened to provide an innovative learning experience where visitors can discover, enjoy and appreciate the many wonders of marine science. The Center houses a wet/dry classroom and lab, gift shop, a sea turtle rehab facility, and a 5,000 gallon artificial reef aquarium, as well as interactive displays on mangroves and whales. Look for science drawers and microscopes. Can you find the guitar fish? How about the psychedelic fish and "Dory" Tang fish in the coral reef? Probably the best part - the turtle rehab tanks are so interesting. Profiles of each rescued turtle help you learn more about their problems surviving our modern world. A boardwalk and nature trail system extends throughout the park allowing for wildlife and habitat observation.

PONCE DE LEON INLET LIGHTHOUSE

Ponce Inlet - 4931 S. Peninsula Drive (US 1 or I-95 to Port Orange exit. East on Dunlawton to Atlantic Ocean, then south six miles) 32127. Phone: (386) 761-1821. www.ponceinlet.org Hours: Daily 10:00am-6:00pm (fall/winter) and 10:00am-9:00pm (summer). Admission: $5.00 adult, $1.50 child.

This is a fine example of a restored maritime museum. Standing 175 feet tall, this lighthouse is the second tallest in the U.S. and the tallest in Florida. Complete with its original lighthouse keeper buildings, it is the only lighthouse in Florida that is recognized as a National Historic Landmark. Begin in the woodshed which is now the video room. The museum houses many nautical artifacts, educational exhibits and a rare Fresnel Lens exhibit. The staff

203 steps to the top - inside it looked like a giant snail shell...

here are known as Fresnel Lens expert restorers. Running the lighthouse was a family job. The kids had to take a boat to the nearest school. An invigorating (yet nice-paced - a landing is on every 22 steps) climb to the top of the 203 steps is rewarded with breathtaking views of the area's coastline. On a clear day, you can see all the way to Cape Canaveral. To commemorate your visit, make time to scour their wonderful gift shop for souvenirs.

SUGAR MILL BOTANICAL GARDENS

Port Orange - 950 Old Sugar Mill Road 32121. www.dunlawtonsugarmillgardens.org Phone: (386) 767-1735. Hours: Daily dawn to dusk, basically 8:00am-6:00pm. Admission: FREE

Stroll amid 12 acres of dense botanical gardens surrounding the ruins of a 19th century English sugar mill. The gardens are also home to 40-year old dinosaur statues erected when the site was known as the Bongoland amusement park. Check out the human sundial - when standing on the sundial, visitors can determine the time of day by their own shadow.

OXBOW ECO-CENTER

Port St. Lucie - 5400 NE St. James Drive   34983. Phone: (772) 785-5833. www.stlucieco.gov/erd/oxbow Hours: Tuesday-Friday 1:00-5:00pm, Saturday 10:00am-5:00pm and Sunday Noon-5:00pm. Admission: FREE

Oxbow Eco-Center offers a rare glimpse of "the real Florida" - a place where geologic history comes alive walking the boardwalk trails of floodplain forest, sandy soils, pine flatwoods and ancient swamps and wetlands. Once a month, they offer Family Nature programs that feature different aspects of the miles of boardwalk, bridges, observation towers and informational kiosks winding through nature without disrupting it. Most all of the property offers self-guided walks, too.

MEL FISHER'S TREASURE MUSEUM

Sebastian - 1322 US 1 32958. Phone: (772) 589-9875.   www.melfisher.com Hours: Monday-Saturday 10:00am-5:00pm, Sunday Noon-5:00pm.   Admission: $6.50 adult, $5.00 senior, $2.00 child (age 5+).

Mel Fisher and family became famous when they became treasure hunters. Mel spent most of the 1990s successfully salvaging the 1715 Fleet, which sank off the Treasure Coast. They then moved towards Key West in search of the Atocha, a 1622 shipwreck estimated to be worth 400 million dollars. Mel's daughter, Taffi, wanted to relocate here and start a museum. The site now houses a working conservation laboratory and museum which displays a vast array of artifacts salvaged from the Atocha, the local 1715 shipwrecks, and other shipwrecks. A window from the museum overlooks the lab so visitors can view ongoing conservation of newly salvaged artifacts before they are displayed in the "recent recoveries" case. View a video presentation featuring Mel's expeditions, too.

RIVER QUEEN CRUISES

Sebastian - 1606 Indian River Drive (1590 US 1) (depart Capt. Hiram's Marina, 2 miles north of SR 510 off US 1) 32958.   Phone: (772) 589-6161.   Admission: $18.00-$22.00 adult, $12.00 child (3-9). Small discount for seniors.

Captain Kathleen welcomes you aboard the River Queen taking you on a journey into the Treasure Coast's scenic waterways. The whole way out and back, you are treated to lots of eco-facts. Every creature sighting includes a run-around watch by all sides of the boat. Learn about pirates and gangs on the water years ago.

Watch the playful antics of resident dolphin and manatee on one cruise (10:00am *Manatee & Dolphin Watch*). The Captain guarantees she'll find a pod of the gentle creatures and they gently maneuver the boat so that you can watch them cavort in the water. Often, you'll see pods (families) working as a team to catch fish for breakfast. Cruise the Sebastian Inlet where the ocean meets the Indian River and around the state park's tidal pool and campground. (Daily except Sunday, 2 - 2½ hours long) The 1:00pm *Sebastian River Cruise* takes you along the narrow banks of the jungle river where you might encounter alligators, turtles, raccoons, dolphins and a wide variety of water fowl. Manatees seek out the warm, shallow waters of the Sebastian River during cooler months and often surface next to the boat. (Daily, 2.5 to 3 hours). The 4:30pm *Pelican Island Cruise* takes you to Pelican Island, the first National Wildlife Refuge in America, where thousands of birds roost, particularly in winter (peak months are November-March). (Daily, 1 1/2 hours).

FOREVER FLORIDA / CRESCENT J RANCH

St. Cloud - 4755 N. Kenansville Road (US 192 to Holopaw, and turn south on US 441. Drive seven and one-half miles, and Forever Florida will be on the east (left) side of the highway) 34773. Phone: (888) 957-9794. www.floridaecosafaris.com Admission: Varies greatly by day of week, overnight, or activities.

Travel a bit west of Melbourne to "Forever Florida" and the Crescent J Ranch, a 4,700 acre cattle ranch and nature preserve. Enjoy a guided elevated coach tour aboard a customized 4-wheel-drive vehicle through prehistoric ecosystems such as wet and dry savannahs, flatwoods, creeks and hammocks. Or, ride in covered wagons behind mules or Belgian horses as the first Floridians did. You may see alligator, otter, gray fox, deer, a bald eagle or two, vultures, hawks - maybe even a caracara or a whooping crane. See how Native Americans and early settlers used the various plants to cure common ailments and learn how these ecosystems are nurtured and protected by fire, flood and drought (commentary by experienced guides). Now that you've built up an appetite, fill up on home-cooked vittles in the beautiful cypress Visitor Center restaurant. The rocking chairs on the veranda overlooking a wildlife pond are tempting to nap off the big meal. That evening, take an overnight trail ride through the wilderness and sleep in their Indian-style, thatched-roof "chickee" for a truly unique and unforgettable overnight.

FLORIDA OCEANOGRAPHIC COASTAL CENTER

Stuart - 890 NE Ocean Blvd. (located on Hutchinson Island across from Stuart Beach) 34996. Phone: (772) 225-0505. www.floridaoceanographic.org Hours: Monday-Saturday 10:00am-5:00pm, Sunday Noon-4:00pm. Admission: $8.00 adult, $4.00 child (3-12).

The 750,000-gallon Game Fish Lagoon, aquariums, touch tanks, stingray tank, and children's activity pavilion with interactive exhibits on mammals, sea turtles, manatees, animal tracks, and a discovery table complete the multitude of hands-on tables and tanks here. Plan your visit during the daily stingray feedings, guided nature walks and boat tours.

AMERICAN POLICE HALL OF FAME & MUSEUM

Titusville - 6350 Horizon Drive (I-95 exit 215. East on SR50 to SR405. SR405 east. or US1 to SR405 east) 32780. Phone: (321) 264-0911. **www.aphf.org** *Hours: Daily 10:00am-6:00pm. Closed major holidays. Admission: $12.00 adult, $8.00 senior & child (age 4+). Law enforcement FREE.*

The Nation's first museum, attraction and memorial honoring all police. This educational attraction offers thousands of items on display such as a crime scene, gas chamber, electric chair and a forensics learning area and several interactive displays. Walk through Auto Alley (from scooters to the future); Wild West stockade; Crime Lab -DNA, fingerprinting and composite drawing; Crime & Punishment area with a real jail cell; and the Kids Discovery and Dress-up area where you try on uniforms and then design your own badge. Other photo opportunities include sitting on police motorcycles or the backseat of a squad car, a jail cell chair, and even Daddy or Mommy sized dress up clothes. Kids who love reading detective novels will engage here! Kids who are a little mischievous might straighten up!

VALIANT AIR COMMAND WARBIRD MUSEUM

Titusville - 6600 Tico Road 32780. Phone: (321) 268-1941. **www.vacwarbirds.org** *Hours: Daily 9:00am-5:00pm. Admission: Adults $12.00 adult, $10.00 senior & active military, $5.00 child (12 and under).*

More than 35 vintage war planes, including Flying Tigers and C-47 Transports, are maintained in top flight condition as tours breeze by eras of military aviation form Sopwith Camel bi-plane days through the P-51 Mustang hardships of World War II.

MERRITT ISLAND NATIONAL WILDLIFE REFUGE

Titusville - State Route 402 (3.5 miles east of town) 32782. Phone: (321) 861-0667. **www.fws.gov/merrittisland/**

The refuge, which shares a common boundary with the Kennedy Space Center, contains more than 500 species of animals (including 21 listed as endangered or threatened). You can find both freshwater and saltwater environs…even sand dunes. The best times to visit the refuge are winter, spring and fall. November is peak bird watching season as white pelicans and peregrine falcons migrate along the coast. Look for Loggerhead sea turtles nesting in May and bald eagles return each September. While you watching, make plans to hike a trail, paddle a canoe or watch for manatees.

SPACE COAST NATURE TOURS

Titusville - Titusville Municipal Marina, 451 Marina Rd, Slip A-23 (Exit off of US 1 on to Marina Rd) 32796. Phone: (321) 267-4551. ***www.spacecoastnaturetours.com*** *Miscellaneous: Shuttle Launch tours when appropriate. Want a natural marine show? Try their seasonal Bioluminesce tours (summer weekend nights). The warm water lights fish like fluorescent mini-light bulbs or fireworks in the water. What a light show - all natural.*

Nestled next to Merritt Island National Wildlife Refuge, the "Skimmer" cruises on the Indian River Lagoon, where dolphins play, eagles soar and alligators lurk. River views of NASA'S massive shuttle assembly building and the towering launch pads uncover the refuge that coexists with the only place in the United States where man is launched into space. You'll get to be the captain for a while. Once you spot some dolphins, you can actually listen to them with an underwater microphone. Why do marine life make sound? The captain and crew are super friendly.

KENNEDY SPACE CENTER VISITOR COMPLEX

Titusville (Merritt Island/Cape Canaveral) - State Route 405 32922. Phone: (321) 449-4444. www.KennedySpaceCenter.com Hours: Opens daily at 9:00am. Closing times vary according to season. Closed Christmas and certain launch days. Admission: Maximum Access Admission is $38.00 adult, $28.00 child (3-11). Other admission packages with fewer add-ons are less expensive. Miscellaneous: Before or after your guided tour, you'll

want to check out the many scheduled programs on site. Maybe take in a space IMAX film or an Astronaut Encounter where you come face-to-face with a real astronaut every day during a half-hour, interactive Q&A session. Fork out some extra bucks ($16.00-$23.00) and have an eventful and yummy Lunch with an Astronaut. Ask a real astronaut what life in space is like. What do your senses experience after lift off - some describe it as a train

Have lunch with a real astronaunt!

wreck! Begin with an excellent buffet and video showing the real life experience of a typical day in space. Our kids reaction after the photo op - "I can't believe I met a real astronaut!"

Kennedy Space Center Visitor's Complex (cont.)

A space theme park - not with rides, but with many visual and 3D attractions. A must-see experience, this tour can begin or end as guests go on a narrated, video-supplemented bus tour of Kennedy Space Center. While traveling to launch pads and rockets, you might see a shuttle being moved to its launching pad. The first stop is the Observation Gantry, where guests enjoy a panoramic view of Kennedy Space Center and the Space Shuttle launch pads, as well as the

...gonna take a ride across the moon...you and me...

rocket launch pads at Cape Canaveral Air Force Station. Buses then drive by the Vehicle Assembly Building (VAB) where the Space Shuttle is stacked for launch, as well as the Orbiter examination area. The second stop is the Apollo/Saturn V Center. Begin in the giant theme-park atmosphere of a simulated mission control room. In the final moments of the presentation, with exhilaration, the Shuttle jets off with a huge powerful thrust. You walk out and behold a marvelous scene. Just to stand beneath the 36-story Saturn V moon rocket invites awe and it's a blast walking through re-creations of modules used as part of the International Space Station. A great souvenir is the photo opportunity shot of weightlessness (additional fee, but sure worth the curiosity it invokes). Want to feel a more extreme simulation? Try The Shuttle Launch Experience (open 2007). Using a custom-designed motion platform as well as multiple video screens, advanced audio effects and special effect seats, the attraction promises to re-create the sensations of blasting into earth's orbit. Back at the main center, the ever-popular Rocket Garden is outdoors featuring several rockets from the past and "climb-in" Mercury, Gemini and Apollo capsule replicas. What are Robot Scouts? Meet the fun robots who take you through a simulated training program assignment with the first to explore new space - robots. The adorable Mad Mission to Mars is 35 minutes of quizzes, antics and aliens! A super kid-friendly live space show and kids (and parents) get to be volunteers. Through all the fun, you'll actually learn about air, gravity and thrust. This was our favorite way to learn about space.

PELICAN ISLAND NATIONAL WILDLIFE REFUGE

Vero Beach - 510 Wabasso Causeway (southern end of Archie Carr Wildlife Refuge) 32960. Phone: (772) 562-3909. www.fws.gov/pelicanisland/

Designated as the first National Wildlife Refuge by President Theodore Roosevelt, the waters and wetlands of Pelican Island National Wildlife Refuge form a complex ecosystem. Over 90 species of birds live within the refuge (including, of course, pelicans!). West Indian manatee, green sea turtle and loggerhead sea turtle. Other wildlife include raccoon, bobcat, marsh rabbit, opossum, river otter, dolphins and many varieties of neotropical and resident songbirds. Visitors are welcome to enjoy year-round bird watching, guided boat tours, kayaking, canoeing and sport fishing within the waters of the lagoon. An observation tower is now available to the public for "birds-eye" viewing from the Centennial Trail boardwalk.

ENVIRONMENTAL LEARNING CENTER

Vero Beach - 255 Live Oak Drive (on Wabasso Island between Vero & Sebastian along the Indian River Lagoon) 32963. Phone: (772) 589-7723. www.elcweb.org Hours: Tuesday-Friday 10:00am-4:00pm, Saturday 9:00am-Noon (extended to 4:00pm in winter), Sunday 1:00-4:00pm. Admission: FREE. Most excursions require a small fee, indoor programs are generally free.

This non-profit nature center on a 51-acre island site develops programs and activities to encourage discovery of nature. They use hands-on exhibits and elevated boardwalks for nature strolls; eco-excursions such as Family birding trips via pontoon boat, wagon rides in a preserve, beach walks; Lagoon Nights sleepovers and weekly canoe excursions. Kids can touch mystery boxes, make bird tracks, try to be an ibis digging for sand crabs, or identifying dozens of birds, seashells and coral. Often, Junior Interpreters are standing by in the Wet Lab exhibit area with a scavenger hunt, live hermit crabs, and other nature activities. Did you know near the high tide watermarks is where you'll find the most interesting treasures? A walk out to the lagoon may warrant a dolphin sighting. On your way onto the boardwalk, take a gander at the giant surprises sitting under the Wet Lab. What will the Gulf Stream bring up next?

MCLARTY TREASURE MUSEUM

Vero Beach - 13180 North A1A (5 miles north of rte. 510 and 20 miles south of rte. 192, at Sebastian Inlet State Park) 32963. www.atocha1622.com/mclarty.htm Phone: (772) 589-2147. Hours: Daily 10:00am-4:30pm (last video shows 3:15-4:00). Admission: $1.00 per person. Miscellaneous; The observation deck outside is shaped like one of the wrecked ships - very clever and adventuresome feelings surface in this environment. Our guys became instant treasure hunters-nothing big yet!

The McLarty Treasure Museum is located on the actual site of the 1715 Spanish Plate Fleet salvaging camp (look for a diorama that visually explains this through the reading of a crew member's journal). From the 1500s to the early 1700s, Spanish explorers mined or stole vast amounts of silver and some gold in the mountains of Mexico and South America. These precious metals were made into coins and ingots and then brought back to Spain in wooden sailing vessels. The fleet encountered a large hurricane along Florida's coast and sank on the shoals between Cape Canaveral and Stuart. In the early 1960s, the wrecks were rediscovered and salvage operations began. The video explains much of this and certainly engages your curiosity. The artifacts the crews recovered are on display including gear from the galleons, weapons and TREASURE! Now that you're trained in what to look for - go out and explore those beaches - people still find treasure washed up on a weekly basis!

RIVERSIDE CHILDREN'S THEATRE

Vero Beach - 3280 Riverside Park Drive 32963. www.riversidetheatre.com Phone: (772) 234-8052.

RCT creates an environment of joy for the theatre for young people. The Pro Series brings the best children's theatrical companies to their stage. About five local shows and 3 professional shows appear on the calendar each year. Look for fun programs like Winnie the Pooh or Stuart Little. (Tickets run $7.00-$8.00).

SUGGESTED LODGING AND DINING

RON JON RESORT CAPE CARIBE - 1000 Shorewood Drive, **Cape Canaveral** (A1A exit South ports). (321) 799-4900 or **www.ronjonresort.com**. Immerse yourself in a Caribbean setting suited to families. A beach and water lifestyle theme is seen throughout the complex. Rooms and spacious suites are decorated with tones of green, orange and yellow...and bright. We loved the large kitchen table - booth style. All suite units come with a full kitchen and utensils. Bring your own food, coffee, etc. or try the Surf Grill with casual caribbean gourmet selections - most everything grilled. One warning, once you start roaming the property, be aware that your kids are not going to want to leave the property to site-see. From the surfing mini-golf, pool, Lazy River, waterslide, children's outdoor playground, to the unique rooftop basketball and tennis courts. And, that's just outdoors. Indoors, look around the corners and plan some playtime Children's Play Center (giant soft play), a video arcade and 50+ seat movie theatre with selections shown nearly all day. Still want more activity? Activities are planned for families all day, every day beginning at 10:00 or 11:00am. From Surfing lessons, scavenger hunts, dance lessons, beach theme bingo, musical chairs and crafts to fee-paid Pen Pals supervised crafts, munchies, pizza and movie nights.

BEST WESTERN AKU TIKI - 2225 South Atlantic Avenue, **Daytona Beach**. (800) 258-8554 or (386) 252-9631 or **www.bwakutiki.com**. Directly on the ocean, overlooking the miles of soft-white sand on the "World's Most Famous Beach", the Best Western Aku Tiki Inn is the affordable, ideally located beach family resort. It is on the quiet strip of shops and eateries and many room's patios face the ocean. All rooms have mini-frig and microwaves and some have kitchenettes. Most rooms have two queen beds. Winter rates hover just over $100.00. They have a large outdoor pool, kiddie pool, sport courts and ping-pong table facing the ocean. Just one half mile down the road is vehicle or bicycle beach access - yes, the sand is hard enough to drive on and most certainly bike on (during low tide only, a $5.00 all day vehicle pass is needed for car driving).

BUBBA GUMP SHRIMP COMPANY - Ocean Walk Shoppes, 250 North Atlantic Avenue, **Daytona Beach**. **www.BubbaGump.com**. This restaurant captures the charm that made Paramount Picture's "Forrest Gump" such a smash hit *(we recommend the TV version for families with parental guidance)*. The restaurant offers quality seafood in a casual, family atmosphere. Steamed shrimp, fried shrimp, coconut shrimp, grilled shrimp…Well, you get the picture. Did you know Americans eat a billion pounds of shrimp a year and it is the nation's most favorite seafood? Other favorites include: Bucket of Boat Trash (much better than it sounds), Shrimp New Orleans and mouth-watering Dixie Style Ribs or Pork BBQ. Kids Menu includes burgers, pizza, fish & chips, mac 'n cheese, chicken strips and Hubba Bubba Fried Shrimp…all around $5.00. Scrawled "Gumpisms" grace the varnished tabletops and guests can try on plaster casts of Forrest's running shoes at the famed bus bench in front of each restaurant. Trivia: What did Mrs. Gump always tell Forrest life was like - purchase a box in their gift shop. Yummy, flavorful food and such a fun staff!

CAPTAIN HIRAM'S RESORT - 1580 US 1, 2 miles north of Rte. 510, **Sebastian**. (772) 589-4345 or **www.hirams.com**. An adorable dockside property with two restaurants serving seafood and steaks. Try Captain Jim's Famous Crab Cake or anything with grilled shrimp. All of their food is so flavorful. The resort also features shops, a marine and a Key West Inn (some suites have bunk bed rooms for kids). Lunch and dinner with moderate Florida seafood prices.

DIXIE CROSSROADS SEAFOOD RESTAURANT - 1475 Garden Street (I-95 exit 220, east 2 miles to corner of Dixie and Garden), **Titusville**. **www.DixieCrossroads.com**. (321) 268-5000. Ever had Rock Shrimp? Well, this place (at least the owners) invented a machine to process these hard shelled shrimp found fresh in these parts. All of their entrees are offered with seasonings including: Old Bay, Key West, Caribbean Jerk (our favorite), Garlic and Salt Free. We strongly suggest a combo and be sure it includes Rock Shrimp! Start with great, hot corn fritters or let the kids color or go out and feed the fish. All their shrimp is fresh from the ocean, not ponds. Oh, and there's fish on the Kids Menu (shrimp, fish or clams) or a hamburger or chicken nuggets, served with fritters, french fries, beverage and chocolate pudding for only $2.99. Lunch and dinner daily. Plan on about $12.00 for most entrees (includes fritters and two sides), bigger appetites and combos with enough to share are around $25.00-$30.00.

DISNEY'S VERO BEACH RESORT - 9250 Island Grove Terrace (A1A north of town), **Vero Beach**. (772) 234-2000 or (800) 359-8000 or **www.dvcresorts.com**. Make yourself at home among the old world architecture of spacious Vacation Homes and stand-alone beach cottages. This beachfront location with a pool (Mickey-shaped w/Pirates Plunge pool slide and a giant lighthouse slide), two restaurants (and poolside take-out), a game room, supervised programming, baby-sitting and a daily list of community hall activities really make a family want to stay awhile. Enjoy organized board games, scavenger hunts, arts and crafts, card games and table-tennis. Play some pinball, rent a bicycle or sporting equipment, play some tennis, get a massage or sign up for a selection of bike tours, bird watching expeditions, nature hikes and evening campfires. Challenge your kids to a round of miniature golf or take to the water from catch and release fishing to snorkeling. All rooms have a full kitchen or a kitchenette and TV/VCRs. Cook your own specialties in your room or at one of the grills located throughout the resort. Mom doesn't want to cook? Try Sonyas or Shutters - both have kids menus with petite size portions of the adult selections so the kids feel grown up. If you need to wait a little for seating or food, they offer a scavenger hunt to complete at the table and in the corridors near the dining hall. Kids can order Shirley Temples and they get a cute dessert with kids meals. Every Saturday they have Disney Character Breakfasts with Goofy and Max. Adults, try anything steak or seafood and be sure to save room for the Celebration dessert. This place is definitely Disney and all Crew Members are super sweet! One of our favorite beaches and kid-friendly resorts to play, go shelling and relax in spacious comfort.

OCEAN GRILL - 1050 Sexton Plaza (A1A to Rte. 60 east to waterfront). **Vero Beach**. (772) 231-5409 or **www.ocean-grill.com**. Originally high on a sand dune, the site now sits right on the water as storms and hurricanes have removed much sand and the dunes. A true ocean-side eatery remains. Lunch weekdays and dinner nightly (fine dining but very casual environment). Fresh fish, duck and grilled shrimp are their specialty. Their coloring and games kids menu includes basics plus fish or steak for kids. Try a sharktooth sundae for dessert.

Chapter 3
Central West (CW) Area

Our Favorites...

* Captain Memo's Pirate Cruise - Clearwater Beach

* Skyway Fishing Pier - St. Petersburg

* Big Cat Rescue - Tampa

* Florida Acquarium - Tampa

* Museum of Science & Industry (MOSI) - Tampa

TECO MANATEE VIEWING CENTER

Apollo Beach - *6990 Dickman Road (I-75 exit 246. Turn west on Big Bend Rd - CR 672 - for 2.5 miles) 33572.* **www.tampaelectric.com/TEEVMVCFront.cfm** *Phone: (813) 228-4289 or (813) 920-4130. Hours: Daily 10:00am-5:00pm (November - mid-April). Admission: FREE*

To observe endangered Florida manatees in their real homes, head to Tampa Electric's Big Bend Power Station, where the manatee are attracted by the power plant's warm water discharge. The Manatee Viewing Center's observation platform allows close-up views of the graceful sea cows. Inside, look for an authentic manatee skeleton and an 11½ foot fiberglass reproduction, with various exhibits, videos, etc. providing insight into the manatee's physical characteristics.

CLEARWATER MARINE AQUARIUM

Clearwater - *249 Windward Passage 33767. Phone: (727) 441-1790 or (888) 239-9414.* **www.cmaquarium.org** *Hours: Monday-Friday 9:00am-2:00pm, Saturday 9:00am-4:00pm, Sunday 11:00am-4:00pm. Admission: $8.75 adult, $6.25 child (3-12).*

This nonprofit marine facility is dedicated to the rescue, rehabilitation and release of injured and sick sea life. Visitors can view sharks from under water, see the splashing dolphin show of Sunset Sam: touch silky stingrays, starfish, sea urchins and snails; and learn about whales, otters and sea turtles.

CAPTAIN MEMO'S PIRATE CRUISE

Clearwater Beach - *25 Causeway Blvd. Slip #3 (SR 60 Clearwater exit west across Old Tampa Bay. The Causeway becomes Gulf to Bay Blvd. to Court St. to Memorial Causeway, over bridge to Roundabout) 33767. Phone: (727) 446-2587.* **www.captainmemo.com** *Admission: $30.00-$35.00 adult, $25.00 senior (65+) and teen (13-17), $20.00 child.*

...everyone's a pirate on a Captain Memo cruise...

Miscellaneous: Metered parking is available in the Marina. Put a quarter in the meter and come buy a half day permit from the ticket booth for $2.00. DO NOT PARK IN THE SPOTS MARKED "NO PERMITS" IN FRONT OF THE MARINA BUILDING.

Hoist the Jolly Roger on this two-hour pirate ship adventure. The ship really looks like a friendly, colorful pirate ship! Quench your thirst at sea with free soft drinks and adult beverages. Cruise away into the fantasy world of swashbucklers aboard the Pirates Ransom featuring pistol battles, water (gun) squirting, cannon firings and storytelling for all. Young ones (and their parents) can go to the lower deck for face-painting, games and line dancing to Caribbean and family party music. Each child receives a pirate hat upon boarding and accumulates treasure, prizes and certificate of successful pirating upon "walking the plank" off the boat at end. The staff are well prepared to make everyone comfortable yet encourage you to explore your fun side. Arrgg! Maties, the photo-ops of our family with pirate "staches" was a hilarious memory.

CRYSTAL RIVER ARCHAEOLOGICAL STATE PARK

Crystal River - 3400 N. Museum Point (travel north on US 19 for two miles; turn west on State Park Street; travel for one mile; turn left on Museum Pointe) 34428. Phone: (352) 795-3817.   www.floridastateparks.org/CRYSTALRIVER/ Hours: Daily 8:00am-sunset. Visitors Center 9:00am-5:00pm. Admission: $2.00 per vehicle.

The Crystal River Archaeological State Park is now surrounded by the CRYSTAL RIVER PRESERVE STATE PARK. This allows the opportunity to uncover a pre-Columbian Ceremonial Complex and hundreds of associated cultural deposits along the coast to be mapped as a layer on a geographical information system. These unearthings may provide additional insight into the lives of people that lived here in ancient times. Already, a burial and temple mound and plaza are preserved. The information gained will likely be rapidly incorporated into indoor and outdoor interpretive exhibits. Programs such as Sifting for Technology and construction of typical pre-historic dwellings continue to be expanded as more information is learned. Undisturbed islands, inlets, backwaters and forests in the preserve are favored by nature lovers. Manatees and whooping cranes appear (in season) at the CRYSTAL RIVER NATIONAL WILDLIFE REFUGE in town.

CALADESI ISLAND STATE PARK

Dunedin - # 1 Causeway Blvd. (Located one mile west of Dunedin off the Gulf Coast) 34698. Phone: (727) 469-5918.   www.floridastateparks.org/caladesiisland/ Hours: Daily 8:00am-sunset.   Miscellaneous: Boaters: From Channel marker #14, just west of Dunedin Causeway Bridge, take an approximately 212-degree heading on your compass for approximately 1-mile. Follow the channel markers into Caladesi Island State Park marina.

From 3 miles of nature trail and a 108-slip marina to the 2nd best natural beach in the Nation, Caladesi Island has something for everyone. Picnic pavilions, bathhouses, and a park concession all make the visit more comfortable. Fishing, shelling, and nature studies are all ways to further enjoy a visit to Caladesi Island State Park.

HONEYMOON ISLAND STATE PARK

Dunedin - One Causeway Blvd.. (extreme west end of SR 586) 34698. Phone: (727) 469-5942. www.floridastateparks.org/honeymoonisland/ Hours: Daily 8:00am-sunset. Admission: $5.00 for up to 8 people per car. Single occupant fee of $3.00. Sunset fee of $3.00 per vehicle starting one hour prior to sunset.

The pioneers called it Hog Island, but it became Honeymoon Isle in 1939 when a New York developer built 50 palm - thatched bungalows for honeymooners. Today, visitors can drive across Dunedin Causeway to enjoy the sun - drenched Gulf beaches, mangrove swamps, and tidal flats. The park boasts several nature trails and bird observation areas. Visitors can swim, fish, and snorkel in the warm waters of the Gulf or picnic while they enjoy the beautiful scenery. Shelling is particularly good here, as the Gulf currents deposit an incredible variety of seashells on the shore. Showers are available and the park´s concession has a gift shop and snack bar. Located at the extreme west end of State Road 586.

YULEE SUGAR MILL RUINS HISTORIC STATE PARK

Homosassa - SR 490, west of US 19 34428. www.floridastateparks.org/Yuleesugarmill/ Phone: (352) 795-3817. Hours: Daily 8:00am-sunset. Admission: FREE

This site was once part of a thriving sugar plantation owned by David Levy Yulee. Yulee was a member of the Territorial Legislative Council, and served in the U.S. House of Representatives and U.S. Senate after Florida statehood. The park contains the remnants of the once-thriving 5,100-acre sugar plantation: a forty-foot limestone masonry chimney, iron gears, and a cane press. The steam-driven mill operated from 1851 to 1864 and served as a supplier of sugar products for southern troops during the Civil War. Bring the family and learn about sugar making from the several interpretive panels stationed around the mill. Across the street, a 6-table pavilion is available to groups on a first-come, first-served basis. Grills and picnic tables are located throughout the picnic area. Best to visit along with group, pre-arranged ranger led tours about the processing of sugar and labor involved through history.

HOMOSASSA SPRINGS WILDLIFE STATE PARK

Homosassa - 4150 S. Suncoast Blvd. (on US 19) 34446. Phone: (352) 628-5343. www.floridastateparks.org/homosassasprings Hours: Open every day of the year from 9:00 a.m. until 5:30 p.m. Last tickets are sold at 4:00 p.m. We recommend that you allow 3 1/2 to 4 hours to tour the park. Admission: $9.00 adult, $5.00 child (3-12).

One of the oldest residential communities on the Gulf Coast, Homosassa Springs has been a tourist attraction since the early 1900s, when passengers from the trains stopped long enough to rest by the spring while fish and spring water was loaded on board. Start your visit with a leisurely boat ride on Pepper Creek or a tram ride along the Pepper Creek Trail and leave your everyday worries behind you as you set out to explore the real Florida. One of its unusual features, the Fish Bowl, is a floating underwater observatory in the spring that provides close range views of manatees. You can meet manatees face-to-face without getting wet. Other native Florida wildlife on display (Wildlife Encounter) include black bear, bobcats, white-tailed deer, alligators, American crocodiles, river otters, and water birds including flamingos. A Reptile House and the Children's Education Center provide close-up viewing native snakes and other reptiles and a chance for children to learn through hands-on activities. Three manatee programs, two Wildlife Encounters and an Alligator/Hippo program are presented throughout the day allowing an opportunity to learn more about the Florida's wildlife.

FORT COOPER STATE PARK

Inverness - *3100 South Old Floral City Road (off US 41, 2 miles south of town) 34480. Phone: (352) 726-0315.* **www.floridastateparks.org/fortcooper/** *Hours: Daily 8:00am-sunset. Admission: $2.00 per vehicle. Camping - Primitive tent camping fee, $4.00/person per day. Miscellaneous: a 2300' long multi-use paved trail that will allow access from the Withlacoochee State Trail directly into Fort Cooper State Park. Please note that the $1.00 per bicycle fee to enter Fort Cooper State Park still applies when entering on the trail extension.*

During the Seminole Indian Wars, a stockade for sick and wounded soldiers stood on the lakeshore. Parts of the stockade wall are standing. There are plenty of activities at the park to enjoy such as paddleboat and canoe rentals, a picnic and playground area and nearly 5 miles of hiking trails.

STARKEY'S FLATWOODS ADVENTURES

Odessa - *12959 SR 54 (9 miles west of U.S. 41 on State Road 54) 33556. Phone: (813) 926-1133 or (877) 734-9453.* **www.flatwoodsadventures.com** *Admission: Safari Tours $10.00-$18.00. Horseback Riding $20.00-$40.00.*

Discover how J.B. Starkey Sr. first realized his love for being a cowboy and how he made his dreams of owning a cattle ranch materialize. Visitors can climb aboard a converted, camouflaged former school bus called a "range buggy" for a city slicker, 2-hour eco-tour of the Anclote River Ranch. You will learn the history of the cow hunters (or "cracker" cowboys as they were called) as well as the techniques used to work the cattle operation today. Visitors ride through pine flatwoods, sand pine ridges and pastureland and walk through a cypress swamp on an elevated boardwalk. Learn about the history of the town of Odessa, native plants and animals and see alligators, egrets, deer and cattle. Provides a hands-on experience with many of the native plants used by the Native Americans and early settlers to survive during those harsh but quiet times. Once a month they conduct full moon hayrides, horseback rides, bonfire and BBQs, where a group setting makes for a more interesting visit.

DINOSAUR WORLD

Plant City - 5145 Harvey Tew Road (I-4 exit 17, 20 minutes from Tampa) 33565. Phone: (813) 717-9865. www.dinoworld.net Hours: Daily 9:00am-6:00pm. Admission: $9.75-$12.75 (age 4+). Miscellaneous: Enjoy a museum, gift shop, and picnic area, playground and hands-on activities for children.

The world's largest dinosaur attraction is located in Plant City. The sight will turn heads as you approach viewing a dinosaur poking out from the foliage beside the highway. In this subtropical garden, visitors can mingle with 160 models of prehistoric beasts. The 12-acre outdoors-educational museum has figures of scaled-down, scientifically accurate models of Brachiosaurus, T-Rex with fiery eyes, Brontosaurus, Stegosaurus and his bumpy backbone, Iguanodon, Triceratops and such. There are little dinos no bigger than a turkey; others rise 25 feet above the ground. Each specimen is identified on a plated description highlighting its habits and habitats. Admire all these prehistoric creatures while skipping along walkways lined with cypress, palm and banana trees. Dinosaur Mountain houses a video theater and an exhibit on how the dinosaur models were made. Families can examine fossils and learn why dinosaur remains are not found in Florida. Then, try your paleontologic skills out digging through the Fossil Dig or Boneyard areas. The simulated sand pit or rock cave areas provide tools to uncover hidden little fossils and one big, life-size Stegosaurus skeleton. Many photo ops here - especially the head of a T-Rex with its mouth open.

FLORIDA INTERNATIONAL MUSEUM

St. Petersburg - 100 2nd Street N 33701. Phone: (727) 822-3693 or (800) 777-9882. www.floridamuseum.org Hours: Monday-Saturday 9:00am-6:00pm, Sunday Noon-5:00pm. Varies some by exhibition. Admission: Varies by each exhibition.

This Smithsonian affiliate hosts a wide variety of rotating American and International traveling exhibitions. Past events include: Diana, Titanic, Cuban Missile Crisis. Each format displays amazing artifacts in an artistic, educational setting.

SALVADOR DALI MUSEUM

St. Petersburg - *1000 3rd Street South (I-175E exit 22 on the right towards Tropicana Field. Right on 4th Street south, left on 11th Avenue South, left on 3rd Street South) 33701. Phone: (727) 823-3767 or (800) 442-3254. www.salvadordalimuseum.org Hours: Monday-Saturday 9:30am-5:30pm, Thursdays until 8:00pm, Sunday Noon-5:30pm. Closed Thanksgiving and Christmas. Admission: $15.00 adult, $13.50 senior (65+), teachers, military, police; $10.00 youth (10-18); $4.00 child (5-9). Discount coupons on website.*

A unique museum housing the most comprehensive collection of the famous artist's works. Surrealistic, original paintings, drawings, sculptures and objects d-art. See Dali's art evolve from landscape to double images and enormous religious paintings. Each summer, the Museum offers week-long "hands-on" workshops for families and children. Featuring artists and educators from the local community, these exploration sessions have included collage, basic print processes, puppet making, story telling and mask making. Because of Dalí's sense of whimsy and fun, a visit to the museum can be a rewarding and enjoyable experience for the entire family. His holograms, optical illusions, and strange dreamlike canvases can engage a child's attention like few other artists can. It is important to remember, however, that Dalí was painting in an artistic tradition and, as such, you and your child may encounter nude or partially-clothed figures or grotesque figures from his Surrealistic period. Read the visitation tips posted on the website.

THE PIER

St. Petersburg - *2nd Avenue NE. 33701. Phone: (727) 821-6443. www.stpetepier.com Hours: Monday-Thursday 10:00am-9:00pm, Friday-Saturday 10:00am-10:00pm, Sunday 11:00am-7:00pm. Admission: FREE*

The Pier, the downtown five-story inverted pyramid structure, offers visitors an array of waterfront things to do and places to eat and shop. Attractions at The Pier include: The Pier Aquarium, the Education Station, Great Explorations Hands-On Children's Museum, Art Galleries and an observation deck with spectacular views of Tampa Bay. Fishing gear, bicycles and jet skis are available for rent.

EGMONT KEY STATE PARK

St. Petersburg - *33711. Phone: (727) 893-2627. www.floridastateparks.org Miscellaneous: Access to the island is by boat only. The park is located at the mouth of Tampa Bay, southwest of Fort DeSoto Beach. To visit Egmont Key State Park, contact one of the ferry services.*

The island of Egmont Key has unique natural and cultural histories which have made it a valuable resource since the time settlers first arrived in Florida. Named in honor of John Perceval, the second Earl of Egmont and member of the Irish House of Commons in 1763, Egmont Key has had Spanish conquistadors and nuclear submarines pass its shores as they entered Tampa Bay. On March 3, 1847, Congress authorized funds to construct a lighthouse on Egmont. At the end of the third Seminole War in 1858, Egmont Key was used by the U.S. Army to detain Seminole prisoners until they could be transported to Arkansas Territory. Visitors can spend the day on the beach sunbathing, swimming in the warm bay waters, walking through the historic ruins of Fort Dade, or walking the brick paths that remain from the days Fort Dade was an active community with 300 residents. A gopher tortoise can be seen at almost every turn as you walk the historic paths (careful, don't step on them).

SKYWAY FISHING PIER STATE PARK

St. Petersburg - 4905 34th St. S (north and south of the Skyway Bridge on I-275 (U.S. 19) 33711. Phone: (727) 865-0668.   www.floridastateparks.org/skyway/ Hours: 24 hours. Lighted at night. Admission: 24 hour fee is: $3.00 per car; $10.00 for RV/Camper; $2.00 per adult; $1.50 for seniors and children 6-12.

Enjoy fishing or sightseeing on the longest fishing pier in the world! View magnificent sunrises and beautiful sunsets from the pier, which is open 24 hours everyday of the year. Fishing supplies, snacks, drinks and bait are all available on both the north and south piers.

HUBBARD'S MARINA

St. Petersburg (Madeira Beach) - 150 John's Pass Boardwalk 33708. Phone: (727) 393-1947.   www.hubbardsmarina.com

For seafaring folk, Hubbard's Marina offers three unique sea adventures:

THE SHELL ISLAND BEACH BBQ takes visitors to an uninhabited barrier island where white sand, warm water and seashells abound for a fun Florida-style barbecue. (1/2 day at $14.00-$27.00 per person)

The tour of EGMONT KEY STATE PARK offers a one-of-a-kind experience on an island only accessible by boat. Visitors can snorkel over the sunken ruins of Fort Dade built during the Spanish-American War and tour one of the few working lighthouses built in 1848. (2 times each morning, $15.00-$30.00 per person)

To observe dolphins, pelicans, egrets, herons, osprey, bald eagles and manatees, visitors can take the DOLPHIN WATCHING NATURE CRUISE where boats coast through natural wildlife habitats, commercial fishing villages and past historic John's Pass boardwalk while touring Boca Ciega Bay. (3 times daily, ~$10.00-$18.00 per person)

Afterwards, sample some fresh local seafood at the Friendly Fisherman Restaurant and enjoy the quaint shops along John's Pass Village.

PIRATE SHIP AT JOHN'S PASS

St. Petersburg (Madeira Beach) - *140 Boardwalk Place West 33708. Phone: (727) 423-7824. www.thepirateshipatjohnspass.com Admission: $30.00 adult, $20.00 child (ages 2-20).*

Visitors board a replica pirate ship where they are entertained with water gun battles, pirate stories, treasure hunts, face-painting, limbo and Caribbean music as they cruise the picturesque waters of Treasure Island, Boca Ciega Bay (this is the best place to spot playful dolphins) and the Gulf of Mexico. And, free beverages are included. Return two hours later to the Pirate Village at John's Pass Boardwalk.

STARLITE CRUISES

St. Petersburg Beach - *3400 S. Pasadena Avenue 33707. Phone: (727) 462-2628 or (800) 444-4814. www.starlitecruises.com*

Starlite Cruises' (Starlite Princess and Starlite Majesty) offer lunch and dinner cruises through the tranquil inland waters of Tampa Bay. In addition, the Princess also offers sightseeing excursions. The Starlite Princess is an authentic paddle wheeler that features a Victorian atmosphere and a charm that is highlighted by crystal chandeliers, brass accents, and rich woodwork. Price ranges $12.00 to $50.00 per person, depending on service.

TAMPA SPORTS TEAMS

TAMPA BAY BUCCANEERS - Super Bowl XXXVII Champions, the Buccaneers have been bringing hard-hitting football action to Tampa for more than 25 years. The red and pewter pirates play 16 regular season games from September to December in the 65,000 seat Raymond James Stadium. **www.tampabaybuccaneers.com**

TAMPA BAY DEVIL RAYS - Tropicana Field in downtown St. Petersburg welcomes you to major league baseball. Training each March at Florida Power Park (Al Lang Stadium), the Devil Rays are the only Major League Baseball team to train in the same city as its regular season stadium. **www.devilrays.mlb.com**.

TAMPA BAY LIGHTNING - Pro Hockey team, won the Stanley Cup in 2004. St. Pete Times Forum arena located on Tampa's downtown waterfront, Channel District. Game season runs October thru April. **www.tampabaylightning.com**.

TAMPA BAY STORM - have won many Arena Bowl Football League championships with a regular season during the summer months of May through July at the St. Pete Times Forum on Tampa's waterfront, downtown. **www.tampabaystorm.com**.

AMERICAN VICTORY MARINERS MEMORIAL & MUSEUM SHIP

Tampa - 705 Channelside Drive (adjacent to Florida Aquarium) 33602. Phone: (813) 228-8766. www.americanvictory.org

BEHIND THE SCENES TOURS OF THE AMERICAN VICTORY - Docent-guided 'Behind the Scenes' Tours get you into some 'out of the way' areas of the ship not open to regular visitors. Call the ship at (813) 228-8766 for more information. 'Behind the Scenes' Tours are $12.00 per person (age 3 and under no charge) and take about 90 minutes

SELF GUIDED RESTORATION TOURS - The ship's popular Self-Guided Restoration Tours allow visitors to view first hand the on-going work to restore this 60-year old icon of America's merchant maritime might. If you haven't visited in a while, do so soon! Restoration Tours are available Tuesday - Saturday, 10:00am-4:00pm and Sundays, 12 Noon-4:00pm. Passengers boarding before 4:00pm may remain onboard until 5:00pm. The last self-guided tours begin at 4:00pm, all days. Tour costs are $8.00 adults, $4.00 for kids 4-12; kids 3 and under are free.

RELIVE HISTORY CRUISE - cruise aboard the S.S. American Victory, the only restored merchant cargo vessel of its class on the East Coast sailing under her own steam. Cruise tickets are $100 per person and include a continental breakfast and hearty box lunch. Ship boarding begins at 8:00am; departure is at 9:00am and return is at 3:00pm on cruise day. See website for details. Passengers can witness vintage aircraft flyovers, touching memorial services and burials at sea, ship tours, weaponry demonstrations, great vistas of Tampa Bay and participate in shipboard routines, like marking time on the ship's bell.

BALCONY TO BACKSTAGE TOURS OF TAMPA THEATRE

Tampa - 711 Franklin Street 33602. Phone: (813) 274-8981. www.tampatheatre.org

Enjoy a balcony-to-backstage tour of Tampa's famous historic movie theatre and one of America's best preserved examples of grand movie palace architecture. Tours are held twice a month, lasting about 1.5 hours, and include a demonstration of the Mighty Wurlitzer Theatre Organ (sounds like music from the early silent movies, kids). Oh, the glamor and drama of such a place! $5.00 donation per person. Look on website for monthly open tours.

FLORIDA AQUARIUM

Tampa - 701 Channelside Drive (I-275 take Exit 45A Downtown East (Jefferson Street). Left on Twiggs to Channelside Dr.) 33602. Phone: (813) 273-4000 or (800) FLFISH-1. www.flaquarium.org Hours: Daily 9:30am-5:00pm. Admission: $17.95 adult, $14.95 senior (60+), $12.95 child (2-12).

Let me tell you about the giant fish I caught...

With more than 10,000 aquatic plants and animals and tons of hands-on stations, this place really exhibits some unique creatures around every corner. Be sure to watch for the white alligator with blue eyes; play alongside otters; unbelievable Goliath Grouper (800 lbs); and our favorite - Trumpetfish - they look like feathers instead of fish. Look for the sea dragon habitat, sea urchin touch tank and Sea Hunt shark exhibit. The downtown waterfront attraction also offers a number of daily shows including dive shows in the "Coral Reefs Gallery" and the Shark Show. You'll encounter creatures with long-range sensors, shape-shifting abilities and bone-crushing teeth. Shark Bay is a 93,000-gallon saltwater exhibit that is home to shark species from around the world including sand tiger sharks, zebra sharks, nurse sharks, black tip reef sharks and a green sea turtle. Try to catch the show labeled from "Fear to Fascination." New adventures at the aquarium allow visitors to put on a wetsuit and "Swim with Fishes" like angelfish and parrotfish. Also new is "Explore a Shore," an adorable outdoor children's play area with water cannons and slides.

SEAPORT ADVENTURE TOUR

Tampa - 651 Channelside Drive, Terminal 2 (I-4 west to exit 1, Ybor. Go south on 21st St., turn right on Adamo/Hwy 60, left on Channelside) 33602. Phone: (813) 905-5131 or (800) 741-2297. www.TampaPort.com Admission: FREE

The catamaran takes you around the Port to see how the Port of Tampa achieves the growth that makes it the greatest economic force in the Tampa Bay area. This one port generates over 10 billion dollars a year in spending and supports 93,000 jobs. Learn about the regional, national and international businesses docked in just one day.

KID CITY - THE CHILDREN'S MUSEUM OF TAMPA

Tampa - 7550 North Blvd. (I-275: Take exit # 48 (Sligh Avenue) west. At the 4th traffic signal (North Boulevard) turn right, past the zoo) 33604. Phone: (813) 935-8441. www.flachildrensmuseum.com Hours: Tuesday-Friday 9:00am-5:00pm, Saturday 10:00am-5:00pm, Sunday Noon-5:00pm. Open holiday Mondays. Admission: $5.00 (age 2+). Note: The museum is raising funds to move to the Riverfront area and greatly expand by 2008.

A miniature outdoor city offering hands-on activities for children. Complete with streets, sidewalks, park benches, shade trees, picnic tables and 14 buildings representing various businesses found in a typical city - a library, restaurant, school, court house, doctor's office, City Hall, police station, firehouse and apartments - can be explored by little hands and wide eyes. Kids pretend and role-play what they want to be when they grow up in Kid City.

LOWRY PARK ZOO

Tampa - 1101 W. Sligh Avenue (off I-275, look for exit signs) 33604. Phone: (813) 935-8552. www.lowryparkzoo.com Hours: Daily 9:30am-5:00pm. Admission: $14.95 adult, $13.95 senior (50+), $10.50 child (3-11). Miscellaneous: River Odyssey Eco Tours on Hillsborough River take visitors on a one-hour boat cruise with a naturalist in search of local wildlife such as alligators, hawks, herons, gopher tortoises and manatees in their natural habitat. The 49-passenger boat makes five cruises a day Wednesday-Sunday.

This 26-acre open-air natural habitat zoo is ranked as one of the top three mid-sized zoos in the country. Home to more than 1,500 animals in lush tropical settings, the zoo includes a free flight lorikeet aviary, children's petting zoo and educational center. One of the zoo's highlights is its "Manatee and Aquatic Center," one of only three rehab facilities in the state of Florida for gentle sea cows. The world's largest living lizard species, the legendary Komodo dragon, is featured in the zoo's Asian Domain. Newer attractions take visitors to Australia and Africa. "Wallaroo Station" is home to Palm cockatoos, kookaburra, kangaroos and wallabies while "Safari Africa" has habitats for elephants, giraffes, bongo, warthogs and camels.

YBOR CITY MUSEUM STATE PARK

Tampa - 1818 E 9th Avenue (I-4 exit 21st/22nd Street, head east a few blocks) 33605. Phone: (813) 247-1434. www.ybormuseum.org Hours: Daily 9:00am-5:00pm. Admission: $3.00 (age 6+) Miscellaneous: TECO LINE STREETCARS (replicas) transport passengers from downtown Tampa through the Channel District/port, the Florida Aquarium, and into Ybor City (stops at 7th Avenue, Centro Ybor and Centennial Park). Traveling 6 MPH, the streetcars take approximately 20 minutes to make 11 stops on the 23 mile track.

This Historical Park's exhibits tell the story of the immigrant life and Ybor's cigar making history. The State Park complex covers approximately one-half city block and includes a garden, the original Ferlita bakery, and multiple restored cigar workers' houses called casitas (meaning little houses). Visitors can tour the interior of one of the casitas to learn about the shot-gun style houses and the families that resided there. A cigar roller works at the Ybor City Museum State Park from 11:00am-1:00pm on Friday, Saturday and Sunday. Although we don't want to promote smoking to youth, chatting (in Spanish) with the cigar maker was interesting and interactive. La Casita is open from 10:00am-3:00pm (except Sunday). Tours are conducted every 30 minutes and are included in the cost of admission to the museum. The workers were not allowed to leave for coffee breaks, so the restaurant next door would bring café con leche to them. What were readers? Why were they so important?

Inside a Cuban stone baking oven

HENRY B. PLANT MUSEUM

Tampa - 401 W. Kennedy Blvd. 33606. Phone: (813) 254-1891. www.plantmuseum.com
Hours: Tuesday-Saturday 10:00am-4:00pm, Sunday Noon-4:00pm. Admission: a donation of $3.00-$5.00 per person.

With splendid Moorish architecture and fancy furniture, this Victorian structure has tropical gardens, a museum and the guided tour of restored rooms of the Tampa Bay Hotel. It takes you back to a romantic time.

RAYMOND JAMES STADIUM TOUR

Tampa - 4201 Dale Mabry Hwy (just S. of Dr. Martin Luther King Blvd.) 33607. (813) 350-6576. www.tampasportsauthority.com/rjs/tours.htm   Admission: $3-5.00/person (age 6+).

Tampa's community football stadium was named Raymond James Stadium at its dedication September 20, 1998. Raymond James Stadium is the home of the NFL's Tampa Bay Buccaneers, University of South Florida Bulls football and the New Year's Day Outback Bowl, as well as concerts and special events. You'll get to go behind the scenes and see the Security area, visit the field through the Bucs tunnel, walk past the Player locker rooms through service level entrance, take a peek at the Club/suite area and then on to the main concourse to the pirate ship. They may take you into the press box and even for a step out onto the field. Doesn't this sound like a great tour for the football fans in your family?

BUSCH GARDENS TAMPA BAY

Tampa - 3605 East Bougainvillea (I-75 to I-275 SOUTH to the Fowler Avenue exit # 51 east to McKinley. Follow signs) 33612. Phone: (813) 987-5000 or (888) 800-5447. www.buschgardens.com Hours: Basically 10:00am-6:00pm. Extended morning and evenings hours during peak Tampa season. Admission: $48.00-$58.00 (age 3+). Discounts for Florida residents and online ticket purchases. Adventure tours are extra (ex. Safari is $33.95 extra tour). Miscellaneous: Serengeti Safari is a must for giraffe lovers. Your flat-bed gated jeep allows you to feed fresh veggies and fruit to several animals found in Africa but most importantly you can hand-feed tall giraffe as they sweep down their long purple tongues! What a photo!

A family adventure park featuring a combination of world-class animal habitats, thrill rides, and live entertainment. The park provides guests with four steel coasters and two newer coasters: Cheetah Chase - cat and mouse style and Shiekra, the country's first "dive coaster" that goes up, down, down and loops around in Stanleyville town. The park has been recognized among the top zoos in North America providing more diverse ways to get up-close to animals than any other place outside of Africa. Guides take families on a Rhino Rally in customized SUVs to see rhinos the size of pick-up trucks, buffalo, elephant and others in the Serengeti Plain. You'll pass under a waterfall and get washed away in a storm on a fun thrill ride. Entertainment includes a 4-D family adventure film and KaTonga, a 35-minute Broadway caliber musical that takes guests to the heart of the jungle. Each month, several venues throughout the park present live music and dance with different themes (ex. Irish dancers). Regular "fair rides" are found scattered throughout the park. Congo River Rapids is a "wet" family raft ride.

ADVENTURE ISLAND

Tampa - 4500 Bougainvillea Avenue (across the street from Busch Gardens) 33617. Phone: (813) 987-5600 or (888) 800-5447. www.adventureisland.com Open daily late-March through early-September and weekends only mid-February through mid-March or mid-September through late October. Admission: $33.00 plus per person (age 3+).

Thirty acres of water-drenched fun in the sun feature the ultimate combination of high-speed thrills and an inviting tropical surrounding of a Key West setting. Corkscrew slides, waterfalls, outdoor cafes, a wave pool and children's play area round out the assortment of rides.

MUSEUM OF SCIENCE AND INDUSTRY (MOSI)

Tampa - 4801 E. Fowler Avenue (I-75 exit 265, Fowler Avenue westbound about 2.5 miles) 33617. Phone: (813) 987-6000 or (800) 995-MOSI. **www.mosi.org** *Hours: Monday-Friday 9:00am-5:00pm; Saturday-Sunday 9:00am-7:00pm. Admission: $19.95 adult, $17.95 senior (60+), $15.95 child (2-12). Admission includes IMAX, Kids in Charge and special exhibit spaces for kids.*

Home to Florida's first IMAX Dome Theater and the Southeast's largest science center, the Museum was designed with input from kids. The scientific playground is filled with over 450 hands-on activities and interactive traveling exhibits. Highlights include the "Gulf Coast Hurricane Chamber" which allows visitors to experience 74 mile per hour winds, and the "Challenger Learning Center" where guests can

Safely inside a hurricane...

assume the role of astronaut or engineer. We absolutely loved the hurricane wind chamber experience! MOSI's "High Wire Bicycle" is the longest high wire bike in a U.S. museum . The Kids In Charge building was so well done - you can tell local kids really have input. The exhibits not to miss are Bed of Nails (we really laid on a real bed of nails!) and the Rope Maze (spider web puzzle). Other features: "BioWorks Butterfly Garden," "The Amazing You: An Exhibition of the Human Body," plus an Avionics Flight simulator, a planetarium and two Diplodocus dinosaurs that stand three stories tall and are the largest articulated dinosaurs ever discovered. This campus is huge.

BIG CAT RESCUE

Tampa - 12802 Easy Street (I-275 to Busch Blvd. exit, head west 9 miles. After you pass under Veteran's Expressway, take Easy Street U-turn left down dirt road) 33625. Phone: (813) 920-4130. **www.BigCatRescue.org** *Admission: Pricing packages range from $10.00-$21.00 for day or kids tours.*

Big Cat Rescue is home to over 148 large, exotic cats, representing 18 different breeds. Here you will meet and learn all about lions, tigers and bearcats! The mission of Big Cat Rescue is to provide the best permanent home for the abused, abandoned and retired cats in their care. The guided tours on this lake-front big cat sanctuary offer behind the scenes operation of the world's largest big cat rescue

and sanctuary in action. Did you know tigers like to swim? Wanna see it? Big Cats have different "voices" than house cats. More squeeks and screams or low roars. Just to hear a cute cub squeal or the lion roar so deep is worth the money alone. And, you get so close to these beautiful animals! On the way out, you may notice the Cool Cat Café and want a bite to eat. Beware, this café is not for human lunches - but tens of pounds of raw meat prepared to be fed to the cats at the rescue. This is truly an amazing place! Please schedule a visit into your travels.

TARPON SPRINGS SPONGE DOCKS

Tarpon Springs - 34689. Phone: (727) 937-6109. www.tarponsprings.com

Greek sponge divers settled here in the early 1900s. Tarpon Springs is known as "the sponge capital of the world". In the 1930s, the sponge industry of Tarpon Springs was very prosperous, bringing in millions of dollars of sponges yearly. But in the 1940s, the sea sponge beds were contaminated and destroyed by bacteria, which led to a decline in the natural sponge industry. The industry was revived in the 1980s when healthy sea sponges were found. Now Tarpon Springs is back to being a leader in the world's natural sponge market. The Sponge Docks offer something of interest for everyone. You can take a leisurely sightseeing cruise down the Anclote River, enjoy a lunch or dinner cruise to the Gulf, or experience a live, sponge diving exhibition. You can also visit the 120,000 gallon salt water aquarium, tour the sponge museum, or go deep sea fishing. Built an appetite? There are a handful or two of Greek restaurants around the docks and downtown - many still owned by the same family for a century.

HILLSBOROUGH RIVER STATE PARK

Thonotosassa - 15402 N US 301 (12 miles north of Tampa and six miles south of Zephyrhills on U.S. 301) 33592. www.floridastateparks.org/hillsboroughriver/ Phone: (813) 987-6771. Hours: Daily 8:00am-sunset. Admission: $4.00 for up to 8 people per car. $20.00 camping fee.

Built in 1936 by the Civilian Conservation Corp. Hillsborough River State Park is steeped in history and natural beauty. Many activities are available at the park by which visitors can access and enjoy this area. Fort Foster, a replica of an original

Second Seminole War military fort, is open for guided tours on Saturdays and Sundays. A visit to the Fort allows visitors to step back in time to the days of when Florida was being settled by pioneers. The Fort Foster Visitor Station houses a display of artifacts from the time period, and provides the visitor with information about the operation of the Fort.

Hikers can walk over seven miles along four nature trails. The Wetlands Restoration Trail accommodates bicyclists and hikers. A popular trail is the Rapids Nature Trail. It meanders through oak hammocks to the edge of the Hillsborough River at the point where an outcropping of limestone rocks has created rapids. For enjoying the river by being on it, the park has canoe rentals for visitors' convenience. Hillsborough River State Park also offers 111 campsites, picnic areas, pavilions, and the Spirit of the Woods Pool Side Café and Gift Shop. A swimming pool with a capacity of 216 swimmers is also within the park.

WEEKI WACHEE SPRINGS

Weeki Wachee - 6131 Commercial Way (US 19, just south of intersection of SR 50) 34606. Phone: (352) 596-2062. www.weekiwachee.com Hours: Daily 10:00am-4:00 or 5:00pm (summertime). Buccaneer Bay is open weekends in September. The rest of the park is open year round - mostly long weekends (spring, fall, winter). See website for current schedule. Admission: $16.00-$22.00 (ages 3+). Online coupon. Parking $3.00. Tube and locker rentals extra. Canoe/kayak rentals available. Miscellaneous: Mermaid Reunion show once each month.

Buccaneer Bay at Weeki Wachee Springs is a water resort that offers mermaid shows, water slides, white sand and a tiki bar.

MERMAID SHOW: The "World Famous" Mermaids of Weeki Wachee Springs have been entertaining audiences since 1947. They perform shows daily in the only underwater theater of its kind! There is no tank or aquarium. The theater is built into the spring itself and the mermaids perform in this natural and pristine spring while visitors enjoy the show 16-feet below the surface of the water. The mermaids perform with Florida's wildlife as a variety of fish, turtles, manatees and an occasional alligator frequent the spring and the show. They put on two performances of "The Little Mermaid" daily and a third called "Fish Tails," a historical retrospective of the springs and mermaids skills set to music.

BUCCANEER BAY: On the other side of the mermaid lagoon is Buccaneer Bay, a natural swimming hole with a lazy river, giant waterslides, beach and lifeguards, all included in the admission price. Lil' Mates Caribbean Cove provides the youngsters with a fun and safe water play area. The springs stay an even 72 degrees year round for swimming - especially refreshing on hot, 90 degree plus days.

Weeki Wachee Springs (cont.)

RIVER BOAT NATURE RIDE: The Wilderness River Boat Cruise takes you down the pristine waters of the Weeki Wachee River where every boat ride provides the opportunity to see Florida wildlife in its natural setting.

RECREATION: Another way to take advantage of the Weeki Wachee River is to rent a canoe or kayak and explore the area's nature preserve and clear water. **www.floridacanoe.com** The flowing river makes it an ideal place to canoe. Even beginners can just flow down river and enjoy the scenery and wildlife. Along the way, people can see manatees, exotic birds, fish and maybe the occasional alligator. Once people travel beyond the preserve, they are encouraged to swim in the water. There are even rope swings set up along the shore.

LITTLE MANATEE RIVER STATE PARK

Wimauma - *215 Lightfoot Road (five miles south of Sun City, off U.S. 301 on Lightfoot Road) 33598. Phone: (813) 671-5005.   www.floridastateparks.org/littlemanateeriver/ Hours: Daily 8:00am-sunset. Admission: $4.00 per vehicle.*

The Little Manatee River begins in a swampy area near Fort Lonesome and flows almost 40 miles before emptying into Tampa Bay. Visitors can fish along the banks of the river or rent canoes at the ranger station. Wildlife enthusiasts can enjoy hiking a 6½ mile trail through the park's northern wilderness area. For those who prefer their hikes on horseback, the park has 12 miles of equestrian trails and four equestrian campsites. Campers can spend the night in a full-facility campground or hike out to a primitive campsite along the trail.

SUGGESTED LODGING AND DINING

SADDLEBROOK RESORT - **Tampa (Wesley Chapel)**. 5700 Saddlebrook Way (one mile east of I-75 exit 279). **www.saddlebrookresort.com**. Saddlebrook Resort is a secluded retreat that offers service and comfort. In the heart of the resort, the Walking Village includes all recreation and dining facilities surrounding the heated SuperPool. Wait 'til your kids see the Super Pool! Guest accommodations border the Walking Village, making transportation needless (valet parking is provided so you're not tempted to "drive" the property). The resort is comprised of 800 deluxe guest rooms, and one-two-and three bedroom suites. Suites include a spacious living/dining room and fully equipped kitchen. Every day is different for children staying at Saddlebrook: Animal Mondays,

Dinosaur Tuesdays, Weather Wednesdays, Underwater Thursdays, Finally Fridays, Sports Saturdays and Science Sundays. Open to kids ages 4-12, S'Kids Club offers a place for young resort guests to meet others their age while allowing mom and dad free time for meetings, golf, tennis or the Spa. Babysitting is provided for kids under age 4. Saddlebrook also offers a variety of other activities for children including the SuperPool featuring racing lanes, water volleyball and basketball. Additional equipment is available for check out at the Swim Shop including board games, bicycles, water toys and fishing gear. Two whirlpools, the Poolside Café and a child's play area surround the pool. Nearby are Junior tennis and golf opportunities. Rates range $100.00-$200.00 per person (age 13+), per night. All nightly rates include breakfast and dinner.

COLUMBIA RESTAURANT - **Ybor City (Tampa)**. 2117 E. 7th Avenue. (813) 248-4961 or **www.columbiarestaurant.com**. This 100 year old plus eatery has old-world charm serving authentic, flavorful Spanish/Cuban cuisine since 1905. The Columbia continues to be owned and operated by the 4th & 5th generation of the Hernandez Gonzmart family and has remained the oldest restaurant in Florida and the largest Spanish restaurant in the world. Kids Menus ($4.95) items offer: steak, Cuban sandwich, grilled cheese or chicken tenders, but the adult menu is what's special. Daily lunch (average $11) and dinner (average $20) are served. Try Cuban sandwiches, grouper, Cuban bread, deviled crab, guava dessert, Spanish bean soup and Crema Catalana with café con leche for dessert. Really, if you want to try several dishes like Mama Gonzmart would cook, try their combos. Our favorites were the gravy, black beans and empanadas on the combo plate. We love when eating can become a cultural education. To get the feel for how this eatery fits into this old city space, take a peek through the Columbia Museum next door.

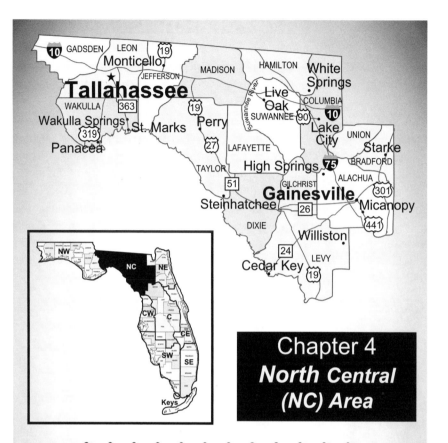

Chapter 4
North Central (NC) Area

Our Favorites...

* Santa Fe Community College Teaching Zoo - Gainesville

* Historic Haile Homestead - Gainesville

* Florida Museum of Natural History - Gainesville

* Devil's Millhopper - Gainesville

* Majorie Kinnan Rawlings SP - Gainesville (Cross Creek)

* Mission San Luis - Tallahassee

* Tallahassee Museum of History & Natural Science

TROY SPRINGS STATE PARK

Branford - 674 NE Troy Springs Road (1.3 miles north of US 27, off County Road 425) 32008. Phone: (386) 935-4835.   www.floridastateparks.org/troyspring Hours: Florida state parks are open from 8:00am until sundown 365 days a year. Admission: $3.00 per vehicle.

Troy Springs is a beautiful first magnitude spring which offers unsurpassed opportunities for swimming, open water diving and snorkeling. While enjoying the refreshing clear, 72 degree water check out the multitudes of turtles, fish and wading birds. For more adventure, you can snorkel over the depths of this spring viewing the remains of the Civil War-era steamboat Madison, scuttled in the spring run in 1863 to keep it from being captured. A recent addition to the state park system, Troy Spring now has an entrance road, rest rooms, an accessible walkway, picnic tables, and a riverside dock for canoeists and boaters on the Suwannee River. Much of the park lands are still under development for hiking trails.

CEDAR KEY MUSEUM STATE PARK & SCRUB STATE PRESERVE

Cedar Key - 12231 SW 166th Court (SR 24 west into town) 32625. Phone: (352) 543-5350. www.floridastateparks.org/cedarkeymuseum/default.cfm Hours: Thursday-Monday 9: 00am-5:00pm. Admission: $1.00 per person (age 6+).

Come visit the St. Clair Whitman house. This house has been restored to circa 1920 - 1930 and is open for tours from 1:00 p.m. to 4:00 p.m. Thursday through Monday. The house depicts life in Cedar Key and focuses on the life of St. Clair Whitman and his collections of natural items. Kids like the unique collection of sea shells and Indian artifacts. Small gray squirrels, doves, mockingbirds, blue jays, woodpeckers, and green tree frogs can be seen on the museum grounds and along the walking trail. Just down the road visit Cedar Key Scrub State Reserve's salt marshes, swamps, forest and scrub offering more opportunities for nature study.

NATURE COAST STATE TRAIL

Fanning Springs - 18020 NW Highway 19 32693. Phone: (352) 535-5181.   Hours: Daylight.   www.dep.state.fl.us/gwt/state/nat/faq.htm

The Trail is part of Florida's Statewide System of Greenways and Trails. Along the highlights is a historic train trestle that allows trail goers to cross over the Suwannee River near Old Town. The trail is also close to nearby FANNING SPRINGS STATE PARK. 32 miles of paved trail.

SANTA FE COMMUNITY COLLEGE TEACHING ZOO

Gainesville - 3000 NW 83rd Street (I-75 exit 390, east on SR 222 to right on NW 91st St., follow until sharp left turn) 32606. Phone: (352) 395-5604. ***http://inst.santafe.cc.fl.us/ ~zoo/*** *Hours: Saturday-Sunday 9:00am-2:00pm or by appointment. Closed school holidays and breaks. Admission: FREE*

Guided tours are led by zoo keepers at the only community college teaching zoo in the nation. The property is the local zoo and the lab for the Zoo Animal Technology Program housing mammals, reptiles, amphibians, birds, and endangered species from Africa, Asia, Australia, Europe and the Americas. Why don't they have lions, tigers and bears? Expense and danger. Because students run this, they learn taking "baby steps" to care for manageable animals on a smaller scale. Some family favorites are the Bald Eagles, Galapagos tortoises, Kangaroos that climb and live in trees or Cranes with mohawks! A great way

Former and current students guide this unique tour...

to peak interest in kids who may want to pursue careers in zoology. Kids really love the selection of smaller animals and the college students interaction on the tour.

HISTORIC HAILE HOMESTEAD AT KANAPAHA PLANTATION

Gainesville - 8500 Archer Road (SR 24. I-75 exit 384 west of town) 32608. Phone: (352) 336-9096. ***www.hailehomestead.org*** *Hours: Saturday 10:00am-2:00pm and Sunday Noon-4:00pm. Open for tours during the week by special appointment. Admission: $5.00 adult, under 12 free.*

One of the oldest houses in Alachua County, this historic home was once Thomas Evans Haile's and his family. The Hailes came here from Camden, South Carolina in 1854 to establish a 1,500 acre Sea Island Cotton plantation which they named Kanapaha. The Homestead later became the site of house parties attended by some of Gainesville's most distinguished citizens. The unusual thing about this family is: they wrote on the walls! Start your tour on the front porch. Kids like to sit on the Boggle Bench – what does it do? Once inside, you can't help but notice the assorted writings on the wall – mostly about parties held here. Why

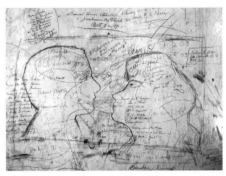

A family was allowed to write on the walls?

were kids and guests allowed to write on the walls? Whose name appears the most? Look for poems and math problems. Measure yourself against the growth chart of the owner's kids (15 of them). Many furnishings are original (like the nursery crib used by all the kids). There's a rock tablet outside you can write on – just to get it out of your system. Although the furnishings are sparce, the student tour slowly introduces you to the "characters" that lived here versus what they owned. This makes for curious questions from kids. And, really, the highlight of the tour are those 12,500 assorted words on the walls! Very interesting...

GAINESVILLE RACEWAY

Gainesville - 11211 North County Road 225   32609. www.gainesvillespeedway.com Phone: (352) 377-0046. Lightning speed and thundering excitement, and home of the NHRA Gatornationals every March, the Raceway hosts a year-round calendar of pro and amateur drag racing, auto shows and motorcycle racing.

FLORIDA MUSEUM OF NATURAL HISTORY

Gainesville - University of Florida Cultural Plaza, Southwest 34th St. and Hull Road. (I-75 exit 284) 32611. Phone: (352) 846-2000. www.flmnh.ufl.edu Hours: Monday-Saturday 10:00am-5:00pm, Sunday 1:00-5:00pm. Admission: Museum - Free, donations accepted. Special exhibits and Butterfly Rainforest: $8.50 adult, $7.50 senior (62+)& Florida residents, $4.50 child (3-12).

Giant fossil shark jaws...

While exploring the natural history of Florida and ancient times, museum scientists made discoveries. The museum showcases and shares these finds. The Northwest hardwood hammock features a life-sized limestone cave and is patterned after the forest at Florida Caverns State Park early spring (walk through an amazingly realistic cave - indoors!). Lift up a log and look for fossils and creatures; crawl in the cave – Look for the Spelunker; and Listen to bird sounds. The pitcher plant bog (coastal), Indian trading scene (river), and boardwalk coastal marsh (barrier islands) showcase many waterways and wildlife. Walk through time beginning when Florida was underwater (scaled 12 times larger!) to fossils and bones of ancient animals. Move the Earth or see a 15-foot-tall ground sloth and a two-foot-tall horse. Investigate South Florida Peoples (Calusa, Miccosukee and Seminole Indians) as you walk thru a full-scale mangrove forest and a Calusa leader's house. The theatrical lighting and recreated environs are spectacular! Engaging and entertaining.

Finally, the **BUTTERFLY RAINFOREST**. At any one time, over 2000 butterflies delicately flutter around. Look for the state butterfly – the Zebra Longwing, or the large, almost neon, Blue Morpho. More butterflies than we've ever seen! The four-story outdoor screened enclosure also has waterfalls, a walking trail, and lush subtropical and tropical plants. As you leave the Rainforest, check in the mirror for "hitchhikers." Their "Wall of Wings" reaches nearly three stories high. Kids can observe scientists

working in labs. Think you know butterflies? What temperature do butterflies prefer? Where do they go when it rains?

UNIVERSITY OF FLORIDA

Gainesville - Visitors Passes at UF's main entrance at Southwest 13th Street (US441) and Southwest 2nd Avenue 32611. Phone: (352) 392-3261. www.ufl.edu

The Historic Campus contains many buildings on the National Register of Historic Places such as University Auditorium. Above the Auditorium, visitors will find Century Tower, a 49-bell carillon that rings on quarter hours. (maps available at the gated entrances) Florida Field at Ben Hill Griffin Memorial Stadium is located directly east of the O'Connell Center and seats 85,000 fans. Affectionately nicknamed "The Swamp" - the Stadium is home to the National Champ "Fightin Gators" football team.

BAT HOUSE: (just past the Natural History Museum, left onto Museum, immediate left into parking lot, walk left to Bat House) They sleep 60,000 plus by day but at sunset – out they all come for a drink and an eating frenzy (30 million bugs each night)! Your family can watch and learn from thousands of live bats. Be sure to be there right at sunset (nights over 60 degrees) for the overwhelming view!

MORNINGSIDE NATURE CENTER LIVING HISTORY FARM

Gainesville - 3540 East University Ave 32641. www.natureoperations.org Phone: (352) 334-2170. Hours: Farm is open daily from 9:00am-5:00pm, with live interpretive experiences offered every Saturday (September-May). Admission: Small admission fee during festivals and reenactments.

At Morningside Nature Center, 278-acres of remnant forest type is preserved along 5 miles of nature trails. Morningside's Living History Farm recreates the single-family rural farm that typified north central Florida during the late nineteenth century. Hogan's Cabin, a long-leaf pine cabin built in 1840, was the centerpiece of a project put at Morningside as part of Alachua County's bicentennial celebration in 1976. Other buildings include Clark's Kitchen, with a wood-burning cook stove, a log twin-crib barn from the late 1800s, a smoke-house, composting privy, and the Half-Moon one-room schoolhouse, built in the 1880s and one of the oldest schoolhouses in Alachua County. The farm is used as a re-enactment most Saturdays, where visitors can view costumed interpretive staff growing crops such as cotton and tobacco in the Cash Crop Field, or medicinal herb, fruits, and vegetables in the Heirloom Garden. They produce the annual supply of syrup from sugar cane grown on property. Interpreters care for live farm animals, leach lye from oak ashes to make soap, spin and weave cotton and wool, hook up the windmill to pump water, split wood for the fireplace, and other chores that were a part of turn of the century living.

DEVIL'S MILLHOPPER STATE GEOLOGIC SITE

Gainesville - 4732 Millhopper Road (2 miles north of town, off SR 232. I-75 exit 390, CR 222 east. At 43rd St., turn left, then left onto Millhopper) 32653. Phone: (352) 955-2008.

We made it to the bottom...

www.floridastateparks.org/devilsmillhopper Hours: Wednesday-Sunday 9:00am-5:00pm. Admission: $2.00 per vehicle. Miscellaneous: guided walks with a Park Ranger are available every Saturday at 10:00am. Otherwise, check out the short intro video and info plaques along the stairway.

Devil's Millhopper gets its unique name from its funnel-like shape. Researchers have learned a great deal about Florida's natural history by studying fossil shark teeth, marine

For updates & travel games visit: **www.KidsLoveTravel.com**

shells, and the fossilized remains of extinct land animals found in the sink (on display in the interpretive center). Legend has it that the millhopper was what fed bodies to the devil, hence the name. Limestone is the foundation on which the surface of Florida sits. Although this stone is very hard, it is easily dissolved by a weak acid. A sink happen suddenly – the first rain after a drought. Each layer of sediment contains a record of events and animals that lived before. Marine animal shells in the lower layers, bones and teeth of land animals found in more "recent" layers. The sinkhole is 120 feet deep and 500 feet across. A one-half mile nature trail follows the rim, and there is a 232-step stairway to the bottom of the sink. Take a picture at the bottom as proof of your easy descent and aerobic ascent!

MILL CREEK FARM

Gainesville (Alachua) - 20307 NW County Road 235A (I-75 exit 399, west on US 441. Just past Santa Fe High School, turn right on CR 235A for 3 miles) 32615. Phone: (386) 462-1001.   www.millcreekfarm.org   Hours: Open Saturday from 11:00am-3:00pm. Admission: 2 carrots, but a 5-pound bag preferred!

Over 80 horses wander the quiet countryside and rolling emerald hills of this farm. This equine sanctuary provides lifetime care to old, rescued, abused, abandoned, circus, police & blind horses. Retired now, these horses are relaxing and kicking up their heels.

MARJORIE KINNAN RAWLINGS HISTORIC STATE PARK

Gainesville (Cross Creek) - 18700 S County Road 325 (between Ocala and Gainesville, off SR 20 east) 32640. www.floridastateparks.org/marjoriekinnanrawlings Phone: (352) 466-3672.   Hours: Rawlings' farmyard, grove, and nature trails (2 short ones) are open 9:00am-5:00pm daily, throughout the year. Admission: $2.00 per vehicle. Guided tours are $2.00-$3.00 per person (age 6+). Miscellaneous: The adjacent county park, which has a boat ramp, playground and picnic facilities, is the site where MKR kept her milk cow.

Famed author, Marjorie Rawlings came to Cross Creek in 1928 where she settled into her new life in this "half-wild, backwoods country," growing oranges, cooking on a wood-burning stove, running a small animal farm, and writing down her impressions of the land and her Cracker neighbors. Visitors may tour the house and farm - kept the way it was in the 1930s - with a ranger in period costume. The ranger will invite you in and quote Miss Rawlings, "bring an open mind and an overnight bag." She sat most often on the wide veranda at her typewriter, writing the books that would endear her to the world and capture the beauty of Florida and the spirit of its people. Rawlings' clunky black typewriter still rests on a table on the front porch (good photo op). Also, look for the giant dictionary and Moe,

Rawling's favorite writing place...

the dog. Marjorie's most famous book, "The Yearling", an American classic and winner of the Pulitzer Prize, is the story of young Jody Baxter's coming of age in the big scrub country forest (a pet deer sounds like fun but there is a sad ending). Learn about the author's life, including her famous dinners with guests such as Ernest Hemingway or her party in the bathroom. The kitchen is a favorite room – did you know Miss Rawlings wrote a cookbook, too? Inspiring and authentic tour.

GAINESVILLE-HAWTHORNE TRAIL STATE PARK

Gainesville (Micanopy) - 100 Savannah Boulevard 32667. Phone: (352) 466-3397. www.floridastateparks.org/gainesville-hawthorne Notes: Parking is provided at three locations, Boulware Springs Park in Gainesville (Mile 0), Lochloosa Trailhead (Mile 15), and the Hawthorne Trailhead (Mile 16.2). Bicycling and skating are permitted everywhere in the park except on La Chua trail.

Gainesville-Hawthorne Trail State Park stretches 16 miles from the City of Gainesville's Boulware Springs Park through the Paynes Prairie Preserve State Park and the Lochloosa Wildlife Management Area. The old rail bed-turned-greenway is both a recreational surface and a grassy path for equestrians. Family bike riding is recommended. The entire trail is a pleasure to ride, and there are even a few hills to climb and speed down. If you take your time, park your bikes and visit La Chua trail in Paynes Prairie, you might even have an opportunity to see bison, wild horses and sandhill cranes.

PAYNES PRAIRIE PRESERVE STATE PARK

Gainesville (Micanopy) - 100 Savannah Blvd. (I-75 exit 374. East on CR 234. Left onto US 441) 32667. Phone: (352) 466-3397. www.floridastateparks.org/paynesprairie Hours: Visitors Center open daily 9:00am-5:00pm. Park open 8:00am to sunset. Admission: $4.00 per vehicle.

Watch the video, "The Level Green Plain," view the exhibits, and enjoy panoramic views of the prairie from the 50' observation tower. You may even catch a glimpse of some of recent spring additions, including 2 bison calves, wild "cracker" horse foals, turkey chicks, and young eagles. From late November to early March, sandhill cranes and migrating waterfowl winter at the prairie basin. Buffalo and wild horses roam. The wild horses are descendants of those brought over by the

Spanish in the early 1500s. For a closer look, explore the 30 miles of trails for equestrians, hikers and bicyclists. Fishing and boating (canoes, kayaks and small boats) and full campground amenities.

DUDLEY FARM HISTORIC STATE PARK

Gainesville (Newberry) - 18730 W. Newberry Road (I-75 exit SR 26 west 7 miles. Between Newberry & Gainesville) 32669. www.floridastateparks.org/dudleyfarm Phone: (352) 472-1142. Hours: Wednesday-Sunday 9:00am-4:00pm. Admission: $4.00 per vehicle.

A 19th century working farmstead features a visitor center, picnic area and a guided or self-guided tour of the 18 historic structures that make up an authentic (no reproduction) farm complex. Staff and volunteers in authentic farm clothing carry on chores and activities much the same as they were in the late 1800s. Buildings include the old general store, a dairy shed, canning house, smokehouse, syrup house, hay barn, tobacco barn, stables and an 1880s kitchen. Livestock includes mules, cracker cows, horses, turkeys, and Barred Rock chickens. You might notice gardens, grape arbors, pecan and fruit trees, pastures, pinewoods, and croplands of peanuts, field peas, and sweet potatoes growing. In the fall, you can experience harvesting, grinding, boiling and bottling of sugar cane. Year-round, you can feed the chickens, walk on the nature trail or enjoy sitting in the rocking chairs on the spacious porches as you watch time go by.

MADISON BLUE SPRINGS STATE PARK

Lee - 8300 NE State Road 6 (10 miles east of Madison on SR 6) 32059. Phone: (850) 971-5003. www.floridastateparks.org/madison/default.cfm Hours: Daily 8:00am-sunset. Admission: $4.00 per vehicle.

Located in one of Florida's newest state parks, this crystal clear, first magnitude spring is a popular spot for swimming. About 82 feet wide and 25 feet deep, the spring bubbles up into a limestone basin along the west bank of the Withlacoochee River. Scenic woodlands of mixed hardwoods and pines create a picturesque setting for picnicking, paddling, and wildlife viewing. Really, most families come here to splash and swim.

SUWANNEE RIVER STATE PARK

Live Oak - 20185 County Road 132 (located 13 miles west of town, off US 90) 32060. Phone: (386) 362-2746. www.floridastateparks.org/suwanneeriver Hours: Florida state parks are open from 8 a.m. until sundown 365 days a year. Admission: An Honor Fee of $4.00 per car or $1.00 per person is payable at the pay station. Miscellaneous: Falmouth Springs, a short drive from Suwannee River State Park, claims to be the world's shortest river. Falmouth is a fifth magnitude spring.

Suwannee River State Park (cont.)

The scenic Withlacoochee River joins the legendary Suwannee River with this State Park. An overlook provides a panoramic view of both rivers and the surrounding wooded uplands. When water level is low, visitors can see springs bubbling from the banks of both rivers. Five trails provide great views of both rivers and access to remote springs. Along the river are long mounds of earthworks built during the Civil War to guard against Union gunboats. Other remnants from the past include one of the state's oldest cemeteries, and a paddle-wheel shaft from a 19th century steamboat. Other activities include fishing, picnicking, and canoeing. The park also has a boat ramp, picnic shelters, and a full facility campground and cabins.

LAFAYETTE BLUE SPRINGS STATE PARK

Mayo - 799 NW Blue Spring Road (from town, drive NW on US 27 for 4.3 miles. Turn right on CR 251) 32066. www.floridastateparks.org/lafayettebluesprings/default.cfm Phone: (386) 294-3667. Hours: Daily 8:00am-sunset. Admission: $4.00 per vehicle.

Located on the Suwannee River, this cool, clear water has attracted people on hot days for thousands of years. The Springs produce up to 168 million gallons of water daily, making it one of the state's 33 first magnitude springs. Swimming or snorkeling in the spring is most popular; river fishing is also a popular recreation activity. Visitors can enter the park by boat from the River as well as by car. Shaded picnic areas.

LETCHWORTH MOUNDS STATE ARCHAEOLOGICAL PARK

Monticello - 4500 Sunray Road South (US 90 east, then turn just south) 32344. Phone: (850) 922-6007. www.floridastateparks.org/letchworthmounds Hours: Daily 8:00am-sunset. Admission: FREE

Visitors to this archaeological site will see Florida's tallest Native American ceremonial mound (46 feet) built between 1100 and 1800 years ago. This is actually one of several mounds located on the site, suggesting the area was an activity center for the Weeden Island culture (Pre-Columbian). The people who built the mound are believed to be a group of Native Americans who lived in North Florida between 200 and 800 A.D! The park offers picnicking, birding, and hiking, too. A nature trail winds around the perimeter of the ceremonial mound. The picnic area and platform viewing area for the mound are wheelchair-accessible. Because there is not a Visitors Center, this park is more noted for the nature trails around the mound vs. historical learning.

GULF SPECIMEN MARINE LAB

Panacea - PO Box 237 32346. ***www.gulfspecimen.org*** *Phone: (850) 984-5297. Hours: Monday - Friday 9:00am-5:00pm, Saturday 10:00am-4:00pm, Sunday Noon-4:00pm. Aquarium is closed to the public on Thanksgiving, Christmas and New Years Day Admission: $5.00 adult, $3.00 child (3-11).*

Get up close and personal with native marine life through interactive touch aquariums and educational programs at this working marine biology lab. The hundreds of plant and animal species include mostly smaller creatures: sea anemones, crabs and jellyfish. Visitors can see and handle life forms that they have never before encountered, such as urchins, octopuses, shrimp and estuarine fish. They invite you to pick up and touch all the starfish, sea pansies, sand dollars, whelks, clams, etc. that are in the shallow trays and tanks, bearing in mind that crabs can pinch! The people looking at them are delighted to finally see a live seahorse or find out what a shrimp actually is before it ends up on a dinner plate or learn what that funny looking blob on the beach is. Unlike the large public aquariums, these are not static exhibits. Shrimpers, crabbers, gill-net fishermen, and collecting staff bring in a constant flow of new creatures.

FOREST CAPITAL MUSEUM STATE PARK

Perry - 204 Forest Park Drive, Hwy 19 South 32348. Phone: (850) 584-3227. www.floridastateparks.org/forestcapitalmuseum/ Hours: Thursday-Monday, 9:00am-Noon and 1:00-5:00pm. Admission: $4.00 per carload.

Forest Capital Museum State Park celebrates the timber that built Florida. The heart of the museum is dedicated to long leaf pines, which grow on the museum grounds, and the 5,000 products manufactured from them. The geodesic-domed museum features a map of Florida's unique woods, including lignumvitae, the hardest wood; leadwood, the heaviest; and buttonwood, the hottest burning. Adjacent to the museum, the Cracker Homestead Interpretive Site showcases daily living in the vast pinewoods that covered north Florida at the turn of the century. A museum complex devoted to wood - interesting take on "Natural Florida."

ST. MARKS NATIONAL WILDLIFE REFUGE AND LIGHTHOUSE

St. Marks - 1255 Lighthouse Road (County Road 59) (3 miles south of U.S. Hwy. 98 at Newport) 32355. Phone: (850) 925-6121. ***www.fws.gov/saintmarks/*** *Admission: $4.00 entrance fee per vehicle.*

The graceful lighthouse and registered historic site overlooking the St. Marks River serves as a nature preserve and winter nesting ground for great northern flocks of Canadian Geese. Students may be found dipping nets in the pond behind the Visitor Center or down at Apalachee Bay, exploring for insects, minnows, shrimp and more. There are 75 miles of marked trails to enjoy, winding through diverse habitats of the refuge. Create Your Own Trail – all levees and woodland roads are open to hiking, bicycling and horseback riding. Make up a trail that meets your family needs.

STEINHATCHEE FALLS RECREATION AREA

Steinhatchee - Falls Road (north on SR 51 for approximately 8 miles turn right on Falls Road, stop at the river) 32347. Phone: (850) 838-1530.   www.steinhatchee.info/falls.htm Hours: Daily 8:00am-7:00pm

Steinhatchee (pronounced Steen-hatchee) has always been a popular spot on the map for fishermen and boaters. This equates to great sport fishing. Scalloping in the summer offers a lot of family fun and a chance for some out door swimming exercise. Bring sun protection! Fall and winter usually provide great fishing in the Steinhatchee River and on the grass flats for speckled trout and redfish. The small waterfall is formed by a limerock outcropping in the river which extends north of the falls and, historically, served as a crossing point for Native Americans and settlers in the 1800s. There are several outdoor parks for picnics and swimming. Hagan's Cove, Keaton Beach, and Dallas Creek Landing are all located nearby. There are trails for hiking and the area is truly a real Florida outback experience. Of course there is the upper river for rafting and canoeing.

CHALLENGER LEARNING CENTER & IMAX THEATRE

Tallahassee - 200 S. Duval Street, downtown, next to Museums 32301. Phone: (850) 645-7827.   www.challengertlh.com Hours: Shows run 11:00am-evening. Usually 1-3 times per day. Admission: $5.50-$7.00 per IMAX show. $4.00-$5.00 for Planetarium shows. Combo prices with Planetarium, discounted. Space Station is priced at a group rate and scheduled in advance.

The huge facility uses aerospace as a theme to encourage interest in math, science and technology careers. They use state-of-the-future Space Mission Simulators and immersion dynamics of the IMAX theatre and a domed high-definition planetarium to create educational entertainment. MISSION CONTROL- The "engineers" (students) working in mission control must complete their tasks, share the information with and direct the astronauts to their next task. Furthermore, the "engineers" in Mission Control are required to maintain constant contact with the astronauts aboard the Space Station. Teammates in the SPACE STATION have the task of physically completing the mission "in space." The glove box with its hands-on experiments is a highlight of every mission and using robotics to manipulate science experiments is just one of many such activities that take place during a mission. Kids apply simple chemistry and physics lessons they have learned. The IMAX THEATRE area is for the general public to be entertained by Science or The Arts films on a five-story surround-immersion screen. Most films run 50-90 minutes.

KNOTT HOUSE THAT RHYMES

Tallahassee - 301 E. Park Avenue 32301. http://dhr.dos.state.fl.us/museum/sites/knotthouse/ Phone: (850) 922-2459. Admission: FREE

Built in 1843, the house served as temporary Union Headquarters in 1865, where Brigadier General Edward McCook announced the Emancipation Proclamation. Physician Dr. George Betton made the location his home and office in the 1880s. Betton assisted in the early medical training of his carriage driver, William Gunn, who became Florida's first African - American physician. In the early 20th century, three Florida Supreme Court judges lived in the house, acquired by William and Luella Knott in 1928. As the wife of a state treasurer, Luella hosted notable social functions, and as a poet, she wrote verses about the home and its furnishings, causing the site to be known as "The House That Rhymes." Rhymes are attached with satin ribbon to chairs, tables, lamps, and other household furnishings in this park-front mansion museum reflecting the social, economic and political history of Tallahassee. Her last poem written is displayed. She wrote of the haunting, sadden death of her husband just days before her own. Intriguing, engaging way to tour an historical home.

LAKE JACKSON MOUNDS ARCHAEOLOGICAL STATE PARK

Tallahassee - 3600 Indian Mound Road (off US 27 , 2 miles north of I-10, take Crowder Road) 32301. Phone: (850) 922-6007.   www.floridastateparks.org/lakejacksonmounds/ Hours: Daily 8:00am-sunset. Admission: $4.00 per carload.

Sacred burial grounds of descendants of Florida's Lake Jackson Indians, forefathers to the Seminole and Creek tribes, where arrowheads and pieces of Indian relics are still being unearthed and found today! The park site was part of what is now known as the Southeastern Ceremonial Complex. Today, it encompasses six earthen temple mounds and one possible burial mound. Artifacts found here include copper breastplates, necklaces, bracelets, anklets and cloaks. Take a short hike past the remains of an 1800s gristmill or picnic in one of the grassy areas.

MARY BROGAN MUSEUM OF ART & SCIENCE (MOAS)

Tallahassee - 350 S. Duval Street (downtown on Kleman Plaza behind City Hall) 32301. Phone: (850) 513-0700. www.thebrogan.org Hours: Monday-Saturday 10:00am-5:00pm, Sunday 1:00-5:00pm. First Friday's of the Month 10:00am - 9:00pm (4:00-9:00pm Admission is FREE!) Admission: $6.00 adult, $3.50 for children (3-17), students(with valid ID), senior citizens (60 and up), and military (with valid ID). Museum admission is free from 4:00pm until 5:00pm everyday.

A few blocks from the Old Capitol sits the three-story MOAS. The hands-on EcoLab Science Center offers touch tanks and turtles to delight young learners, while the first and third floors of the museum feature traveling world-class art and interactive science exhibitions such as light sculptures and musical robots. Watch yourself forecast the weather or play with light and color in the Close-Up Classroom. New Mind Games boggle your brain. Build a model of a crane or wishing well or design your own simple machine creation at Exploration Station. Dali to Dinos, Picasso to Plants...diverse and ever-changing.

OLD & NEW CAPITOL BUILDINGS

Tallahassee - Downtown, S. Duval Street or S. Monroe Street (at Apalachee Parkway) 32301. www.flheritage3.com/museum/sites/oldcapitol   Phone: (850) 488-6167 (New) or (850) 487-1902 (Old).   Hours: Monday-Friday 8:00am-5:00pm (New). Monday-Friday 9:00am-4:30pm, Saturday 10:00am-4:30pm, Sunday & Holidays Noon-4:30pm. Admission: FREE

The Capitol buildings are a good starting point for exploring Tallahassee. Built in 1845 and restored to its 1902 grandeur, the Old Capitol is filled with antiques and politics of old - and is open to the public. The American Renaissance appearance has red candy-striped awnings and a dome of stained glass, which sits under towering live oaks just steps away from the New Capitol. In the New, chambers of the House and Senate buzz with political zeal during the March though May legislative session. Special legislative viewing galleries are open during the legislative sessions. The 22nd floor observatory reveals a spectacular, panoramic view of the rolling hills of the county all the way to the shimmering Gulf of Mexico. The tower is the tallest structure in the city; by law, no other building can be built higher. Check out the hallway and Chamber murals. Can you find Florida's great seal?

SAN MARCOS DE APALACHE STATE HISTORIC SITE

Tallahassee - 1022 Desoto Blvd. (off SR 363 on Old Fort Road) 32301. Phone: (850) 922-6007 or (850) 925-6216. ***www.abfla.com/parks/SanMarcos/sanmarcos.html*** *Hours: Thursday-Monday 9:00am-5:00pm. Closed on Tuesdays, Wednesdays, Thanksgiving, Christmas and New Years Day. Admission: FREE*

To escape hostile Indians in 1528, Spanish explorer Narvaez was the first "white man" to build a boat in the United States. The fort was built in 1679 to protect Spanish missionaries. Today, a visitor center containing exhibits and artifacts covering the area's history is built on the foundation of the old marine hospital. Pottery and tools unearthed near the original fort are on display. A trail takes visitors on a journey through the historic fortification ruins.

MISSION SAN LUIS

Tallahassee - 2021 Mission Road (FL-263 S / Capital Circle NW via Exit 196 toward Regional Airport. Turn left onto US-90 E / FL-10 E / W Tennessee Street. 32304. Phone: (850) 487-3711. ***www.missionsanluis.org*** *Hours: Tuesday-Sunday 10:00am-4:00pm. Admission: FREE   Miscellaneous: Workshops and kids Camps sound so interesting – check that out if you live in the area.*

Mission San Luis was the western capital of Spanish Florida from 1656 to 1704. In addition to more than 1400 Apalachee Indian residents, San Luis was home to several hundred Spaniards, including friars, soldiers, and civilians – all living together in one community. It is the only reconstructed mission of the more than 100 such settlements established in Spanish Florida during the 16th and 17th centuries. Today, families can meet the people of San Luis going about the tasks that sustained life centuries ago. Ask them where they're from and who their neighbors are. Walk the plaza where the Apalachees played their traditional ball games. Superior ball players became pampered celebrities in their villages – just like super athletes today. Visit the most

Chatting with the "local" residents...

important structure in the Apalachee village, the council house. The Apalachee council house is the largest known Indian building in the southeast. It served as a hotel and ceremonial quarters. Visitors are welcomed at the church built under the supervision of Franciscans, and at the friary where they lived. Why is the Church unique? Notice there are no chairs or benches. Opened late 2006, the Castillo de San Luis is the authentic fort rebuilt from data found during archeological digs. Kids love running around in the fort. The staff and recreated village is very impressive and extremely educational and interactive! Plan to visit for at least one half day.

TALLAHASSEE AUTOMOBILE MUSEUM

Tallahassee - 3550 Mahan Drive 32308. Phone: (850) 942-0137. www.tacm.com Hours: Monday-Saturday 10:00am-5:00pm, Sunday 1:00-5:00pm. Admission : $7.50 adult, $5.00 youth (11-15), $4.00 child (under 11).

From political figures and premier "Prowlers" to polished chrome, the museum holds one of the most extensive car collections in the world with two Batmobiles, the first Prowler to role off the assembly line, the hearse that carried President Lincoln to his final resting place and the Tucker from "A Man and His Dream." Pedal cars, boat motors, Indian artifacts, too.

ALFRED MACLAY GARDENS STATE PARK

Tallahassee - 3540 Thomasville Road (one-half mile north of I-10 on US 319) 32309. Phone: (850) 487-4556. www.floridastateparks.org/maclaygardens Hours: Florida state parks are open from 8 a.m. until sundown 365 days a year. Admission: $4.00 per group for up to 8 people. Miscellaneous: High blooming season is from January 1 - April 30 with the floral peak in mid-to-late March. During these months, the Maclay house is open daily, 9:00am-5:00pm

These beautiful ornamental gardens were first planted in 1923 by Alfred B. and Louise Maclay after they purchased the property for their winter home. A great place to take the kids in strollers, the gardens feature a picturesque brick walkway, a secret garden, a reflection pool, a walled garden, and hundreds of azaleas and camellias. Lake Hall provides opportunities for swimming, fishing, canoeing and kayaking (especially spring and summer). Only boats without motors or with electric motors are allowed. Pavilions and grills along the lake shore provide the perfect setting for a picnic and there's always a cool breeze there. For walking enthusiasts, two short nature trails meander through the woods overlooking the lake. Hikers, bicyclists, and equestrians can enjoy five miles of multi-use trails winding through the woods surrounding Lake Overstreet, located on park property adjoining the gardens.

TALLAHASSEE MUSEUM OF HISTORY & NATURAL SCIENCE

Tallahassee - 3945 Museum Drive (follow Capital Circle SW to Lake Bradford Road (Springhill Road); a sign will direct you to the Museum) 32310. Phone: (850) 576-1636. www.tallahasseemuseum.org Hours: Monday-Saturday 9:00am-5:00pm, Sunday 12:30-5:00pm. Admission: $8.00 adult, $7.50 senior (65+) and college, $5.50 child (4-15).

At this museum, you can see a real live Florida panther, the state's official animal, and other native wildlife like red wolves (extinct in the wild) and alligators. On its beautiful, 52-acre lakeside setting, the museum combines a natural habitat zoo, a collection of historical buildings and artifacts, and an environmental science center - all linked along shaded paths. HISTORIC COMPLEX: Kids into electronics will want to rent the self-guided audio tours that take you back in time to an authentic 1880s Cracker farmstead, replete with farm animals and a veggie garden (often the site of living history demos). Kids can also tour the 1924 Florida East Coast Railroad caboose, the 1890s Concord schoolhouse established to educate the children of former slaves, and an 1840s manor home moved here from a cotton plantation. Wander past a Cypress Swamp. Lastly, check out the Turpentine Factory Company Store where workers shopped.

DISCOVERY CENTER: Enter the magical world of microscopes and unveil life's tiniest plants and animals. Use a stereoscope to examine 19th century people and places. Watch videos, slides, puppet shows, and creative performances. Become an environmental scientist, and discover what lives in an aquarium, vivarium, and terrarium, and touch some of the creatures if you dare! Crawl through a replica of a 12-foot oak tree. See yourself in the clothes of a bygone era and play with penny banks at the Victorian Corner.

MUSEUM OF FLORIDA HISTORY

Tallahassee - 500 S. Bronough Street, R.A. Gray Building (corner of W. Pensacola & Bronough, downtown) 32399. Phone: (850) 245-6400. www.flheritage.com/museum/ Hours: Monday-Friday: 9:00am - 4:30pm; Saturday: 10:00am - 4:30pm; Sunday and holidays: Noon - 4:30pm. Admission: FREE Miscellaneous: Ask for the audio tour or the kids scavenger hunt to make it interesting.

As the state history museum, it focuses on artifacts and eras unique to Florida's development and on roles that Floridians have played in national and global events. Standing nine feet tall, Herman, a skeletal prehistoric mastodon originally weighing about five tons, was pulled from Wakulla Springs in the 1930s. The museum "mascot" oversees the Prehistoric Florida Exhibit. Pull a lever to re-enact

Every citrus crate label had
a "story to tell"

ancient sea levels. Then, head through the Ice Age. Touch replicas and observe mega fauna. Spanish Treasures explores the quest for gold. Why are some coins and some jewelry? War relics areas include a thought-provoking area outlining southern reconstruction – now that slavery was gone, Floridians used prisoners for labor. Kids especially like the recreated Citrus factory hands-on stations, Grandma's Attic, and the walk-on riverboat.

ECONFINA RIVER STATE PARK

Tallahassee (Lamont) - (end of SR 14, S of US 98) 32301. Phone: (850) 922-6007. www.floridastateparks.org/ecofinariver/ Hours: 8:00am-sunset.

Spectacular vistas and scenic beauty await visitors to this large preserve located on the Gulf of Mexico. Primary recreational activities include picnicking, canoeing, boating, and fishing in the varied surroundings of pine flatlands, palm forests and salt marshes dotted with pine islands. Unimproved hiking and equestrian trails are also available.

WAKULLA SPRINGS STATE PARK AND LODGE

Wakulla Springs - 550 Wakulla Park Drive (14 miles south of Tallahassee on State Road 267 at the intersection with State Road 61) 32327. Phone: (850) 224-5950. www.florida stateparks.org/wakullasprings/Activities.cfm Hours: Daily 8:00am-sunset. Admission: $4.00 per vehicle. Guest Rooms $85.00 - $105.00 Miscellaneous: You can enjoy cuisine and a beautiful view through the arched windows of the Ball Room Restaurant. The dining room features daily specials, fresh seafood and many local favorites including "World Famous" Navy bean soup plus fried chicken. To reserve a guest or meeting room, please call the park.

Home of one of the largest and deepest freshwater springs in the world (185-feet), this park plays host to an abundance of wildlife, including lazy alligators, snake birds, turtles, deer, and birds. The surroundings may look familiar - many of the early Tarzan movies and the Creature From the Black Lagoon were filmed here. Swimming is a popular activity during the hot summer months at the head of the spring. A nature trail offers a leisurely walk along the upland wooded areas of the park. The Wakulla Springs Lodge was built in 1937 and the dining room offers breakfast, lunch and dinner. Daily guided jungle riverboat tours provide a closer view of wildlife, and glass bottom boat tours are offered when the water is clear.

GLASS-BOTTOM BOAT TOUR is a 30-minute trip over the spring. Safaris aboard the glass-bottomed and jungle cruise boats whisk visitors within arm's length of "The Other Florida." Peering down through the clear water to a depth of 125 feet, Park Rangers will share the mysteries and history of this unique natural area. Large fish are observed, as well as, the catfish convention. One of the highlights will be observing the antics of " Henry, The Pole Vaulting Fish". Stories will be told of local folklore and passengers will see prehistoric Mastodon bones on the bottom of the spring basin.

RIVER BOAT TOUR is a 40 minute trip taking a different route. Park Rangers navigate the boat for the 3-mile round trip down the Wakulla River introducing you to the "Real Florida".

STEPHEN FOSTER FOLK CULTURE CENTER STATE PARK

White Springs - Post Office Drawer G (I-75 to SR 136 (Milepost Exit 439 - Old Exit 84), travel east on SR 136 for 3 miles. Turn left on U.S. 41) 32096. Phone: (386) 397-2733. www.floridastateparks.org/stephenfoster Hours: Museum, Tower and Gift Shop are open from 9:00am-5:00pm, daily. Admission: $4.00 per vehicle. Cabin Fee - $90.00 per night. Camping Fee - $16.00 per night per campsite. Nelly Bly's Kitchen - $60.00 per day.

Situated on the banks of the legendary Suwannee River, this center honors the memory of American composer Stephen Foster, who wrote "Old Folks at Home," the song that made the river famous. This Cultural Park offers a permanent year-round craft village. In Craft Square, visitors can watch demonstrations of quilting, blacksmithing, stain glass making, and other crafts, or visit the gift shop. Listen to the melodies flowing from the Memorial Carillon Tower, and see 10 wonderfully detailed dioramas illustrating the famous songs of composer Stephen Foster. Rare pianos and priceless musical instruments also are on exhibit. Guided tours of the Museum and Tower are offered daily. Although he never visited the area, his song about the Suwannee River is legendary. The park has wooded trails that are easily accessible for hiking and cycling. Take a canoe or kayak trip on the Suwannee River sure to promise a leisurely adventure. Check into one of the riverside cabins, complete with a kitchenette, outdoor grill and sleeping accommodations for six people. Camp or simply relax and watch the Suwannee River go by…

SUWANNEE RIVER WILDERNESS TRAIL

White Springs - (The Wilderness Trail is accessible from "hubs", boat ramps, and public parks along its entire 207 mile length, beginning in White Springs) 32096. Phone: (800) 868-9914. www.suwanneeriver.com/ www.floridastateparks.org/wilderness Hours: Staff at the Nature and Heritage Tourism Center are available to provide information about

*the Suwannee River Wilderness Trail 8:00 am to 5:00pm seven days a week, 365 days a
year. Miscellaneous: Suwannee River Diner - southern comfort food and historic murals
on walls. Access to the river tubing is from the ICHETUCKNEE SPRINGS STATE PARK.
Tubing and canoeing. Canoes and tubes are available from vendors outside the park. Tubes
generally rent for $3.00 to $5.00 per day. Several options are available for length of tube
run. (12087 SW US Hwy 27, Fort White, Florida 32038 Phone: 386-497-2511). Several
other Springs are commercially operated along the Trail including HART SPRINGS & BLUE
SPRINGS (www.purewaterwilderness.com). Both have boardwalk trails along the River.*

The SRWT runs 207 miles from the northern most extent of rural north Florida to
the Gulf of Mexico and encompasses activities such as canoeing, camping, boating,
hiking, biking, birding and horseback riding. The Suwannee River boasts over 70
crystal clear springs - most found in the Middle area. The springs range in size
from small fissures to first magnitude springs with an average water flow of over
65 million gallons per day. On hot summer days, spring hopping is a popular sport
for paddlers and boaters who stop at the cooling waters of different springs along
the trail. The average temperature of the spring water is 72 degrees year round.
In the Lower Suwannee, a rail-trail through the greenway provides views of old
Florida. Little River Springs marks the trail's western end while the Ichetucknee
River is on the eastern end. (12 mile long trail) ICHETUCKNEE SPRINGS
STATE PARK, FANNING SPRINGS STATE PARK and MANATEE SPRINGS
STATE PARK are all along this lower Suwannee trail portion. Houseboats make
a fine vehicle for cruising the lower 70 miles of the Suwannee River Wilderness
Trail and visitors can rent one from Miller Marina (training included) for several
days (www.suwanneehouseboats.com). The Upper Suwannee area is included in
the listing for the Suwannee River State Park.

SUGGESTED LODGING AND DINING

HOLIDAY INN WEST HOTEL - 7417 Newberry Road (I-75 exit 387),
Gainesville. **www.gainesvillehotelconferencecenter.com**. (800) 551-8206.
Home of the University of Florida Gators, they offer modest-sized rooms and
the kids eat free in the restaurant (yummy, reasonably-priced breakfast buffet).
The highlight of the property has to be the large outdoor heated pool in the center
courtyard. It welcomed us every evening after a day of touring and we easily spent
hours playing in and around the huge pool area.

MOE'S SOUTHWEST GRILL – 3832 Newberry Road or 3443 SW Archer
Road. **Gainesville**. (352) 337-2850 or 367-8565 or **www.moes.com**. Moe's
knows burritos – huge burritos, tacos, quesadillas and stuff. You tell them what
you want – which fillings, meats, veggies so everybody gets a custom product.

Try their chips and queso dip but save room for the burrito! The owner told us many adults order from the kids menu cause the food is so big (stuffed). Try Puff the Magic Dragon, MooMoo Mr. Cow or Mini-Me that include cookie and drinks. Most items are $4.00-$6.00 and the Kids menu is all under $4.00.

ANDREW'S CAPITAL GRILL – 228 South Adams Street, across from the Supreme Court building. (850) 222-3444 or **www.andrewsdowntown.com**, **Tallahassee**. Lunch and Dinner. Dine amongst politicians. Great hot and cold sandwiches but their best feature is the hot/cold salad bar for around $8.99 at lunchtime. Not only fresh greens, but wonderful prepared salads, too. We especially recommend their homemade quiche, mac 'n cheese or lasagna hot dishes. Quality service and food and within walking distance of all the museums and state buildings to tour.

BARNACLE BILLS – 1830 North Monroe Street (US 27/SR63). (850) 385-8734, **Tallahassee**. Start off with Smoked Salmon Dip (kids say it tastes like bbq'ed tuna salad) or Fried Pickles. We loved the presentation of the Monster Seafood Bucket. Be sure to try their homemade cocktail sauce (outstanding) with the shrimp and oysters. Lots of healthy protein here! Non-seafood lovers can order chicken or steamed veggies. Look for the photo-op mermaid and sailor poster and the live aquarium to amuse the kids while they wait for the meal. Kids Menu with some seafood items plus spaghetti and chicken.

HAMPTON INN & SUITES - 3388 Lonnbladh Rd, (I-10/Thomasville Rd, exit 203, east side of town), **www.hamptoninnandsuitestallahassee.com**. **Tallahassee**. (850) 574-4900. Features 122 rooms, 37 are studio suites including microwaves and refrigerators, outdoor pool, fitness center and business center with complimentary Wireless Internet Access throughout the hotel. Amenities include their new complimentary ''Make It Hampton'' hot breakfast with tons of fresh food. The pool area is inviting and popular. One of the nicest moderately priced hotels we've ever visited.

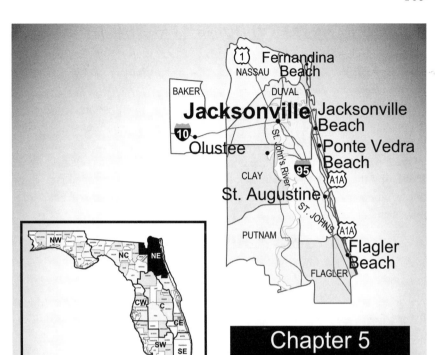

Chapter 5
North East (NE) Area

Our Favorites...

* Museum of Science & History - Jacksonville
* Jacksonville Beach
* GTM Environmental Education Center
- Ponte Vedra Beach
* St. Augustine Lighthouse - St. Augustine
* St. Augustine Old Jail - St. Augustine
* Old Town Trolley Tours of St. Augustine & St.
George Street - St. Augustine
* Ponce De Leon's Fountain of Youth - St. Augustine
* Schooner Freedom - St. Augustine

BULOW PLANTATION RUINS STATE HISTORIC SITE

Bunnell - Old Dixie Highway, north of Ormond Beach (3 miles west of Flagler Beach on SR 100, then south on CR 2001) 32136. Phone: (386) 517-2084. ***www.abfla.com/parks/bulowplantation/ bulowplantation.html*** *Hours: 9:00am-5:00pm daily. Admission: $2.00 /vehicle.*

Here are the remains of what was once known as Bulowville. Founded in 1821, the plantation cultivated sugar cane, cotton, indigo and rice before its destruction in the Seminole Indian War. Bulow Plantation is one of the area's few preserved coquina-rock sugar mill ruins. The once cleared fields have been reclaimed by the forest, and the area looks much as it did in the 1800s. Also included is a spring house, an open-air museum featuring Seminole Indian relics and artifacts, canoe rentals and picnic facilities.

AMELIA RIVER CRUISES

Fernandina Beach - 1 Front Street 32034. ***www.ameliarivercruises.com*** *Phone: (904) 261-9972.*

A visit to Amelia Island is incomplete without a tour of the waterways. Amelia River Cruises & Charters provides many opportunities to do just that. All of the tours are fully narrated and you may explore the backwaters of Amelia Island, and Cumberland Island, cruise up Egan's Creek to the Amelia Island Lighthouse or spend the day in historic St. Mary's, Georgia. The narrated one hour tour will take you past the historic waterfront of Fernandina where the modern shrimping industry was born. Cruise Tiger Basin -- an oasis of salt marshes - then Cumberland Sound where dolphins blow around the boat, sea turtles catch their breath and the endangered manatee spend the summer. Learn about Fernandina's rich history... from Old Town and the former site of Fort San Carlos to Fort Clinch, an 1850's brick fortress which stands guard between the Amelia River and the open sea. Observe North Florida's snowy egrets, spoonbills, herons and pelicans as they fly over or wade near shore. Experience the break-taking views of Cumberland Island and watch as wild horses graze on the island's south end, much like their ancestors did when Cumberland was inhabited by some of America's most prominent families. Watch as crabbers and fishermen bring in their bounty.

FORT CLINCH STATE PARK

Fernandina Beach - 2601 Atlantic Avenue (north of the city, off A1A) 32034. Phone: (904) 277-7274. ***www.floridastateparks.org/fortclinch/*** *Hours: Daily 8:00am-sunset. Admission: $5.00 per vehicle.*

Pre-Civil War coastal fort listed on the National Register of Historical Places. Daily tours with period re-enactors depicting garrison life bring the fort to life for visitors. Sunbathing, swimming, and beachcombing are popular activities at the beach. Anglers can fish from the pier or take advantage of excellent surf fishing. Hikers and bicyclists can enjoy a six-mile trail through the park. Self-guided nature trails provide opportunities to learn about and observe native plants and wildlife. Sixty-two campsites. 1,363 acres of beach, dunes, maritime forest and tidal marsh.

GAMBLE ROGERS MEMORIAL STATE RECREATION AREA AT FLAGLER BEACH

Flagler Beach - 3100 South A1A (I-95 exit 91) 32136. Phone: (386) 517-2086. www.floridastateparks.org/gamblerogers/ Hours: Daily 8:00am-sunset. Miscellaneous: NORTH PENINSULA STATE PARK is just 4 miles south of Flagler Beach (www.florida stateparks.org/northpeninsula/) and offers more than two miles of beautiful, unspoiled Atlantic beaches.

A windswept beach named for Florida folk singer Gamble Rogers and railroad baron Henry Flagler. Bordered by the Atlantic Ocean to the east and the Intra coastal waterway to the west this 144 acre park offers coastal camping, picnicking, swimming, fishing and scenic relaxation. A1A Ocean Shore Scenic Highway spans a seven-mile stretch of Flagler County's beach between quiet Flagler Beach and Beverly Beach. A bicycle/pedestrian path parallels the scenic corridor and provides recreation for the cyclist, jogger and peace-loving stroller. At night, during the months of May through early September, endangered and threatened Loggerhead, Green and the rare Leatherback sea turtles crawl on the beach to nest and lay their eggs as they have done for thousands of years. A wide variety of bird life can be observed during the fall, winter and spring months.

JACKSONVILLE SPORTS

JACKSONVILLE JAGUARS - www.jaguars.com. One Alltel Stadium Place. NFL home games in the Stadium.

JACKSONVILLE SUNS - www.jaxsuns.com. Jacksonville Suns professional baseball team. Members of the "AA" Southern League, affiliated with the Los Angeles Dodgers. The Suns play 70 home games from April-August at the new Baseball Grounds of Jacksonville.

FORT CAROLINE NATIONAL MONUMENT

Jacksonville - 12713 Fort Caroline Road 32099. ***www.nps.gov/foca/index.htm*** *Phone: (904) 641-7155. Hours: Daily except Christmas 9:00am-5:00pm. Admission: FREE*

Fort Caroline on the banks of the St. John's River was settled by the French Huguenots in 1564 and is the site of the first Protestant colony in the New World. The 130-acre memorial is located in East Arlington off Fort Caroline Road. It features a replica of the original fort, a museum with French and Indian artifacts and several nature trails which provide excellent hiking. The nearby Roosevelt Area has additional nature trails.

JACKSONVILLE MUSEUM OF MODERN ART (JMOMA)

Jacksonville - 333 N. Laura Street (on historic Hemming Plaza next to City Hall) 32202. Phone: (904) 366-6911. ***www.jmoma.org*** *Hours:Tuesday-Friday 11:00am-5:00pm, Saturday 11:00am-4:00pm, Sunday Noon-4:00pm. Open until 9:00pm on Wednesdays and Thursdays. Admission: $4.00-$6.00 (student plus). Wednesday evenings are FREE.*

JMOMA is the largest modern & contemporary art museum in the Southeast. Film series and lectures are offered in the 125-seat theater. Family fun in the fifth floor ArtExplorium Loft. Café Nola is open for lunch, weekdays. Jacksonville Museum of Modern Art's ArtExplorium Loft is a family learning center that offers an alternative to the traditionally hands-off approach of museum visits. The Loft offers hands-on activities inspired by the Museum's collection. This vibrant and colorful space features 16 stimulating learning stations where children and adults alike can learn more about modern and contemporary art. An interactive setting, ArtExplorium Loft allows for multiple learning styles and encourages families to foster cultural awareness, arouse curiosity, and learn about modern and contemporary art cooperatively.

CUMMER MUSEUM OF ART

Jacksonville - 829 Riverside Ave. (north bank of the St. Johns River) 32204. Phone: (904) 356-6857. ***www.cummer.org*** *Hours: Tuesday-Saturday 10:00am-5:00pm, Sunday Noon-5:00pm. Open some evenings until 9:00pm. Admission: $8.00 adult, $5.00 senior and child (ages 6+). Admission is FREE on Tuesday nights.*

The Cummer is the largest fine art museum in Northeast Florida. Noted for Old Master and American paintings, beautiful formal gardens and renowned collection of Meissen porcelain. National award-winning art education center enhances the cultural experience of more than 150,000 visitors annually. The newly renovated Art Connections contains hands-on, interactive exhibits designed to raise visitors' understanding of the art in the museum's permanent collection. There are exhibits that are high tech and low tech, exhibits that allow for individual exploration and group interaction, and exhibits that encourage physical activity and quiet contemplation. In Art Connections, it is possible to walk through a painting, create patterns through dance, make a collage, listen to a sculpture, or paint with a virtual paintbrush.

MUSEUM OF SCIENCE AND HISTORY (MOSH)

Jacksonville - 1025 Museum Circle (I-95 Main Street Bridge exit north one block, left on Museum Circle) 32207. Phone: (904) 396-MOSH. **www.themosh.org** *Hours: Monday-Friday 10:00am-5:00pm, Saturday 10:00am-6:00pm, Sunday 1:00-6:00pm. Admission: $8.00 adult, $6.50 senior and active military, $6.00 child (3-12).*

Don't you love the life-size Right Whale that greats you in the beautiful Atlantic Tails room? Because it's life-size (giant), it's a little intimidating. Dolphins and Manatees are displayed here, too, as you interact with this hands-on exhibit space. In other spaces, kids (and their adults) can find out how much water they use or how much water content is in their body. Next, maybe launch a hot air balloon, test your skills on the gravity table, send a rocket soaring, or make loud music. Check the list of Planetarium and Science Theater shows for cosmic, electrifying and explosive science demonstrations. Like live animals? They have plenty, indoors and out. Visit live snakes, birds, spiders,

That's "music" to my ears ...

alligators, frogs, lizards and turtles (such cuties) native to Northeast Florida. Tonca, the 120-pound alligator snapping turtle has a new, improved exhibit house. A scary, intriguing creature. MOSH's oldest resident, the dino Allosaurus skeleton, is here and more history is in Currents of Time: A History of Jacksonville and Northeast Florida. Journey through 12,000 years of regional history as this exhibit displays colonization, war time, the Great Fire and the 50s.

TREE HILL NATURE CENTER

Jacksonville - 7152 Lone Star Road 32211. Phone: (904) 724-4646.   www.treehill.org
Hours: Monday-Saturday 8:00am-4:30pm.   Admission: $1.00-$2.00 per person (students and above).

Tree Hill, Jacksonville's Nature Center, is comprised of 53 acres of urban wilderness. Tree Hill's exhibits on energy, natural history and native wildlife species are all located in the pyramid museum. An interactive exhibit on solar energy teaches our visitors about electricity and energy conservation. Photovoltaic panels on the buildings exterior convert sunlight to electricity and power the displays. Dioramas depicting life 12,000 years ago in Florida are accompanied by fossils and replicas of ancient animal life. Do Bears Live in Florida? Yes! Florida is home to the Florida Black Bear, which is a subspecies of the American Black Bear. Outside, roam the acres of trails using a self-guided map from the center.

JACKSONVILLE ZOO AND GARDENS

Jacksonville - 8605 Zoo Parkway (I-95 North: Take exit number 358A to Zoo Parkway/ Heckscher Drive East) 32218. Phone: (904) 757-4463.   www.jaxzoo.org Hours: Daily 9:00am-5:00pm. Extended until 6:00pm on weekends and holidays.   Admission: $11.00 adult, $9.50 senior (65+), $6.50 child (3-12).

Escape to the Jacksonville Zoo and Gardens for the only walking safari in Northeast Florida. Each year, it seems, they're targeted to add something new. Check in at the Main Camp, then it's off to the Bird Aviary (free flight enclosure) and the Plains of East Africa. Walk along the 1,400 foot boardwalk overlooking the Plains and see the native animals like: Nile Crocodile, the warthog, gazelle, cheetah, the white rhino, or the zebra along the walk. Lions, monkeys and leopard reside here, too. Take a close-up look at Great Apes then back to Wild Florida natives like black bears, otters, bobcats, alligators, and Florida panthers. The alligators are located near the Reptile House and are fed every Saturday at 2:00pm during the warm weather (do we really need to see this?) The Australian Adventure attraction includes beloved kangaroos, wallabies and the koalas. A highlight of this attraction is the lorikeets that can be fed by visitors. Range of the Jaguar focuses on a neotropical rain forest setting and, of course, highlights jaguar. Our adored capybaras (giant guinea pigs) live around here, too. The Giraffe Overlook was redesigned to allow guests to get eye to eye with the tall giraffes. Finally, kids wild to play? Try the Wildlife Carousel or the Kids Play Zone (a splash zone area, forest play area, a maze and discovery building). Kids play while watching the antics of playful otters and monkeys.

KINGSLEY PLANTATION (TIMUCUAN ECOLOGICAL AND HISTORIC PRESERVE)

Jacksonville - *13165 Mount Pleasant Road (I-95, exit on Heckscher Drive (FL 105); follow Heckscher East to Florida 9A, just north of the Mayport car ferry) 32225. Phone: (904) 251-3537.* ***www.jacksonvilleflorida.com/parks/kingsleyplantation.asp*** *Hours: Daily 9:00am-5:00pm. Admission: FREE Miscellaneous: One trail takes visitors from the planter's home to the slave quarters; the return trail winds slightly through the forested landscape. The total loop is approximately one-third mile. The site is self-guiding and a staff member is available throughout the day. Scheduled Ranger talks are posted on-site.*

The oldest plantation still in existence in Florida is now a National Park Service historic site. The location includes the plantation house, which has ranger guided programs and extensive grounds, including the ruins of the slave quarters. Families will be curious to learn more about the fact that the Kingsley operated under a "task" system, which allowed slaves to work at a craft or tend their own gardens once the specified task for the day was completed. Proceeds from the sale of produce or craft items were usually kept by the slaves. Purchased as a slave, Kingsley's wife, Anna Madgigine Jai, was freed in 1811. She was active in plantation management and became a successful business woman owning her own property. As an American territory, Florida passed laws that discriminated against free blacks and placed harsh restrictions on African slaves. This prompted Kingsley to move his family, impacted by these laws, to Haiti, now the Dominican Republic, where descendants of Anna and Zephaniah live today.

AMELIA ISLAND STATE PARK

Jacksonville - *12157 Heckscher Drive (seven miles north of Little Talbot Island State Park on State Road A1A, or eight miles south of Fernandina Beach) 32226. Phone: (904) 251-2320.* ***www.floridastateparks.org/ameliaisland/*** *Hours: Open 24 hours a day. Admission: $1.00/person entrance fee. Miscellaneous: While enjoying Amelia Island, please remember that bird nesting season starts April 1st and sea turtle nesting season starts May 1st. By following posted signs they can safeguard the valuable natural resources.*

Located where Nassau Sound meets the Atlantic Ocean, Amelia Island State Park offers visitors incredible recreational opportunities in a picturesque natural setting. The point at the southern tip of Amelia Island provides a stunning panorama of land and sea. If you really want an exceptional beach experience, visit Kelly's Seahorse Ranch and take a beach tour by horseback! This park is one of the few locations on the East Coast that offers horseback riding on the beach, a 45-minute riding tour along the shoreline. Visitors can also stroll along the beach, look for seashells, or watch the wildlife. For horseback tour reservations, contact Kelly

Seahorse Ranch at (904) 491-5166. Tours are given four times daily. Fishing is popular from the shore of Amelia Island State Park as well as from the adjacent George Crady Bridge Fishing Pier State Park that spans Nassau Sound.

FORT GEORGE ISLAND CULTURAL STATE PARK

Jacksonville - 12157 Heckscher Drive (16 miles east of downtown Jacksonville on SR A1A, or three miles south of Little Talbot Island State Park) 32226. Phone: (904) 251-2320.   www.floridastateparks.org/fortgeorgeisland/ Hours: Daily 8:00am-sunset. Admission: FREE

A site of human occupation for over 5,000 years, Fort George Island was named for a 1736 fort built to defend the southern flank of Georgia when it was a colony. Today's visitors come for boating, fishing, off-road bicycling, and hiking. There is a three-mile hiking/biking trail on Fort George Island. The trail runs through the interior of the former Fort George golf course. A successional process is returning the golf course land back to its natural state and restoring the maritime forest habitat. The trail is suitable for large tired bikes. Fort George Island Cultural State Park offers a loop bicycle ride through history. Pick up a copy of the Saturiwa Trail guide at the Little Talbot Island Ranger Station or in the brochure rack in front of the Ribault Club on Fort George Island. The loop is 4.4 miles and consists of paved road and hard packed gravel. And don't forget about the Virtual Ranger Tour of the Saturiwa Trail on Fort George Island. All you need is a car CD-player and an interest in "old Florida". The tour follows the narrow road around Fort George Island, a setting rich in natural and cultural significance. Visitors have the option of checking out a CD audio guide, or downloading a written version of the Virtual Ranger Tour from this website. Both the audio and text versions are designed to be self-guiding, allowing visitors to do the tour at their own pace.

TALBOT ISLANDS STATE PARKS

Jacksonville - 12157 Heckscher Drive (20 miles east of downtown Jacksonville on A1A North, immediately north of Little Talbot Island State Park) 32226. Phone: (904) 251-2320.   www.floridastateparks.org/bigtalbotisland/ Hours: Daily 8:00am-sunset. Admission: $1.00-$4.00 per vehicle.

Talbot Islands State Parks is a chain of barrier islands, located north of the St. John's River. Come out and enjoy the pristine Big Talbot shoreline this spring from the overlook at the Bluffs. From this comfortable vantage visitors can enjoy the weather and view the water sculpted trees that line the shore. A quick 10-minute walk along the trail will give you access to the shoreline where you can walk among these once mighty oaks and pines that have fallen victim to nature's storms and erosion. Little Talbot has one of Florida's most pristine beaches with over 5 miles of shoreline along the Atlantic Ocean. Visitors can fish, surf, search for seashells, or watch the birds while basking in the springtime Florida sun. The parks offer miles of beautiful beaches, kayaking, horseback riding, fishing, camping, hiking and nature trails, and picnic pavilions.

ALHAMBRA DINNER THEATRE

Jacksonville - 12000 Beach Blvd. 32246. www.alhambradinnertheatre.com Phone: (904) 641-1212. Shows: Evenings Tuesday-Sunday; matinees Saturdays and Sundays. Admission: $35.00-$46.00 general; Teen Matinees $21.00; Children's Matinees $7.00 (bring your own lunch).

Fine dining and an off-Broadway show serving meat, chicken, and seafood entrees with many sides and dessert. Shows include hits like Hello Dolly, Oklahoma and Beauty and the Beast.

JACKSONVILLE BEACH

Jacksonville Beach - Eleven North Third Street 32250. Phone: (904) 247-6268. www.jaxbch.govoffice.com Miscellaneous: ADVENTURE LANDING (On Beach Boulevard just east of the Intracoastal Waterway) The park includes a water park with slides and a riverway, a go-kart track, miniature golf, laser tag arena batting cage and an arcade with a wide variety of games. A full snack bar is available for refreshments. The park is open seven days a week from 10:00am-2:00am. Prices vary for different activities. For information call (904) 246-4386.

Discover northeast Florida's best-kept secret, Jacksonville Beach. Tucked away on a barrier island east of Jacksonville on Florida's famous A1A, you'll find miles of un-crowded white sandy beaches. With the Intracoastal Waterway, St. John's River and the Atlantic Ocean to choose from, Jacksonville Beach offers lots of opportunities whether you are a fisherman, a golfer, or a family looking for good clean fun.

Play in the ocean, walk or collect seashells along the beach, or stroll along the Sea Walk and watch for porpoise year-round or the northern right-whales each winter off the coast. At the Sea Walk Pavilion, you'll find concerts or festivals nearly every weekend from April through October. In May and June, the SeaWalk area shows classic films on the giant screen (Moonlight Movies - free). The best part

- park your vehicle and walk the well-maintained beachfront and splash and play in the water. Our experience was a less crowded, family setting. Occasional foot showers and restrooms available. The small boardwalk area (SeaWalk) is the best place to brush off the sand and grab a bite to eat or do some light shopping.

OLUSTEE BATTLEFIELD STATE PARK & MUSEUM

Lake City (Olustee) - (13 miles east of Lake City, I-10 exit US 90 west) 32072. Phone: (386) 758.0400. www.floridastateparks.org/olustee Hours: The park is open every day from 8 a.m. until dusk. The Interpretive Center is open daily from 9:00am-5:00pm. All facilities are available free of charge.

Olustee Battlefield Historic State Park was built to preserve the site of the state's largest Civil War battle, which took place February 20, 1864. More than 10,000 cavalry, infantry, and artillery troops fought a five-hour battle in a pine forest near Olustee. Three U.S. Colored Troops took part in the battle, including the now famous 54th Massachusetts. The battle ended with 2,807 casualties and the retreat of Union troops to Jacksonville until the war's end just 14 months later. A small interpretive center, a one-mile interpretive trail, and monuments to the Union and Confederate armies are open to the public free of charge. The interpretive center contains historical information and artifacts related to the Battle of Olustee.

OSCEOLA NATIONAL FOREST

Olustee - US Hwy 90 32072. Phone: (386) 752-2577 or (386) 752-0147 Visitors Center. www.fs.fed.us/r8/florida/recreation/index_osc.shtml

Visitors enjoy quiet, peaceful woodlands named in honor of the famous Seminole Indian warrior, Osceola. These forested woodlands and swamps provide many opportunities for a wide range of visitor experiences such as camping, hiking, swimming, fishing, hunting, wildlife viewing and many more. A 23 mile section of the Florida National Scenic Trail meanders its way through the Osceola National Forest. There are 20 boardwalks located on this section of the hiking trail that offer a drier view of swamps and wetland habitat. A primitive camp shelter is located along the Florida National Scenic Trail and is available on a first come first served basis. The trail also passes through the Olustee Battlefield. Olustee Battlefield is a state Historic Site where Confederate soldiers pushed back Union troops in route to Tallahassee (see separate listing). Olustee Beach is located on the south side of Ocean Pond and provides visitors the opportunity to fish, swim, boat and picnic along the scenic shores of Ocean Pond. A white sandy beach, showers, flush toilets, drinking water, boat ramp, picnic tables, a covered shelter and grills are available for day use. ($2.00 per vehicle charged for beach access).

MURALS OF PALATKA

Palatka - Downtown Buildings 32177. Phone: (386) 328-6500. www.conleemurals.org
The Mural City of North Central Florida has dozens of murals to show off - mostly on buildings, some indoors. Various town artists try their hand at depicting local historical, cultural and natural resources about the town. Check out the 3D dimensions of Bygone Days or the stark red mud color in Heartbeat of Palatka.

WASHINGTON OAKS GARDENS STATE PARK

Palm Coast - 6400 N. Oceanshore Blvd. (two miles south of Marineland on State Road A1A) 32173. Phone: (386) 446-6780.   www.floridastateparks.org/washingtonoaks/ Hours: Daily 8:00am-sunset. Admission: $4.00 per vehicle.
The park features formal gardens and a unique shoreline of coquina rock on its Atlantic beach side. A number of short trails provide opportunities for hiking and bicycling. Visitors can learn about the park's natural and cultural resources in the visitor center.

GTM ENVIRONMENTAL EDUCATION CENTER

Ponte Vedra Beach - 505 Guana River Road (A1A north of Vilano Beach 8 miles) 32082. Phone: (904) 823-4500.   www.gtmnerr.org Hours: Daily 9:00am-4:00pm and closed State holidays. Admission: $2.00 adult, $1.00 child (10-17).
The Guana Tolomato Matanzas (GTM) National Estuarine Research Reserve's Environmental Education Center (that's a sentence-full) includes interpretive exhibits, aquariums, and a 15-minute introductory video allowing visitors to learn about the importance of the estuary and the animals that call it home. What is an estuary? Estuaries are places where freshwater from the rivers mix with saltwater from the ocean. What creatures like this environment? You can't miss the life-size models of a North Atlantic right whale mother and calf, manta ray and cobia looming overhead. Discovery drawers and pull doors add to understanding of smaller creatures. The Center also offers scavenger hunts for the kids to complete while viewing the exhibits and nature movies on the weekends. Now go into the GUANA RIVER STATE PARK adjoining ($3.00 per vehicle admission) to explore the extensive salt marshes, 42 miles of pristine beaches and fascinating ecosystem outdoors. Hiking and biking are popular along the more than nine miles of nature trails and old service roads that wind through the hammock. The Shell Bluff trail is a favorite.

ANASTASIA STATE PARK & ST. AUGUSTINE BEACH

St. Augustine - 1340 A1A South (on Anastasia Island) 32080. Phone: (904) 461-2033. www.floridastateparks.org/anastasia/

Located on Anastasia Island, this 1,700-acre bird sanctuary is rich with miles of beach, lagoon waterways, wildlife and sweeping sand dunes. A self-guided nature trail offers an opportunity to walk ancient sand dunes covered by a coastal hammock of live oak, red bay and Southern magnolia trees. Sabal palms and sea oats grow wild on 20-foot-high dunes. The 24-miles of unspoiled, sandy beaches on the island are a surprise for visitors…and you may not pass many visitors at all for a stretch. The park offers seaside facilities for camping, hiking, fishing, picnics, barbecues, nature walks and beach volleyball. Flanked by the Atlantic Ocean on the east, pleasant year-round weather encourages exploration of **St. Augustine Beaches**, just up the road. Their beaches have some vehicle access areas towards the south end. Public access areas are well marked and the beach sand is piled high and sugary clean on the dunes and full of seashells near the water. If you can tear yourself away from the water and beach, try a friendly game of miniature golf and have an ice cream at **Fiesta Falls**. This pirate and water-themed mini-golf and picnic facility serves ice cream treats and has a well-maintained course with putting holes that are really unusual and fun to figure out.

FORT MATANZAS NATIONAL MONUMENT

St. Augustine - 8635 A1A South (south on A1A, 15 miles south of St. Augustine) 32080. Phone: (904) 471-0118. www.nps.gov/foma Hours: Daily 9:00am-5:30pm except Christmas day. Admission: FREE

A tiny, tough fort...but it never saw a battle!

On this site in 1565, the Spanish in a struggle killed 245 French Huguenots over control of Florida (Matanzas means "place of slaughter"). In 1742, the Spanish built Fort Matanzas here, a small-fortified watchtower that guarded the Southern entrance to St. Augustine. This fort is one of two remaining watchtower forts made from coquina rock. Hardly used, it did play a small part in passage of Spanish treasure fleets on their way back from the Caribbean to Spain. If you can climb the rooftop ladder, you'll get a great view from the top. The short boat ride (5 minutes long) runs about every hour and there is a good historical interpretation just outside. If you want, explore the boardwalk nature trail (about 1/2 mile) or beaches and fishing in the bay.

MARINELAND

St. Augustine - 9600 Oceanshore Blvd. (located ocean front on A1A, 20 minutes south of St. Augustine) 32080. Phone: (904) 471-1111. **www.marineland.net** *Hours: Daily 9:00am-4:30pm Admission: $5.00 adult, $2.50 child (under 12).*

Set to reopen after hurricane damage with a full schedule of authentic, original marine park shows and exhibits in 2006. The newest focus - more research orientation and a special project with special needs kids. Check their website for current offerings.

ST. AUGUSTINE ALLIGATOR FARM ZOOLOGICAL PARK

St. Augustine - 999 Anastasia Blvd. (South A1A) (2 miles south across the Bridge of Lions) 32080. Phone: (904) 824-3337. **www.alligatorfarm.com** *Hours: Daily 9:00am-5:00pm. Admission: $17.95 adult, $9.95 child (5-11).*

See all 23 species of crocodilians (that's fun to say) from around the world including rare white alligators. Shows every hour include the "Rainforest Review", featuring macaws and cockatoos and Alligator Feedings twice daily. The natural rookery is home to hundreds of egret, ibis, heron and other wading birds and is part of the Florida Birding Trail. The park is home to many exotic and endangered animals, too.

ST. AUGUSTINE LIGHTHOUSE AND MUSEUM

St. Augustine - 81 Lighthouse Avenue (on A1A, one mile south of downtown) 32080. **www.staugustinelighthouse.com** *Phone: (904) 829-0745. Hours: Daily 9:00am-6:00pm. Admission: $7.75 adult, $6.75 senior (55+), $5.00 child (6-11). You can save a couple of dollars off admission if you do not wish to climb the lighthouse stairs.*

Discover St. Augustine's rich maritime history at the site of Florida's first lighthouse. Climb 219 steps to the top of the 165-foot tower for a breathtaking view of historic downtown and the beaches. An interpreter is waiting for you up

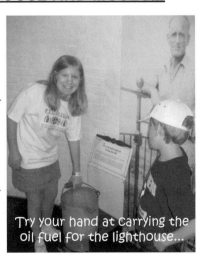

Try your hand at carrying the oil fuel for the lighthouse...

top to answer questions and explain the different views. There are exhibits to look at in the restored keepers' house pertaining to the Coast Guard in WWII, shipwrecks, and the lives of the keepers and their families. Hands-on activities include touching a real cannon ball or learning to make knots with real sailor's rope. Want to engage the kids more? Be sure to pick up a pencil and Scavenger Hunt challenge. Do not leave one stone un-turned or one display board unnoticed because answers are all around you. Read about the story of the cat who fell from the top of the lighthouse and lived (although he wasn't happy with his master for some time). The lighthouse keepers museum covers a lot of ground without getting too detailed for kids. The museum store carries lots of lighthouse-themed gifts. Honestly, this is one of the best maintained lighthouse facility and safest climbing stairs we have explored.

CASTILLO DE SAN MARCOS, THE OLD FORT

St. Augustine - One S. Castillo Drive (I-95 exit Rte. 16 downtown to US 1, turn right for 2 miles, left on Castillo) 32084. Phone: (904) 829-6506. www.nps.gov/casa Hours: 8:45am-5:15pm every day of the year except December 25. (The ticket booth closes at 4:45pm) Admission: $6.00 Adults, age 16 and above (7 day pass)

This national monument reflects the prevalent Spanish heritage and the impenetrable fort is the nation's oldest masonry fortress with Spanish soldier re-enactors firing cannons. Here lies a history of the forces and events which have shaped world history. Be sure to listen in on a costumed soldier's tales and climb the stairs to the roof for great photo ops and views. Did you know they recently discovered a secret room in the fort? It's open to crawl into, if you dare.

COLONIAL SPANISH QUARTER

St. Augustine - 35 St. George Street 32084. www.historicstaugustine.com Phone: (904) 825-6830. Hours: Daily 9:00am-5:30pm. Admission: $4.00-$7.00 (ages 6+), Family rate around $14.00.

Within the restored historic area lies the Spanish Quarter, a living history museum featuring settlers clad in 1740s style britches and bonnets busy blacksmithing, spinning and woodworking and also soldiers who tell of life long ago. Talk with the townsfolk. Meet the mother outside on her porch sewing. Why are the shelves up high on rope and why aren't there any windows on the north end of any building? Ever met a treesmith? Watch crafters turn small parts of trees into wooden utensils and tools.

FORT MOSE

St. Augustine - Saratoga Blvd. 32084. www.floridastateparks.org/fortmose/ Phone: (904) 461-2033. Hours: Daily 8:00am-sunset. New Visitor Center hours posted on website. Admission: During reconstruction, no fees. Check website for updates on openings and fees.

The new Fort Mose Visitor Center is a visual beginning to the outdoor original site. The boardwalk provides a fantastic view into a tidal salt marsh and ends at a benched platform with expansive views of the original Fort Mose sites, a bird rookery, and miles of salt marsh. In 1738, the Spanish governor of Florida chartered Fort Mose as a settlement for freed Africans who had fled slavery in the British Carolinas. When Spain ceded Florida to Britain in 1763, the inhabitants of Fort Mose migrated to Cuba. As the first free African American settlement in what is now the United States, Fort Mose represents a story of courage, determination, and perseverance. The stories of Africans fleeing to freedom and of Native American Indians who aided them, as well as tales of the many other people touched by Fort Mose tend to inspire folks.

LIGHTNER MUSEUM

St. Augustine - 75 King Street (corner of King and Granada Sts) 32084. Phone: (904) 824-2874. www.lightnermuseum.org Hours: Daily 9:00am-5:00pm. Admission: $8.00 adult, $2.00 youth (12-18). Children under 12 free with paying adult.

Experience Florida's Smithsonian. Henry Flagler's former Alcazar Hotel holds 19th century artifacts including natural history exhibits, Tiffany glass, a Victorian Village and antique mechanical musical instruments. They don't charge much for kids admission (if at all) because this is a mostly look, don't touch collection. Ask your trolley guide when they play the mechanical music boxes each day.

OLD FLORIDA MUSEUM

St. Augustine - 254 D San Marco Avenue (I-95 exit 318, go 7 miles, just one block past US 1) 32084. Phone: (904) 824-8874 or (800) 813-3208. www.oldfloridamuseum.com Hours: Daily 10:00am-5:00pm. Admission: $5.00-$6.00 (age 4+). Included in admission ticket for trolleys.

St. Augustine's only hands-on history museum. Games, weapons, foods and tools convey how life changed and how it has remained somewhat the same from Indian to pioneer times. Guests actually get to try their hand at daily chores such as corn grinding, tabby making, or quill pen writing. Everyone can actually touch a silver bar from Spanish treasure. Kids like the General Store shopping for old-fashioned toys from days gone by (no batteries required). It's small and cute and very family-friendly to learn from.

OLD JAIL

St. Augustine - 167 San Marco Avenue (US 1 just one mile north of the Old Fort and Historic District) 32084. Phone: (904) 829-3800. Hours: Daily 8:30am-4:30pm. Closed Easter, Thanksgiving, Christmas. Admission: $4.00-$6.00

...our jailbirds

"You're Goin to Jail" cries the jailkeeper. Experience a first person tour as the sheriff and his staff incarcerate your group tour. Completed in 1891, the jail housed prisoners for over 60 years. It is one of the few surviving 19th century jails. Explore the sheriff's quarters where he and his wife lived adjacent to 72 prisoners. The guest "prisoners" are led by costumed wardens from room to room. Do you know where the name "jailbirds" comes from? Try being one in the giant bird cage cell outside. Lady inmates worked all day in the kitchen while men had to work the chain gang. You can almost set your watch by the morning jailbreak at the Old Jail. Seasonally and most weekend mornings, a 1908-era inmate (in their black-white striped attire) tries to flee aboard a trolley filled with passengers. The fact that the escape ends with being re-captured by the sheriff and his deputies doesn't seem to dim the prisoners' enthusiasm for their rollicking run through the parking lot. Our kids loved this site - especially the actor guides - who, at some points, were so believable, I think the kids really felt like they might have to do some hard time. It's light enough, mixed with humor, that it shouldn't scare kids, though. Before you leave, visit the gift shop and purchase some fun re-enacting clothes and hats to use for dress-up when you get home.

OLD ST. AUGUSTINE VILLAGE

St. Augustine - 149 Cordova Street (south of the plaza, enter on Cordova St. near Bridge St. one block south of King St) 32084. Phone: (904) 823-9722. **www.old-staug-village.com** *Hours: Monday-Saturday 10:00am-4:30pm, Sunday 11:00am-4:30pm. Admission: $5.00-$7.00 (age 6+).*

On just one city block, discover over 400 years of history hidden amongst courtyards of historic houses original to the site. Inside these homes, you'll find exhibits reflecting the town's history. We liked the variety of time periods from Spanish Colonial to American Territorial to a Prince's home and, our favorite, "the crooked house" - the red, leaning Carpenter House. There are not interpreters so this may be boring to children who do not like to read many placards.

OLD TOWN TROLLEY TOURS OF ST. AUGUSTINE

St. Augustine - 167 San Marco Avenue (I-95 to SR 16, left on US 1, left at Ford Dealership) 32084. Phone: (904) 829-3800 or (800) 868-7482. **www.trolleytours.com** *Hours: Daily 8:30am-5:00pm Admission: $18.00 adult, $5.00 child (6-12). Free parking. Tickets good for 3 days of unlimited trolley service and admission to the Beach Bus and Florida Heritage Museum, next to the Old Jail.*

The tours provide historically accurate information accented by anecdotes and tales of the colorful parts of the city's history. Historical characters of the past whose legacy endures include Ponce de Leon and his Fountain of Youth, and renowned Spanish explorer Pedro Menendez de Aviles, who founded the city more than 435 years ago. Did you know this town is the oldest, continuously occupied European settlement in the continental United

...step back in time on
St. George Street

States? Notice several different architectural stylings ranging from simple tabby cottages along brick lanes to more modern structures capped by towers, turrets and red clay roofs. St. Augustine is home to some of the oldest original structures and sites in the U.S., including The Oldest House (1704), The Oldest Wooden Schoolhouse (1804), the Oldest Store Museum (1840) and the Old Jail (1891). The tour covers over 100 sights of interest and has 19 stops where you can hop on or off to sightsee, shop or dine. Look for the green and orange trolleys at the Old

Jail complex to start at "stop one". This is, by far, the best way to learn about the town and not have to find parking (difficult on small historic streets). Go around the tour once, completely, to determine what you want to get off and see on the next round. The trolleys pick up at each stop every 15 minutes so it's easy on and off. Our favorite stops were the Old Jail and **St. George Street**. Looking for something different for lunch? Try the **Columbia Restaurant** on St. George for authentically prepared Cuban food.

OLDEST HOUSE MUSEUM COMPLEX

St. Augustine - 14 St. Francis Street (US 1 to King Street East, right on Avenida Menendez, right on St. Francis) 32084. Phone: (904) 824-2872. www.oldesthouse.org Hours: Daily 9:00am-5:00pm. Admission: $8.00 adult, $7.00 senior, $4.00 child (6+), $16.00 family.

The Oldest House Museum Complex features the Gonzalez-Alvarez House, Florida's oldest Spanish Colonial dwelling and the Manucy Museum, and the Museum of Florida's Military. This block was a haven for sea captains, writers, rebels, tourists and travelers. Learn about Seminoles and statehood, food and fashion, bathing and bed bugs. Trace more than 400 years of the city's history, soldiers, gardens and a museum store. Guided tours are every half hour.

OLDEST WOODEN SCHOOL HOUSE IN THE USA

St. Augustine - 14 St. George Street 32084. Phone: (904) 824-0192 or (888) 653-7245. www.oldestwoodenschoolhouse.com Hours: Daily 9:00am-5:00pm. Admission: $2.00-$3.00 (age 6+).

Let your first lesson in history start here. This *first* school is over 200 years old and made of red cedar and cypress. Sit with the animated schoolmaster and the pupils as they show you what school life was like in the 1700s. Why the dunce cap? Compare your school days with those of the old days. If you pay attention, you can get a diploma as a souvenir of your visit. This is a really cute site and worth a quick visit.

PONCE DE LEON'S FOUNTAIN OF YOUTH

St. Augustine - 11 Magnolia Avenue (right behind the Ho-Jo Hotel or the Old Jail) 32084. Phone: (904) 829-3168 or (800) 356-8222. www.fountainofyouthflorida.com Hours: Daily 9:00am-5:00pm. Admission: $6.50 adult, $5.50 senior, $3.50 child (6-12).

Ponce de Leon's Fountain of Youth National Archaeological Park exhibits foundations and artifacts of the first St. Augustine mission and colony. This is the REAL legendary eternal spring! And, at the end of your tour, you are provided the opportunity to sip from the Fountain of Youth! Kids generally can't handle the odor (slight sulfur smell) of the mineralized water but adults drink it up quick (I wonder why?). In the Spring Room, you'll also learn about the authentic stone cross found during excavation of the site. Ponce de Leon's personal journey papers were found here - documenting his journey and findings. Other areas include the Explorers Globe and the Navigators'

Fountain of Youth samples ...try it!

Planetarium. Here, you can visualize the Age of Exploration and discover the clever ways navigators used the stars to find their way to new lands. Outdoors, visitors can go through Christian Indian burial grounds and see the Smithsonian site documented as the first original colony. They have several exhibits with moving, life-sized dioramas depicting the Indian Town and the Historic Landing of Ponce de Leon's fleet and meeting the giant Timucuan Indians. Once you see the life-size Indian chief statue, you'll understand why short Spaniards felt the native's secret was in the water! Really interesting place - a must see in town.

POTTER'S WAX MUSEUM

St. Augustine - 17 King Street (just west of the Bridge of Lions) 32084. Phone: (904) 829-9056 or (800) 584-4781. www.potterswax.com Hours: Sunday-Thursday 9:00am-5:00pm; Friday-Saturday 9:00am-9:00pm. Admission: $9.00 adult, $8.00 senior, $6.00 child (6-12).

"The first wax museum founded in the U.S." has received acclaim for its authenticity and unique costuming. Holding more than 160 life-size figures, view characters from historical, political, royal and motion picture fame. From Beethoven to Sylvester Stallone's "Rambo". You'll catch some poets, composers, authors, artists, explorers, and religious leaders, too. See the world's only working wax studio on display to the public. There are some horror scenes and the characters are more adult-friendly movie and TV stars. Note: This may not be as much fun for pre-teens and younger and it's not super big. Parents will probably get the most from the museum.

RIPLEY'S BELIEVE IT OR NOT! MUSEUM

St. Augustine - *19 San Marco Avenue (I-95 exit 31B/SR 16, travel east for 5 miles to US 1, turn south one mile to Castillo Drive east) 32084. Phone: (904) 824-1606.* ***www.staugustine-ripleys.com*** *Hours: Daily 9:00am-7:00pm. Admission: $12.95 adult, $8.95 senior, $7.95 child (5-12).*

Explore over 800 exhibits of crazy, unique and very strange oddities. The site is Castle Warden, an Historic Moorish Revival style mansion filled with fun mind benders and exciting action and creepy sounds. Look for a family favorite - the giant erector set (almost three stories) ferris wheel. Every Ripley's is as bizarre as the next…this one happens to be the original. Parking is available but it's very easily accessible by trolley or train tour, too (it's one of their stops).

ST. AUGUSTINE SCENIC CRUISE

St. Augustine - *(directly south of the Bridge of Lions at the St. Augustine Municipal Marina) 32084. Phone: (904) 824-1806 or (800) 542-8316.* ***www.scenic-cruise.com*** *Admission: Varies by cruise, consult website.*

Relax and enjoy a one hour and 15-minute cruise aboard the Victory III. Enjoy a view of historic downtown from the water. Narrated tours provide information on historic landmarks and natural sites of interest.

ST. AUGUSTINE SIGHTSEEING TRAINS

St. Augustine - *170 San Marco Avenue (I-95 exit 318/SR 16 east about 5 miles, continue one block east of US 1 to Old Sugar Mill) 32084. Phone: (904) 829-6545 or (800) 226-6545.* ***www.redtrains.com*** *Hours: Open daily 8:30am-5:00pm. Admission: $18.00 adult, $5.00 child (6-12).*

A good way to explore historic St. Augustine. The scenic 7-mile tour stops at several of the city's most popular attractions, historic sites, restaurants and shops. The entire tour takes approximately one hour - but you may step on and off the train at any of the 20 stops - and your ticket is good for 3 consecutive days of travel. The trolley and the train stop at nearly the same spots. If you're wanting to easily visit (discounted) the Florida Museum and the Old Jail (highly recommended), we'd suggest the Trolley tours instead (their depot is right in front of the Old Jail).

SCHOONER FREEDOM

St. Augustine - 111 Avenida Menendez (departs from City Marina, next to Bridge of Lions) 32085. Phone: (904) 810-1010. www.schoonerfreedom.com Admission: $35.00 adult, $20.00 child (4-16). Seniors 10% discount. Tours: 2 hours long, Ghost cruise is one hour.

The 72-foot Schooner Freedom, St. Augustine's only Tallship, departs daily for cruises. Take a step back in time and experience the romance and adventure on the high seas while sailing the waters adjacent to historic St. Augustine. Dolphins, seabirds, pilot whales (wintering) and manatees are among the creatures encountered on the guided tours. The sunset tour is excellent and the kids get to help raise the sails, heave lines and take the helm. Dolphins often make playful escorts as gentle sea breezes fill the ships sails. The sunset tour offers a beautiful dusk view of the historic city!

Sailing buddies...

FAVER-DYKES STATE PARK

St. Augustine - 1000 Faver Dykes Road (15 miles south of town near I-95 and US 1) 32086. Phone: (904) 794-0997. www.floridastateparks.org/faver-dykes/ Hours: Daily 8:00am-sunset. Admission: $3.00 per vehicle for up to 8 people. Camping and canoe rentals.

Noted for its pristine condition, this tranquil park borders Pellicer Creek as it winds along Florida's east coast highways down to the Matanzas River. Fishing, picnicking, and nature walks are popular activities. Pellicer Creek is a designated state canoe trail and visitors can rent canoes at the park. A full-facility campground is available for overnight stays.

WHETSTONE CHOCOLATES FACTORY TOUR

St. Augustine - *100 Whetstone Place (US 1 south to SR 312 E, to Coke Road. From I-95, take exit 311, N on SR 207 to SR 312) 32086.* **www.whetstonechocolates.com** *Phone: (904) 825-1700. Admission: FREE admission, FREE sample.*

Enjoy the introductory 15-minute video, then walk through the factory to watch chocolates being made. Kids get to activate a robot and see 500 lbs. of melting chocolate. Visit the gift shop at the end of the tour.

WORLD GOLF HALL OF FAME & IMAX THEATER

St. Augustine - *1 World Golf Place, World Golf Village (I-95 exit 323) 32092. Phone: (904) 940-4123 or (800) WGVGOLF.* **www.wgv.com**

The World Golf Hall of Fame presents golf's story in more than 70 separate exhibits that combine historic artifacts with the latest in golf interactive technology. Historical and interactive exhibits enable visitors to experience some of golf's most exciting moments and players. The adjacent IMAX Theater is a larger-than-life adventure where the visitor becomes part of the experience.

SUGGESTED LODGING AND DINING

HOWARD JOHNSON EXPRESS INN - 137 San Marco Avenue, **St. Augustine**. (I-95 exit 318, SR 16 east 5 miles, then right on San Marco for one mile). (904) 824-4641 or **www.hojo.com/staugustine**. The Howard Johnson Express Inn is located in the heart of St. Augustine's beautiful downtown Historic District, directly in front of the world-renowned Ponce De Leon's Fountain of Youth. It is the only hotel included on the route of the Old Town Trolleys and the St. Augustine Sightseeing Trains as they cruise through the grounds to view the magnificent "Old Senator", a 600 year old Live Oak Tree, which stands as a silent witness to Don Juan Ponce De Leon's discovery and naming of the continent La Florida in 1513. Free Continental Breakfast daily and Outdoor Pool with heated Jacuzzi. Each room includes a micro/frig and the average room rate is around $100.00. For a little more, you can rent a family suite with a private bedroom. The hotel is directly in front of the Fountain of Youth and you never know, they may have secretly tapped into the Fountain's water supply. So, when you take your shower or bath…you'll might lose 10 years - please be careful!

BARNACLE BILL'S - 13 Castillo Drive (downtown), **St. Augustine**. (904) 819-0030 or **www.barnaclebillsonline.com**. Restaurant favorites include: Homemade Onion Rings, Fried Shrimp, Clam Chowder, Matanzas Shrimp, Shrimp Menendez Salad, and Banana Delight for dessert. They have their own sauces that you can purchase if you get hooked. The Kids Menu is mostly seafood (fried) and a burger or chicken fingers (average $6.00 includes 2 veggies). We think their appetizers and combos offer the best variety and average about $12.00 for dinner entrees with all the fixins. Ask them to prepare their grouper Matanzas style - so good! We loved the Datil pepper sauce they've concocted, too - sweet hot pepper sauce - actually, all of their sauces and service staff are excellent.

CONCH HOUSE MARINA - 57 Comares Avenue, **St. Augustine**. (800) 940-6256 or **www.conch-house.com**. Come and visit the Conch House Restaurant and take a little trip to the Caribbean. Sit down under a palm tree on their outside deck or dine in unique grass huts out over the water. If the weather isn't cooperating, the covered patio overlooking beautiful Salt Run is the place to be. They specialize in seafood and Caribbean style cooking, offering fresh seafood, steaks, great chicken dishes, and delightful salads. Try anything Caribbean or their award-winning conch chowder or fritters. Kids Menu ranges from $4.00-$7.00 with fries. Lunch, $10-15.00, Dinner, $22.00 average. The state of the art 200 slip marina is conveniently located on Salt Run just off the Intracoastal waterway and 1000 ft. from the St. Augustine Inlet.

HARRY'S SEAFOOD BAR & GRILLE - 46 Avenida Menendez, **St. Augustine**. (904) 824-7765 or **www.HookedOnHarrys.com**. Enjoy seafood, steaks, pasta and authentic New Orleans dishes indoors or out on the multi-level courtyard across from St. Augustine's bayfront. Specialties include New Orleans-style shrimp, shrimp etouffee and pasta chicken Louisianne. Anything with Harry's, New Orleans or Jazzy in the name is super flavorful and the portions (even appetizers) are large. The Kids Menu has puzzles and the varied entrees run around $4.00 and include fries and a souvenir cup soda. Nightly courtyard entertainment. Great Key Lime pie, too. Lunch ~ $10.00, dinner ~$16.00-$21.00.

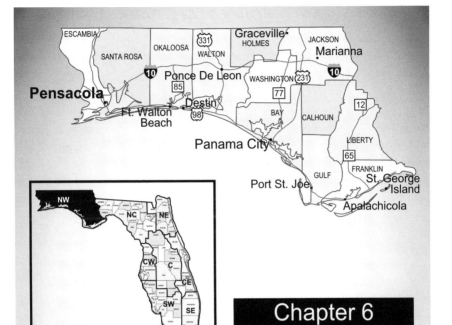

Chapter 6
North West (NW) Area

Our Favorites...

* Dolphin Cruises - Destin & Panama City

* Gulfarium - Ft. Walton Beach

* Okaloosa Island Boardwalk & Pier - Ft. Walton Beach

* National Museum of Naval Aviation - Pensacola

* Gulf Islands National Seashore - Pensacola Beach Area

* St. Joe Peninsula State Park - Port St. Joe

BALD POINT STATE PARK

Alligator Point - 146 Box Cut (off U.S. 98, one mile south of Ochlockonee Bay. Take State Road 370 for 3 miles to Bald Point Road) 32346. www.floridastateparks.org/baldpoint/ default.cfm Phone: (850) 349-9146. Hours: Daily 8:00am-sunset. Admission: $3.00 per vehicle.

Bald Point State Park is an excellent area to catch a glimpse of the rare Florida black bear. Sometimes the bears swim at the beach at Bald Point to the delight of park visitors. Fishing can be done from the beach or a small fishing pier. If you enjoy hiking or bicycling, Bald Point has many trails to explore. For canoeing, they have many freshwater lakes, tidal creeks, Ochlockonee Bay and the Gulf of Mexico. Every fall, bald eagles, other migrating raptors, and monarch butterflies are commonly sighted as they head south for the winter. Bald Point offers access to two Apalachee Bay beaches for swimming, sunbathing, kayaking, windsurfing, and hiking.

ORMAN HOUSE STATE PARK

Apalachicola - 177 5th Street (North Market Street) 32325. Phone: (850) 653-1209. www.floridastateparks.org/ormanhouse/default.cfm Hours: Thursday-Monday 9:00am-5:00pm, closed for one hour lunch at Noon.

Two-story Greek Revival structure built by Thomas Orman in 1838 is one of the oldest in the area. Built in 1838 by Thomas Orman, this antebellum home overlooks the Apalachicola River, and was used for both business and social gatherings. Orman was a cotton merchant and businessman in Apalachicola from 1840 to the 1870s. He helped the tiny town become one of the Gulf Coast's most important cotton exporting ports during the mid-19th century.

JOHN GORRIE MUSEUM STATE PARK

Apalachicola - (6th Street and Avenue D, one block east off US 98) 32329. Phone: (850) 653-9347. www.floridastateparks.org/johngorriemuseum/default.cfm Hours: Thursday-Monday 9:00am-5:00pm. Admission: $1.00 per person (ages 7+).

John Gorrie State Museum contains a replica of the ice machine created by Dr. John Gorrie in an attempt to cool the rooms housing yellow fever patients. Gorrie also served as postmaster, city treasurer, town councilman, and bank director. He became a pioneer in the field of air conditioning and refrigeration by inventing a machine that made ice, and received the first U.S. Patent for mechanical refrigeration in 1851. There are many other exhibits chronicling the colorful history of Apalachicola, which played an important role in Florida's economic development. Did you know this area produces 90% of Florida's oysters?

PANHANDLE PIONEER SETTLEMENT

Blountstown - (west on Route 20 to signs for Sam Atkins Park) 32324. Phone: (850) 674-3050. ***www.panhandlepioneersettlement.org*** *Hours: Tuesday, Thursday, Friday & Saturday Noon - 4:00 p.m. CST (September-May). Tuesday, Thursday & Saturday 9:00am-1:00pm CST (June-August). Admission: $4.00 adult, $3.00 senior (60+), $2.00 child (5-12). Miscellaneous: Best to visit during festival or group tour event.*

The Pioneer Settlement is accessed from Atkins Park by a 700 foot boardwalk across a creek, natural swamp and wet land. This walk alone will provide many opportunities to observe and learn about trees, plants, birds, reptiles and insects. Both the boardwalk and the Pioneer Settlement are handicapped accessible. They welcome families and School children are encouraged and especially 4th grade, to learn Florida history in a living museum setting. As visitors and school children step back in time for a whole century, teachers, senior citizens and craftsmen will be teaching and demonstrating the every day skills rural pioneers found necessary to survive in that time before electricity. The children get some hands-on experience by shelling corn, making whirly birds and washing clothes on a scrub board, etc. They watch the Blacksmith and sample homemade biscuits baked in a wood stove while they learn how a pioneer kitchen operates.

TORREYA STATE PARK

Bristol - 2576 NW Torreya Park Road (west on County Road 1641 off State Road 12, 13 miles north of Bristol) 32321. ***www.floridastateparks.org/torreya/default.cfm*** *Phone: (850) 643-2674. Hours: Daily 8:00am-sunset. Admission: $2.00 per vehicle. Extra $1.00-$2.00 for home tour.*

The park is named for an extremely rare species of Torreya tree that only grows on the high bluffs along the Apalachicola River. See a restored antebellum mansion and nature preserve, claimed to be the Garden of Eden because of the magnitude of plants indigenous to the park. Developed by the Civilian Conservation Corps in the 1930s, Torreya is popular for camping, hiking, and picnicking. Adventurers hike past ravines, river swamps and remains of Confederate gun pits. Forests of hardwood trees provide the finest display of fall color found in Florida. The main campground offers full-facility campsites and a YURT (Year-round Universal Recreational Tent). Primitive campsites and a youth campground are also available.

FALLING WATERS STATE PARK

Chipley - 1130 State Park Road (north on SR 77A, south of I-10, 3 miles south of town) 32428. Phone: (850) 638-6130. www.floridastateparks.org/fallingwaters Hours: Daily 8:00am-sunset. Admission: $4.00 per vehicle.

Trees line the boardwalk leading to Florida's tallest waterfall, which drops 73 feet into a 100-foot deep sinkhole. The water's final destination remains unknown! Visitors can see beautiful native and migrating butterflies in the butterfly garden, take a dip in the lake, or have a family picnic. Park rangers host interpretive programs in the amphitheater. Full-facility campsites are nestled in a shady pine forest.

BIG KAHUNA'S WATER & ADVENTURE PARK

Destin - 1007 Highway 98E   32541. Phone: (850) 837-4061.   www.bigkahunas.com Admission: $29.00-$35.00 waterpark; $5.00 plus per amusement ride or around $45.00 for both parks. (seasonal).

This oversized water park offers more than 40 exciting water attractions, including three tropical mini golf courses, two wild and fast go-kart tracks and three high-thrill rides.

HENDERSON BEACH STATE RECREATION AREA

Destin - 17000 Emerald Coast Parkway 32541. Phone: (850) 837-7550. Hours: Daily 8:00am-sunset. www.floridastateparks.org/hendersonbeach/

Henderson Beach State Recreation Area has one of Florida's greatest natural assets- sugar white sand beaches (6,000 feet of them). Swimming, surf fishing and picnicking are popular pastimes. Visitors wishing to try their luck in the surf may catch popular species such as pompano and whiting. A picnic pavilion is conveniently located nearby and bathhouses with outside showers are also provided.

MOODYS EMERALD MAGIC DOLPHIN CRUISES

Destin - 194 Hwy 98E (1/2 mile east of Destin Bridge) 32541. Phone: (850) 837-1293. www.moodysinc.com Hours vary by season and weather. Admission: $15.00 adult, half price for kids.

These two hour boat cruises highlight dolphins and other wild things. The smoke-free cruise serves tropical drinks and snacks while you watch "dinnertime" dolphins feeding (tons of them)!

SAILING SCHOONER - DANIEL WEBSTER CLEMENTS

Destin - *(on Highway 98 at the intersection with Benning Drive, 2 lights from the Destin bridge) 32541. Phone: (850) 837-7245. www.sailingsouth.com*

SNORKEL AND SAIL: Why just go snorkeling when you can go snorkeling AND sailing!! This cruise departs around noon depending upon the tidal currents and winds forecasted for that particular day. When currents are favorable they prefer to visit a favorite snorkel spot just under the Destin Bridge. Sometimes they'll go outside the Pass just to the West side of the Jetties. After a refreshing swim, you cast off, raise the sails, and enjoy an exhilarating sail in the Bay or Gulf.

SUNSET CRUISE: set sail in late afternoon and return to the dock at sundown. Sail out the East Pass, through the rock jetties, past the sea buoys and out into the Gulf. Huge white sails will tower overhead as you sail out quite a way or "tack" up and down the coastline depending on the wind direction. The sounds and feel of the wooden ship underway will take you back centuries to the days sailing vessels ruled the seas. You can join in sailing the ship or simply sit back and relax while taking this all in and listening to your favorite "island" tunes played softly on deck. Dolphin generally come to the boat and swim alongside or you may see a big sea turtle lumber by. As on all of their charters, you are welcome to bring your own drinks or purchase water, juice and soft drinks for only a dollar. You can even bring a picnic snack, but they'll have you back to the dock in time for your dinner reservations.

SOUTHERN STAR GLASS BOTTOM BOAT

Destin - *HarborWalk Marina, Highway 98E (To the left of the Lucky Snapper restaurant) 32541. Phone: (850) 837-7741 or (888) 424-7217. www.dolphin-sstar.com Admission: $22.00 adult, $17.00 senior, $10.00 child (3-12). Coupon for adult admission discount on website.*

Family-run with a family focus, the 2 hour relaxing cruise includes Dolphin Watching, Bird Feeding, and music. "Southern Star" embarks on a cruise in search of the coastal bottlenose dolphin. You will experience the beauty and grace of these incredible marine mammals up close and personal. Watch the dolphins swim alongside the boat, having almost as much fun as you will. Snacks and restrooms are on-board and the kids even get to steer the boat, if they like. You can bring your own cooler on board, too. The cruises are fair-weather friendly meaning the captain goes the direction of the most protected waters to avoid seasickness. Begin cruising around the harbor, then venture into the Gulf or along the Bay.

EMERALD COAST SCIENCE CENTER

Fort Walton Beach - 139 Brooks Street   32548. Phone: (850) 664-1261 or www.ecscience.org. Admission: $3.50-$5.00 (age 4+).

Stimulating the imagination, the center has interactional fun like a reflecting Castle of Mirrors, "adult-sized" bubble makers, a literally hair-raising generator, an electrifying Illuma Storm and more.

GULFARIUM

Fort Walton Beach - 1010 Miracle Strip Pkwy. SE   32548. Phone: (850) 244-5169. www.gulfarium.com   Hours: Daily 9:00am-4:00pm. Extended to 6:00pm summers. Admission: $17.50 adult, $15.50 senior (55+), $10.50 child (4-11)

America's second oldest marine park hosts Atlantic bottlenose dolphin and sea lion shows. Dolphin stars Princess and Delilah delight with feats from comedic soccer and football games to 18-foot leaps toward the clouds. Ever seen Dolphin Disco? They have a very unique Scuba Living Sea Show. Here, a diver descends into the water and demos diving techniques and then points out various fish found in the Gulf. You will love how manageable each show is to see. There are 30 minutes between alternating shows to allow for a look at tropical penguins, alligator, sharks or giant turtle exhibits. Maybe dare yourself at the TouchPool area where they have sea urchins, horseshoe crab, and seashell crab you can touch all you want. This park is very do-able for grandparents because the park is small and the shows are short (keeping the kid's attention span in tact). We loved the simplicity of this place...and the animal antics!

INDIAN TEMPLE MOUND AND MUSEUM

Fort Walton Beach - 139 SE Miracle Strip Pkwy.   32548. Phone: (904)-243-6521. Hours: Monday - Saturday 10:00am - 4:30pm. Sundays Noon-4:30pm in June and July. Admission: $3.00-$5.00 per person (age 4+).

The indoor/outdoor exhibit showcases America's largest collection of Southeastern Indian ceramic artifacts through 10,000 years of four prehistoric tribes. In the museum, you'll see lots of hands-on tools and ancient rug weaving that kids can do. The largest Indian mound discovered along saltwater (1400 A.D.) stands guard beside the museum. Learn about excavations and find out who lived on top of the mound. Approximately how many chiefs are buried in this mound? You might even find burials of their pet dog!

learning ancient rug weaving...

OKALOOSA ISLAND BOARDWALK & FISHING PIER

Fort Walton Beach - 1030 Miracle Strip Pkwy. 32548. Phone: (850) 244-1023. Hours: Dawn to dark.

The Boardwalk on Okaloosa Island has the ideal family setting complete with three beach accesses, playground, beach volleyball courts, restrooms, showers, shopping, restaurants, and pavilions. The restaurants all around here have kids menus and many have beach playgrounds for the kids to romp around while you wait for your food order. For $1.00 you can walk the pier and fish or just chat with the fisherman (it's even lit for night fishing). You'll find someone catching something every few minutes in the "Luckiest Fishing Village in the World." A great place to hang out!

BLACKWATER RIVER STATE PARK

Holt - 7720 Deaton Bridge Road (15 miles northeast of Milton, off U.S. 90) 32564. Phone: (850) 983-5363. www.floridastateparks.org/blackwaterriver/default.cfm Hours: Daily 8:00am-sundown. Admission: $3.00 per vehicle.

The river is one of the purest sandbottom rivers in the nation, making this park a popular place for swimming, fishing, camping, and paddling. Bring your canoes or tubes to truly enjoy the beauty of the Blackwater River. Local vendors offer trips and rentals. Shaded campsites are just a short walk from the river, and visitors can enjoy a picnic at a pavilion overlooking the river. Nature enthusiasts will enjoy strolling along trails through undisturbed natural communities.

FLORIDA CAVERNS STATE PARK

Marianna - 3345 Caverns Road (I-10 west to exit 142, turn right on Hwy 71 N to Hwy 90, turn left. Follow brown park signs. 3 miles north of town on SR 166) 32446. Phone: (850) 482-9598. www.floridastateparks.org/floridacaverns Hours: Daily 8:00am-sunset. Admission: $4.00 per vehicle. Cave Tour Fees: Age 13 and up $8.00, Age 3 to 12 $5.00.

This is one of the few state parks with dry (air filled) caves and is the only Florida state park to offer cave tours to the public. The cave has hundreds of formations of limestone stalactites, stalagmites, soda straws, flowstones, and draperies plus clear underground pools and unusual cave-dwelling creatures. Florida Caverns is also popular for camping, swimming, fishing, picnicking, canoeing, boating, hiking, bicycling, and horseback riding (The park does not rent horses.). Tour several miles of multiuse trails while viewing natural wonders such as floodplains, sinkholes, and rivers. Located near the campground, a river vent rises to create the Blue Hole swimming area. This favorite warm weather attraction provides a great way to cool down during the hot summer months. The Visitor Center provides historical interpretation in its walk-through museum and large screen video tour of the caverns. Stables are available for equestrian campers.

JUNIOR MUSEUM OF BAY COUNTY

Panama City - 1731 Jenks Avenue 32405. Phone: (850) 769-6128. www.jrmuseum.org Hours: Monday-Friday 9:00am-4:30pm, Saturday 10:00am-4:00pm. Sunday and Major Holidays, Closed. Admission: FREE. Suggested donations are $5.00 for Adults and $3.00 for Children under 12.

This Children's Museum is a hands-on site established to inspire and educate children with interactive exhibits and programs that focus on science, history, cultural studies and the environment. What do a super-sized ViewMaster, a See-Saw and an Archimedes Screw have in common? They are all part of a new multilingual exhibit that teaches children how six simple tools can help them work, play and solve problems in everyday life. Kids can also learn about the human body; fill and launch a hot air balloon; go pretend-fishing off a real boat; search for the world's biggest hissing cockroaches inside at Nature's Corner; take a walk along the nature trail on a boardwalk through a swamp; and visit the pioneer farm with a log cabin, gristmill, barn and smokehouse.

COCONUT CREEK FAMILY FUN PARK

Panama City Beach - 9807 Front Beach Road   32407. Phone: (850) 234-2625.
www.coconutcreekfun.com Hours: Open daily at 9:00 a.m. weather permitting, year
round. Closed on Christmas Eve and Christmas. Admission: $8.50 per activity or $15.00
all day unlimited ticket. Children under 6 play free. Discount coupon on website.

Approximately the size of a football field and the first giant human maze of its
kind in the U.S. - it's the Gran Maze. Experience the excitement of discovery
as you step upon a maze-version of the South Pacific islands of FIJI, TAHITI,
SAMOA, and BALI, the four checkpoints you must find to successfully complete
the grand maze. Use your best navigational skills to find these islands and return
to home port, just as Captain James Cook did over two hundred years ago when he
first sailed the great Pacific Ocean and discovered these islands. If you have more
time, try one of two African Safari.

SHIPWRECK ISLAND WATERPARK

Panama City Beach - 12000 Front Beach Road (located on the left side of Alf Coleman
Road) 32407. Phone: (850) 234-3333.   www.miraclestrippark.com Waterpark: Daily
10:30am-5:00pm (Memorial Day Weekend - first weekend in August). Weekends only (late
April, May, August, early September) Admission: Waterpark $18.00-$28.00 (35" tall and
up). Pre-schoolers (less than 35" tall) are FREE.

The area's only waterpark has Tadpool Hole for the little ones but loads of fun
rides for those over 35" tall. Family rides include a Wave Pool, Lazy River and
Flume raft rides. Thrill rides includes Tree Top Drop, Raging Rapids and Pirate's
Plunge.

ZOO WORLD ZOOLOGICAL & BOTANICAL PARK

Panama City Beach - 9008 Front Beach Rd.   32407. www.zoo-world.us/index.html
Phone: (850) 230-1243. Hours: Opens 9:00am daily. Admission charged.

Home to approximately 300 beautiful and exotic animals. Lions, Tigers, Bears,
Kangaroo, Giraffe, Orangutans, Snow Leopards just to name a few. Lots of
playful and funny monkeys and even a Kookaburra. These exotic animals live in
a beautiful setting of botanical gardens including 250 species of tree and plant life
from around the world. Zooworld also features a Petting Zoo where you can hand
feed Sidney the friendly giraffe.

CAPT. ANDERSON II DOLPHIN GLASSBOTTOM BOAT CRUISE

***Panama City Beach** - 5550 N. Lagoon Dr. 32408. **www.captandersonsmarina.com/ shellisland.htm** Phone: (850) 234-3435.*

The Glass Bottom boat is the only excursion vessel that features "Sea School" which includes: underwater viewing, dolphin encounters, a tour of Shell Island, crab trapping, bird feeding, shrimp netting and other sights of interest around the beach on daytime tours. A shorter tour is offered near dinnertime with just the focus on underwater viewing the dolphin.

SEA DRAGON PIRATE SHIP CRUISE

***Panama City Beach** - 5325 N. Lagoon Drive (Next to the Boatyard Restaurant at Lighthouse Marina) 32408. Phone: (850) 234-7400 or (866) YOHOHO1. **www.piratecruise.net** Miscellaneous: Drinks, snacks and souvenirs are available for purchase.*

Cruise away into the fantasy world of friendly swashbucklers and spirited pirates aboard the 80' authentic, and very colorful, pirate ship. Your journey cruises within cannon shot range of the shores of Shell Island. Frequent sightings of playful dolphin, gliding seagulls, pelicans, and other mysterious marine life just are noted by the captain. BEWARE MATEYS! You may be required to do a little sword fighting or steer the gallant ship. After you and the other pirates have discovered the treasure and take your share of the loot, you will be invited to party hearty with festive music, games, and dancing all the way back to dock. Assorted treasures are given out to the little pirates aboard. These are so fun - especially if you begin to look like a pirate on board - you'll see.

SEA SCREAMER SPEEDBOAT CRUISE

***Panama City Beach** - 5325 N. Lagoon Drive (at Lighthouse Marina, next to the Boatyard Restaurant) 32408. Phone: (850) 233-9107 or (877) 233-9107. **www.seascreamer.net** Admission: $16.00 adult, $14.00 senior (60+), $12.00 child (3-11). Coupon on website. Miscellaneous: Reservations are recommended 1-3 days in advance. Or, when you arrive in town, come to the ticket booth located next to the famous Boatyard Restaurant. The Sea Screamer is docked behind the restaurant.*

Come ride the World's Largest Speedboat. They have Day Cruises and Sunset Cruises to enjoy. Narrated journeys past beautiful Shell Island and the jetties, then go for a refreshing ride in the Gulf of Mexico alongside the world's most beautiful beaches and resorts. Breath-taking dolphin and marine life sightings make this a smooth-sailing way to see Panama Beach sites.

ST. ANDREWS STATE PARK

Panama City Beach - 4607 State Park Lane (3 miles east of town, off State Road 392 (Thomas Drive) 32408. Phone: (850) 233-5140. www.floridastateparks.org/standrews Hours: Daily 8:00am-sunset. Center open 9:00am-4:00pm. Admission: $5.00 per vehicle.

The park is known for rolling, white sand dunes separated by low marshes. Hike the Blue Heron Trail that starts at a reconstructed Cracker turpentine still and winds through a lush plants. The Gator Lake Trail provides visitors with a beautiful vantage point for spotting alligators and many waterfowl, wading birds and small creatures. The 1.5 miles of beach on the Gulf of Mexico offer swimming and snorkeling in the Gulf waters. Two fishing piers, boat ramp and concession stands are nearby. Two campgrounds loop the pinewoods near the Grand Lagoon. The new Environmental Interpretative Center is open to the public daily.

AIRBOAT ADVENTURES

Panama City Beach - 14852 Bayview Circle (Highway 79 at West Bay Bridge, just north of the beach) 32413. Phone: (850) 230.3822. www.swampvette.com Admission: $18.95 adult, $11.95 child (one half hour tour). Add $10-$15.00 for one hour or sunset tours. Coupon on website.

Come see the REAL, Florida - not what you see from the beach. You'll tour the back waters of West Bay, rivers, creeks and marshlands in search of native Florida wildlife. American Bald Eagles, Ospreys, Heron, Dolphins, Alligators and more. Also, enjoy the beautiful scenery as you glide along on just inches of water in a real Everglades style airboat. The 18 passenger "SWAMPVETTE" and 6 passenger "MUDSTANG" are sure to get your heart thumping when you hear those big block Chevy engines ROAR!

GULF WORLD MARINE PARK

Panama City Beach - 15412 Front Beach Road (From Highway 79: Turn Left on Front Beach Road, Approximately 2 miles East) 32413. www.gulfworldmarinepark.com Phone: (850) 234-5271. Hours: Opens daily at 9:00am and last ticket sold by 2:00pm. (except a more limited schedule in January). Admission: $24.00 adult, $15.00 child (5-11). Miscellaneous: Swim with a Dolphin: Summer Season (Memorial Day Weekend – Labor Day Weekend): $150.00. Spring/Fall/Winter Seasons: $125.00 (includes park admission). $65.00-$149.00 for other programs.

The 2,000 seat Dolphin Stadium that by day features dolphin performances, and by night is the setting for an electronically orchestrated laser light show that ends with a spectacular patriotic salute. Gulf World features more than 25 shows and exhibits featuring sharks, sea turtles, stingrays and sea lions; and, also offers a Dolphin Encounter, Trainer for a Day and Day Camp (separate admission for encounters and camps). As you're walking the park, stop and take in the unusual tropical flowers, plants, fountains, waterfalls and pools.

BIG LAGOON STATE PARK

Pensacola - 12301 Gulf Beach Highway (on County Road 292A, 10 miles southwest of Pensacola) 32507. www.floridastateparks.org/biglagoon/default.cfm Phone: (850) 492-1595. Hours: Daily 8:00am-sundown. Admission: $4.00 per vehicle.

Big Lagoon separates the mainland from Perdido Key and the Gulf of Mexico. Beaches, shallow bays, nature trails, and open woodlands offer splendid opportunities for nature study. The park also beckons visitors with opportunities for camping, swimming, fishing, boating, canoeing, and hiking. Crabbing in the shallow waters of Big Lagoon is a popular activity as well.

NATIONAL MUSEUM OF NAVAL AVIATION

Pensacola (N.A.S.) - 1750 Radford Blvd. (I-10 east or west to exit 7, Route 297. Go about 1.5 miles to Blue Angel Pkwy. Turn right and drive about 12 miles to the back (west) gate of N.A.S.) 32508. Phone: (800) 327-5002. www.naval-air.org Hours: Daily 9:00am-5:00pm, except for Thanksgiving Day, Christmas Day, and New Year's Day. Admission: FREE Miscellaneous: Enjoy lunch at the CubiBar Cafe, decorated with over 1000 squadron and unit plaques reassembled from the historic Officers' Club at Cubi Point in the Philippines.

This Museum, preserving the history of Naval Aviation, is the most visited museum in the State of Florida. From wood and fabric biplanes, to the frontiers of space, the Museum captures Naval Aviation's heritage and brings its story of challenge, ingenuity, and courage to you. See over 140 beautifully restored aircraft representing Navy, Marine Corps, and Coast Guard Aviation. Retrace the first flight across the Atlantic;

courtesty of visitpensacola.com

stand on the flight deck of the USS Cabot. Fly an F/A-18 mission in Desert Storm using a motion-based flight simulator. See The Magic of Flight IMAX® film projected on a seven-story high screen, and feel like you've had a bona fide ride with the Blue Angels. Take the Flight Line Bus Tour on a free 20-minute tour of the approximately 40 aircraft displayed on the flight line behind our Restoration hangar. Kids of all ages love strapping into the many cockpit trainers for pretend test flights or trying their hands at defending a ship from Cabot's anti-aircraft gun battery. Tons of giant aircraft everywhere and many areas to play pretend.

GULF ISLANDS NATIONAL SEASHORE

Pensacola Beach Area - *(south side of Hwy 98) 32507. Phone: (850) 934-2600.*

On the western point of Santa Rosa Island, home to today's Pensacola Beach, the U.S. built the mammoth Fort Pickens in 1830. Now part of a national park, its well-

preserved ruins sit among the magnificent pure-white sand dunes and salt-dwarfed vegetation of GULF ISLANDS NATIONAL SEASHORE. At Pensacola Beach's east end, more such surreal beachscape is preserved at a long stretch known as SANTA ROSA NATIONAL SEASHORE Day Use Area (includes GRAYTON BEACH STATE PARK & DEER LAKE STATE PARK, 357 Main Park Rd, **www.floridastateparks.org/ graytonbeach**). In between, the town maintains a low-key profile with modern seafood restaurants, name-brand resorts, tidy beach shops, miniature golf and a couple of full-facility beach parks with watersports and fishing piers. One pier takes over the old bridge that once crossed to mainland.

The town of Gulf Breeze lies between the beach and Pensacola on a peninsula at the mouth of the bay. To the east, small town NAVARRE BEACH (off U.S. 98) crosses a bridge to Santa Rosa Island. A new state park (**www.floridastateparks**

courtesty of visitpensacola.com

.org/navarrebeach/) opened recently across from the beach, where a 900-foot fishing pier is central to activities, acclaimed for its stellar spring catches.

Still more fort ruins lie on PERDIDO KEY (off State Road 292, $8.00 per vehicle - 7 day pass), an out-of-the-way island that meets up with Alabama at the famous Flori-bama Lounge. Here you can take a long, secluded shoreline stroll along the deserted, powder beaches of another part of the National Seashore.

EDEN GARDENS STATE PARK

Point Washington - (off U.S. 98 on CR 395) 32454. www.floridastateparks.org/ edengardens/default.cfm Phone: (850) 231-4214. Admission: $3.00 per vehicle. $1.50-$3.00 per person for house tour.

Surrounded by moss-draped live oaks and ornamental gardens, the white-pillared Wesley house inspires visions of hoop skirts and gentlemen callers. The park is part of the estate owned in the 1800s by the Wesleys, a wealthy Florida timber family. In 1963, Lois Maxon bought and renovated the home, creating a showplace for her family heirlooms and antiques. The collection of Louis XVI furniture is the second largest in the United States. Guided tours of the house are available hourly Thursday through Monday (including holidays). Visitors can enjoy the grounds, gardens, and picnic area daily from 8:00am-sunset.

PONCE DE LEON SPRINGS STATE PARK

Ponce de Leon - 2860 Ponce de Leon Springs Road (one-half mile south of US 90 on CR 181A) 32455. Phone: (850) 836-4281. www.floridastateparks.org/poncedeleonsprings/ default.cfm Hours: Daily 8:00am-sunset. Admission: $3.00 per vehicle.

This beautiful spring is named for Juan Ponce de León, who led the first Spanish expedition to Florida in 1513 (as legend has it) in search of the "fountain of youth." You may feel invigoratingly younger after taking a dip in the cool, clear waters of Ponce de Leon Springs where the water temperature remains a constant 68 degrees Fahrenheit year-round. Snorkeling is available in some areas. Visitors can also take a leisurely walk along two self-guided nature trails through a lush, hardwood forest and learn about the local ecology and wildlife. Rangers also conduct seasonal guided walks. Picnicking is a popular activity at the park; grills and pavilions are available. Anglers will enjoy fishing for catfish, largemouth bass, chain pickerel, and panfish.

CONSTITUTION CONVENTION MUSEUM STATE PARK

Port St. Joe - 200 Allen Memorial Way (off US 98) 32456. Phone: (850) 229-8029. www.floridastateparks.org/constitutionconvention Hours: Thursday-Monday 9:00am-Noon and 1:00pm-5:00pm. Closed on Thanksgiving, Christmas and New Year's Day. Admission: $1.00 per person.

The museum commemorates the work of the 56 territorial delegates who drafted Florida's first constitution in 1838. Following four more constitution conventions, Florida was finally admitted to the Union in 1845 as the 27th state. Visitors can take a self-guided tour through displays and exhibits of 19th century life in St.

Joseph. Life-size, audio-animated mannequins in the replicated convention hall demonstrate the debate and process of drafting a state constitution. These life-size, audio-animated mannequins bring a realistic touch to the pomp and circumstance of drafting a state constitution.

ST. JOSEPH PENINSULA STATE PARK

Port St. Joe - *8899 Cape San Blas Road (On US 98 (heading East) turn onto SR30-A, travel to SR30E, turn and travel to the park 32456. www.floridastateparks.org/stjoseph/ default.cfm Phone: (850) 227-1327. Hours: Daily 8:00am-sunset. Admission: $4.00 per vehicle. Camping and cabin fees.*

Miles of white sand beaches and striking dunes are the big appeal. The 2,500 acre park is bounded by the gulf and St. Joe Bay. Sunbathing, snorkeling, and swimming are popular activities along the Gulf of Mexico and St. Joseph Bay. From offshore, canoeists and kayakers can take in a superb view of the high dunes and sand pine scrub. Outdoor enthusiasts can enjoy camping, fishing, hiking, and bicycling. As a coastal barrier peninsula, St. Joseph provides excellent opportunities for bird watching; over 240 species have been sighted in the park. A boat ramp is located at Eagle Harbor on the bay side. Campers can stay in a full-facility campground, a short walk from the beach, or at primitive campsites in the wilderness preserve. Eight cabins on the bay side offer alternative overnight accommodations. Voted #2 beach in the nation by Dr. Beach.

TOPSAIL HILL PRESERVE STATE PARK

Santa Rosa Beach - *7525 W Scenic Hwy 30A (on Route 30A approximately 10 miles east of Destin) 32459. Phone: (850) 267-0299. www.floridastateparks.org/topsailhill/ Hours: Daily 8:00am-sunset. Admission: $2.00 per vehicle.*

Topsail Hill Preserve is a secluded beach area in Santa Rosa Beach, Florida that is made up of over three miles of white sand beaches, massive sand dunes, lakes, unique plant and animal life, wetlands and more. Visitors will find that Topsail Hills Preserve State Park offers numerous activities, including swimming, bicycling, rollerblading, fishing, hiking on the nature trails, bird-watching, picnicking and more. Explore the famous Topsail Hill dune which stands nearly 25 feet above sea level. A variety of overnight accommodations are available at Topsail Hill Preserve State Park, including full facility, cabin and RV camping.

THREE RIVERS STATE PARK

Sneads - *7908 Three Rivers Road 32468. www.floridastateparks.org/threerivers/* Phone: *(850) 482-9006. Hours: Daily 8:00am-sunset.*

Three rivers meet here serving abundant recreational activities centering on the Apalachicola, Chattahoochee and Flint Rivers as well as Lake Seminole. Fishing and boating are most popular, with a 100-foot fishing pier helping even landlubbers test the waters. A leisurely walk along the nature trail is an ideal way to enjoy both wildlife and natural features of the park - especially wildflowers and birds.

ST. GEORGE ISLAND STATE PARK

St. George Island - *1900 E. Gulf Beach Dr. 32328. Phone: (850) 927-2111. www.floridastateparks.org/stgeorgeisland/default.cfm* Hours: *Daily 8:00am-sunset. Admission: $5.00 per vehicle. Camping fees.*

Nine miles of undeveloped beach, pristine shoreline, majestic dunes and bay forest, sandy coves and salt marshes. A series of hiking trails, boardwalks and observation platforms great for hiking, camping or a leisurely stroll. Few parks offer better opportunities for gulf coast shelling and birding.

SUGGESTED LODGING AND DINING

DESTIN WEST BEACH AND BAY RESORT. 1515 Miracle Strip Pkwy. (850) 654-4747 or **www.beachguide.com** (Dale Peterson Properties). Great beachview condo rentals with spacious master suite, guest suite, bunk beds, full kitchen, washer/dryer units, and large lanai. Comfortable, exotic island furnishings. The heated pool is extra large with a spa, exercise room, beach service and video rental available on property. Rates around $150.00-$200.00 per night.

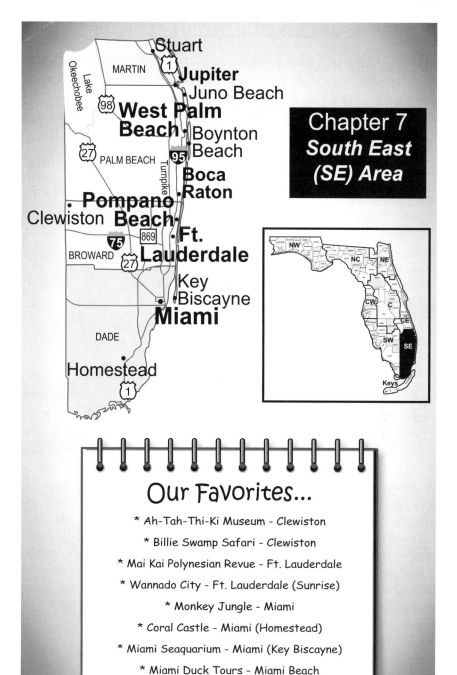

Stuart
MARTIN
Jupiter
Juno Beach
West Palm Beach
Boynton Beach
PALM BEACH
Boca Raton
Clewiston **Pompano Beach**
BROWARD **Ft. Lauderdale**
Key Biscayne
Miami
DADE
Homestead
Lake Okeechobee
Turnpike

Chapter 7
South East (SE) Area

NW
NC NE
CW C
CE
SW SE
Keys

Our Favorites...

* Ah-Tah-Thi-Ki Museum - Clewiston

* Billie Swamp Safari - Clewiston

* Mai Kai Polynesian Revue - Ft. Lauderdale

* Wannado City - Ft. Lauderdale (Sunrise)

* Monkey Jungle - Miami

* Coral Castle - Miami (Homestead)

* Miami Seaquarium - Miami (Key Biscayne)

* Miami Duck Tours - Miami Beach

SPORTS IN SOUTHEAST FLORIDA

FLORIDA PANTHERS - This popular National Hockey League team heats up the ice October to April each year at the Office Depot Center. One Panther Pkwy, Fort Lauderdale (Sunrise). (954) 835-PUCK or **www.floridapanthers.com**.

FLORIDA MARLINS - Catch all the excitement of Major League Baseball action as the Florida Marlins play April-September in Dolphins Stadium. 2267 Dan Marino Blvd, Miami. (305) 626-7400 or (877) MARLINS or **www.floridamarlins.com**.

DAVIE RODEO - Visit a Wild West rodeo the fourth Saturday of every month (except December) at 8:00pm. 4271 Davie Road, Fort Lauderdale (Davie). (954) 680-3555 or **www.fivestarrodeo.com**.

MIAMI DOLPHINS - From August to January this 40-year old championship football team plays in Dolphins Stadium. 2269 Dan Marino Blvd, Miami. (305) 632-6100 or (888) FINS-TIX or **www.miamidolphins.com**.

MIAMI HEAT - NBA Basketball October-April at American Airlines Arena. 601 Biscayne Blvd, Miami. (786) 777-HOOP or **www.heat.com**.

GUMBO LIMBO NATURE CENTER

Boca Raton - 1801 N. Ocean Blvd. 33432. Phone: (561) 338-1473. www.gumbolimbo.org
Hours: Monday-Saturday 9:00am-4:00pm, Sunday Noon-4:00pm. Admission: Suggested donation of $3.00.

Seawater is pumped directly into large outdoor aquariums filled with representatives of native marine fauna. Indoor and outdoor classrooms, interpretive displays, aquariums, visual presentations, a butterfly garden, a 40-foot high observation tower, an elevated boardwalk through the hammock and mangrove communities offer unique opportunities for environmental education. Rare and endangered species such as the manatee, the brown pelican, the osprey and sea turtles can often be observed on or from the facility. Coastal relics like a shell midden from the Pre-Columbian Indians and Pond Apple trees from the original freshwater body (known as the Spanish River) can be seen. A cannon and anchors have also been found on the shore of Red Reef park. All these assets give Gumbo Limbo a unique blend of living history.

SCHOOLHOUSE CHILDREN'S MUSEUM

Boynton Beach - *129 E. Ocean Avenue (1/4 mile east of Boynton Beach Blvd. South on Seacrest Blvd, 2 Blocks, then East on Ocean Avenue) 33435. Phone: (561) 742-6780.* **www.schoolhousemuseum.org** *Hours: Tuesday-Saturday 10:00am-5:00pm, Sunday 1:00-4:00pm. Admission: $3.00-$5.00 (age 2+).*

Children learn about Florida's vibrant history through hands-on interactive exhibits. Begin your experience at the Schoolhouse museum by relaxing and enjoying an exciting ten-minute introductory film about Boynton Beach History. Dozens of actual photos embedded into this refreshing, upbeat show set the tone for the fun and learning to follow in the galleries. Step back in time and see for yourself how South Florida grew. Get a ticket at the train depot, pack up a suitcase, and take a ride on the Orange Blossom Express. Dress up like a conductor or a train passenger, ring the bell, shovel coal into the steam engine or read about trains while traveling in the passenger car library. Through imaginary play, students and parents together learn about Palm Beach County's rich cultural heritage. Four main exhibit areas, Time Travels, Family Farms, Water World and Main Street provide props and dress-up clothes for children to imagine themselves as Florida pioneers. Photos and wall displays in every area explain the historical characters and places that inspired each exhibit.

LOXAHATCHEE, ARM NATIONAL WILDLIFE REFUGE

Boynton Beach - *10218 Lee Road (I-95 north to FL 806, turn left heading west about 7.5 miles to FL7/US441 and turn right. Travel north 3.1 miles to Lee Road) 33437. Phone: (561) 734-8303.* **http://loxahatchee.fws.gov/home/default.asp** *Hours: Park open sunrise to sunset. Visitors center open Wednesday-Sunday 9:00am-4:00pm except winter holidays. Admission: A fee of $5.00 is charged to private vehicles entering the refuge.*

Loxahatchee National Wildlife Refuge is home to the American alligator and the endangered Everglades snail kite. In addition to being a home to wildlife, the refuge offers many recreational opportunities. Walking trails, a canoe trail, bike trail, boat ramps, fishing platform, observation towers, butterfly garden, and a visitor center are available. Not quite all of the 147,392 acre refuge is Everglades habitat. A four hundred acre cypress swamp is the largest remaining remnant of a cypress strand that once separated the pine flatwoods in the east from the Everglades marshes. A boardwalk into the swamp gives the visitor a chance for an up-close swamp experience without getting his or her feet wet.

AH-TAH-THI-KI MUSEUM

Clewiston - HC-61, Box 46 (I-75W to exit 49, then 17 miles north on County Road 833 to West Boundary Road) 33440. Phone: (863) 902-1113. **www.seminoletribe.com/museum** *Hours: Tuesday-Sunday 9:00am-5:00pm. Admission: $4.00-$6.00.*

Ah-Tah-Thi-Ki means "a place to learn". Just three miles from Billie Swamp Safari, this museum exhibits rare artifacts showing how Seminole ancestors lived in the Florida swamps and Everglades. The museum film, *We Seminoles*, tells their story in their own words, including the dramatic struggle to remain in Florida (Seminole Wars). At the center of all chickee huts, you see a fire ring of four or more logs facing east, west, north and south. Soft fires burn at many locations and the smoke wafts in the air. What meaning do the beads have? Notice the huge family canoes. Did you know their hats are also their blankets? See a diorama re-enacting a seasonal Corn Dance (like their family reunions). Kids will be surprised to learn of their customs for youth discipline. Learn about their favorite sport - stick ball - a lot different than our baseball. Nature trails will take you throughout the beautiful 60-acre cypress dome to a living village where you can witness authentic Seminole Tribal members preparing traditional arts and crafts.

BILLIE SWAMP SAFARI

Clewiston - (I-75W to exit 49, then north on CR 833 for 19 miles to park entrance) 33440. Phone: (800) 949-6101. **www.seminoletribe.com/safari** *Hours: Daily 8:30am-6:00pm.*

Museum 9:00-5:00pm (except Mondays). Shows: Alligator 2:15pm daily. Swamp Critters 1:15pm daily. Admission: Swamp Buggy (leaves every hour / on the hour) $15.00-$25.00. Air boat Ride (every 1/2 hour) $15.00. Alligator or Swamp Critter Show $4.00-$8.00 each. $35.00 chickee hut rental. Discounted packages available. Miscellaneous: Complete camping facilities with all amenities are available on the Reservation just a short ride from the safari. Dine in the full service restaurant, the Swamp Water Café, and sample Seminole specialties such as gator nuggets, frog legs, catfish and fry bread with honey (yum), or make a selection from a regular American-style menu.

Take a ride on a "swamp buggy", see native and exotic animals from around the world, sleep in a Seminole chickee, listen to Indian folklore around the campfire, or skim across a grass-and-water world in an airboat. Try a day or night in Native Florida...on a real Seminole Reservation. Billie Swamp Safari opens 2,200 lush acres of its Big Cypress Reservation to the public. Sightings of deer, water buffalo, bison, wild hogs, swamp chickens, blue heron, hawks, eagles other rare birds and alligators are common - there are even Florida panthers in the area. Tours are provided aboard swamp buggies, customized motorized vehicles specially designed to provide visitors with an elevated view of the frontier while comfortably riding through the wetlands and cypress heads. The buggies are camouflage colored, with padded seats and a canopy cover so that it really looks like a safari vehicle - are you ready for some adventure? Also, visitors may choose to take an exhilarating airboat ride or take a walk through the cypress dome boardwalk nature trail.

JOHN U. LLOYD BEACH STATE PARK

Dania - 6503 N. Ocean Drive 33004. www.floridastateparks.org/lloydbeach/default.cfm Phone: (954) 923-2833. Visit the beautiful beach on the ocean side, or see a mangrove lined inlet on the island side shore.

INTERNATIONAL SWIMMING HALL OF FAME

Fort Lauderdale - One Hall of Fame Drive 33004. Phone: (954) 462-6536. www.ishof.org Hours: Daily 9:00am-5:00pm. Admission: $2.00-$5.00 per person or $10.00 per family.

Since 1965, ISHOF has promoted swimming, diving, water polo, synchronized swimming, open water swimming, water safety and aquatic art by honoring the great achievements and events in aquatic history. The Museum chronicles feats of famous swimmers and divers, from Esther Williams to Greg Louganis. Located on the ocean side of the complex, the International Swimming Hall of Fame Museum and Exhibition Hall, an elevated wave-shaped building occupying over 7,500 square feet, adorns the entrance to the Hall of Fame Aquatic complex. Johnny Weissmuller's Olympic medals are a part of the world's largest collection of aquatic Olympic medals, pins, badges, diplomas and certificates. Mark Spitz's starting block used to win six of his seven 1972 Olympic gold medals is on view as are over 60 Olympic, national and club uniforms, warm ups and swim suits. The first automatic timing machine to determine the results of close races can be seen along with the modern system used today. The visitor may play the role of both the starter and timer in a hands-on tribute to timing automation.

HUGH TAYLOR BIRCH STATE RECREATION AREA

Fort Lauderdale - *3109 East Sunrise Blvd. (off A1A) 33304. Phone: (954) 564-4521. www.floridastateparks.org/hughtaylorbirch Hours: Daily 8:00am-sundown.*

The former site of an oceanfront estate, this rambling preserve has woodlands containing the last significant remnant of a maritime hammock (tropical hardwood) forest in the county and is home to several endangered and threatened animals. Visitors can rent a canoe and paddle along a mile-long freshwater lagoon or fish from the seawall. Nature lovers can hike along two short trails and learn about local plants and wildlife while bicyclists and skaters glide along the paved park road. Visitors can access the beach via the pedestrian tunnel under A1A.

MAI KAI POLYNESIAN REVUE

Fort Lauderdale - *3599 N. Federal Hwy (on US 1, north of Rte. 816) 33308. Phone: (954) 563-3272. www.maikai.com Hours: Restaurant open Daily at 5:00pm for dinner. Show Times: (Dinner served before the show): Sunday - Thursday 7:00pm and 9:30pm; Friday and Saturday 7:00pm and 10:00pm (Times may vary with season) Admission: Showcharge: $9.95 per person. Children under 12 years old enjoy the show at no charge. Dinner Kids Menu (avg. $13.00), Adult Menu varies but the best value is the package for $45.00. Miscellaneous: During the summer months (June through September), the Mai-Kai features a Kids Show every Sunday evening. Children, ages four to twelve, interpret stories of Polynesia's rich heritage through graceful dance movements.*

What fun! Take a trip to exotic countries without leaving the Florida Coast. The Mai-Kai authentically recreates a Polynesian Village, complete with tiki torches, a thatch roof, gardens, babbling brooks, waterfalls and more. Each room reflects a different region of Polynesia. After your South Pacific feast, add the Mai-Kai Islander

SO COlOrful...SO fun!   Revue, performed by Polynesian

dancers and musicians in colorful hand sewn costumes. The Samoan fire dance spectacular had the kids in awe! Watch with delight as the brave warriors juggle, twirl and even lick or touch the flaming fire-torches without even a scorch. The ladies competitive drum dance was another favorite. How do they move like that? The Mai-Kai dancers invite audience members to hop on stage and learn some new dance moves. Each child receives a lei and a Polynesian activity book on family Sunday nights. In addition, the Mai-Kai has a special menu tailored to children's tastes including Captain Hook's Ribs, Society Island Shrimp, Bora Bora Beef and Kon Tiki Chicken. Did you hear your car make thunder as you entered? That's just one of their "tricks" to make guests escape to Polynesia.

MUSEUM OF DISCOVERY & SCIENCE

Fort Lauderdale - 401 SW Second Street, downtown 33312. Phone: (954) 467-6637. www.mods.org   Hours: Monday-Saturday 10:00am-5:00pm. Sunday Noon-6:00pm. Call for showtimes at IMAX Theater. Admission: $8.00-$10.00 (age 2+). Combo ticket discounts pared with IMAX film. Miscellaneous: DISCOVERY CENTER - Children seven and under will enjoy this hands-on play and learning center designed especially for them.

Explore interactive exhibits, experience live encounters with resident animals and learn about Florida's unique ecosystem. Launch a space vehicle and discover how much force it takes to escape Earth's gravity. Or, take a simulated trip to the Moon or Mars. Check your watch with the Gravity Clock. See sharks and the largest living Atlantic coral reef in captivity or hang out with bats. Listen to the sound and watch the bright lights of a Kaleidascope or play with Gizmos and gadgets. Outdoors, explore the 11,000 square foot nature trail and learn about Florida's amazing Everglades in the Living in the Everglades exhibit.

OLD FORT LAUDERDALE MUSEUM OF HISTORY

Fort Lauderdale - 231 SW 2nd Avenue (Riverwalk, downtown) 33312. Phone: (954) 463-4431. www.oldfortlauderdale.org Hours: Tuesday-Friday 11:00am-5:00pm, Saturday-Sunday Noon-5:00pm.

Located where Henry Flagler's East Coast Railway crosses the New River on Riverwalk, where the city began, it includes three historic buildings, a replica of the first schoolhouse in Broward County and a modern research and collections facility. Old Fort Lauderdale Village is easily recognized with historic markers, a white picket fence, Victorian lighting and landscaping that matches the lush tropical beauty of a bygone era. Guides take you through the 1899 Replica Schoolhouse and the 1907 King-Cromartie House, a pioneer home.

FORT LAUDERDALE ANTIQUE CAR MUSEUM

Fort Lauderdale - 1527 SW 1st Avenue 33315. www.antiquecarmuseum.org Phone: (954) 779-7300. Hours: Monday-Friday 9:00am-3:00pm Admission: $8.00 adult, $5.00 senior, under 12 free.

The museum houses a permanent display of 22 Packard automobiles from 1900 to the 1940's, along with a gallery dedicated to the late President Franklin D. Roosevelt plus several special collections of automobile memorabilia.

JUNGLE QUEEN RIVERBOAT

Fort Lauderdale - 801 Seabreeze Blvd. (located near the Bahia Mar Resort docks) 33316. Phone: (954) 462-5596. www.junglequeen.com Admission: $31.95 evenings, $13.95 daytime.

Step back in history aboard this sternwheeler that cruises the Intracoastal and New River on day and evening sightseeing cruises. Cruise to an island for BBQ dinner and variety show nightly at 7:00pm. Narrated sightseeing cruises are 10:00am and 2:00pm.

SEA EXPERIENCE GLASSBOTTOM BOAT & SNORKELING TOURS

Fort Lauderdale - 801 Seabreeze Blvd. Bahia Mar Resort docks - 100 yards north of the Jungle Queen) 33316. Phone: (954) 467-6000. www.seaxp.com Admission charged based on tour.

Discover the underwater world of south Florida. Swim through the clear waters of the warm Atlantic and experience the colorful fish and marine life that lie beneath the surface. To name just a few, you might see French, Grey and Queen Angelfish, Blue Parrotfish, Trumpetfish, and many others. The crew's favorite snorkeling spot, named the Fort Lauderdale Twin Ledges, is located about a half mile off of Fort Lauderdale beach in 10 to 20 ft. of water. The water temperature is warm all year-round making it an ideal spot for snorkeling. For first time snorkelers the crew is more than happy to provide lessons and to make it a pleasurable experience for all. And if you don't want to get wet, you can enjoy the view from aboard the glass bottom boat!

WATER BUS

Fort Lauderdale - 1850 SE 17th Street, Suite 106A 33316. Phone: (954) 467-6677. www.watertaxi.com

See the "Venice of America" via scheduled on-time service Water Taxis. Water Bus is a unique alternative to traditional transportation, providing a comfortable and relaxing way to avoid traffic and congested roadways. Take a ride along Ft. Lauderdale's wet streets and see the sights and sounds of Ft. Lauderdale's waterways. Daily from 17th Street to Oakland Park Blvd. And west to downtown Fort Lauderdale. All day pass is $7.00.

BUTTERFLY WORLD

Fort Lauderdale (Coconut Creek) - 3600 W. Sample Road (in Tradewinds Park) (exit at Sample Road and head west. Enter into Tradewinds Park on the south side of Sample Road, only a quarter of a mile west of the Florida Turnpike) 33073. Phone: (954) 977-4400. www.butterflyworld.com Hours: Monday-Saturday 9:00am-5:00pm, Sunday 1:00-5:00pm. Admission: $18.95 adult, $13.95 child (3-11).

One of the most unusual "zoos" in the world, the Butterfly World is dedicated to the study, care and display of astonishingly beautiful butterflies from all over the globe. The site includes a farm, where the delicate creatures are raised, several aviaries where thousands of butterflies fly freely, a tropical rain forest, hanging gardens, a museum, a hummingbird exhibit, an English Rose Garden, a Secret Garden and a gift shop. You'll also find fish, lorikeet and insects here. The butterflies are best in the morning until about 3:00pm, so make sure you arrive early.

FISHING HALL OF FAME & MUSEUM (IGFA)

Fort Lauderdale (Dania Beach) - 300 Gulf Stream Way (located next to Bass Pro Shops) (I-95 to Griffin Road Exit 23; west on Griffin to first light (Anglers Ave.); south to Gulf Stream Way; left at Sportsman's Park) 33004. Phone: (954) 922-4212. www.igfa.org Hours: Daily 10:00am-6:00pm. Closed only Thanksgiving and Christmas. Admission: $5.00-$6.00 (age 3+).

The galleries and marina displays here are full of fish. Meet live alligators, too. Start your adventure with Journeys, an exciting cinematic experience that you can see, hear, and feel! Try "on" reels. Kids might like to feed the fish or try the virtual fishing simulator (sport fishing without getting wet). Younger ones like the Discovery Room where kids dress up and "fish" from a fun boat. Along the Wetlands walk, you might find iguanas, lizards and birds amongst the mangroves. In the Hall of Fame, you'll find the world's largest life-size collection of fishing world record holders. Some are stationed as photo ops so you can go home and tell some fish stories about your big catch!

BUEHLER PLANETARIUM & OBSERVATORY

Fort Lauderdale (Davie) - 3501 SW Davie Road (Broward Community College, central Campus) 33314. Phone: (954) 201-6681. www.iloveplanets.com Admission: $4.00-$5.00 per person.

Explorations through all of space. Enjoy programs that explore the wonders of the Universe. Most of the public programs involve the stars and folklore. Observatory open to Public on Wednesday, Friday, Saturday 8:00pm-10:00pm for free.

FLAMINGO GARDENS

Fort Lauderdale (Davie) - 3750 S. Flamingo Road (Take I-595 West to Flamingo Road. (Exit #1B) Turn South) 33330. Phone: (954) 473-2955. **www.flamingogardens.org** *Hours: Daily 9:30am-5:30pm. Closed Mondays June-September. Admission: $15.00 adult, $8.00 child (4-11). Discounts for seniors, military and students w/ID. TOUR BY TRAM: Adults $4, Children (4-11) $3, Miscellaneous: Flamingo Café.*

Once a spectacular estate, this Garden is now a refuge housing a free flight aviary, alligators, flamingos, bobcats and injured animals. Rare, exotic and native plants, a 200-year old oak hammock, citrus groves, wetlands and a tropical flowering tree walk balance out the botanical gardens. A nice living example of Florida's natural history.

ANNE KOLB NATURE CENTER

Fort Lauderdale (Hollywood) - 751 Sheridan Street (West Lake Park) 33019. Phone: (954) 926-2480. Hours: Rentals daily 9:00am-5:00pm. Park open daylight hours.

Over 1,500 pristine acres of wilderness and mangrove wetlands are minutes from the beach. Visitors can enjoy a variety of activities including hiking, biking, canoeing, fishing, tennis and racquetball. There are abundant nature and canoe trails with wildlife viewing areas, an exhibit hall and observation tower. Sports equipment rentals and narrated boat tours are available at the marina (extra fee)

WANNADO CITY

Fort Lauderdale (Sunrise) - 12801 W. Sunrise Blvd., Sawgrass Mills Mall (Merge onto 595 West. Exit on Flamingo Road and make a right, going north. At Sunrise Boulevard, make a left, going west) 33323. Phone: (954) 838-7100 or (888) WANNADO. **www.wannadocity.com** *Hours: Friday-Sunday 10:00am-8:00pm. Weekday hours vary. Generally 10:00am-5:00pm. Call or web check for hours. Admission: $29.95 child (3-13), $15.95 adult. Late afternoon and Florida resident discounts. Miscellaneous: Parents, enjoy your time here by being interviewed by a kid journalist, taken to court or even made into a circus clown. Share in your kid's adventures by watching from numerous storefront windows. Grown-ups can refresh and recharge at The Eagle's Nest. Enjoy free high-speed Internet access and digital cable television, or relax with a gourmet coffee, pastry or dessert. IMPORTANT: Although they have a sophisticated SafetyZone arm bracelet monitor system for parents to locate their kids throughout the day, it isn't full proof. We experienced numerous false locations that were a little unsettling. Maybe have your kids carry a cell phone if you plan to relax in the lounge vs. tagging along with the kids. The armbands ARE secure for exits. Only the whole party linked to each family's code is allowed to exit together.*

In addition to the large variety of shops and restaurants, Sawgrass Mills is also home to Wannado City, a multi-million dollar indoor recreation center ranking as the first indoor role-playing theme park of its kind in the United States. Whata Ya Wanna Do? This scaled-down, kid-sized City allows children to role-play in up to 100 careers, in 40 venues from TV anchor to lawyer, doctor, firefighter, banker, police officer, chef and beyond in VERY realistic settings (ex. Real medical equipment in the hospital, real water in hoses to put out a fire). Upon entering Wannado City, each "kidizen" will receive a check for Wongas, the city's

Learning what it takes to make Coca Cola...fun!

official currency. He or she can enjoy the option of setting up a bank account, spending his or her "cash" at the various city entertainment options or earning more at the numerous career choices. Kids gain money management savvy by deciding how to spend "earnings" and a sense of empowerment as they use their own ATM card. Our kids favorite areas on their first visit: The Crime Lab (look for clues using a briefcase and scratch pad to secure observations) and the Coca-Cola bottling factory (which team can clean, fill and cap the fastest?). This is an Amazing place - parents will want to be a kid again!

EVERGLADES NATIONAL PARK

Homestead - 40001 State Road 9336 33034. Phone: Visitor Information (305) 242-7700.
www.nps.gov/ever Hours: The main park entrance (near Homestead and Florida City) is open 24 hours a day. Park waters are open 24 hours a day. NOTE: during and after hurricanes that hit south Florida, be aware that most often the park entrances and facilities close for some time. Admission: $10.00 per private vehicle for a 7 day pass.

VISITOR CENTERS

ERNEST F. COE - Phone: 305-242-7700. Located at the main park entrance west of Homestead and Florida City. Exhibits: Educational displays, orientation films, brochures, and information are available. No trails start from this visitor center. The Long Pine Key Campground and Picnic Area is six miles further west, and is surrounded by an abundance of hiking trails.

Everglades National Park (cont.)

ROYAL PALM - Open All Year 8:00am-4:15pm. Phone: (305) 242-7700. Located on the east side of the park, four miles west of the main entrance station. Special Programs: Anhinga Amble: join a ranger on a leisurely stroll to find out why this trail is an attraction to wildlife; anhingas, alligators and Florida gar can all be seen along this trail. Offered most days at 10:30 a.m. Artist Charles Harper's stylized images of Everglades wildlife are on display with recorded messages that interpret the park's unique ecosystems. The Anhinga and Gumbo Limbo trails begin here.

SHARK VALLEY - Open All Year 9:00am-5:00pm. Phone: (305) 221-8776. Shark Valley is located along US 41 (Tamiami Trail) on the northern border of the park. The small visitor center contains educational displays. Shark Valley lies in the heart of the "river of grass". Wildlife abounds here in a freshwater ecosystem of sawgrass marsh and tree islands. A 15-mile (24 km) tram road (not open to private motorized vehicles) extends into the marsh, offering one of the best opportunities to view alligators. A two hour narrated tram ride provides an overview of the freshwater Everglades. Bicycles are available to rent. Those wishing to explore alone can walk the short trails and portions of the tram road, or bike. An observation tower located halfway around the tram road provides a spectacular view into the sawgrass coves.

FLAMINGO - Phone: (239) 695-2945. Flamingo is 38 miles (61 km) southwest from the main entrance at the southern end of the park. Open intermittently during the summer. Natural history exhibits and information in the Florida Bay Museum. A restaurant, gift shop, lodge, and campground are nearby. Boat tours and canoe & kayak rentals are available at the marina. Several hiking and canoeing trails begin at Flamingo or nearby, including the south end of the Wilderness Waterway. Abundant wildlife may be found here year-round.

LOGGERHEAD MARINELIFE CENTER

Juno Beach - 14200 US Hwy. One 33408. Phone: (561) 627-8280. www.marinelife.org Hours: Tuesday-Saturday 10:00am-4:00pm, Sunday Noon-3:00pm. Closed all federal holidays. Admission: Small admission fee. Miscellaneous: Park amenities include a guarded beach, nature trails, picnic pavilions.

The new campus is comprised of 10,000 square feet of indoor space which will include a visitor center, marine laboratory, sea turtle veterinary hospital, and learning center. A 3,000 square foot outdoor exhibit 'yard' houses marine turtle rehabilitation tanks, shark exhibit, and a marine touch tank. Exhibits include a giant Leatherback sea turtle, salt water aquaria and displays of local wildlife, as well as educational displays about south Florida's marine environment. The nature center includes a marine-oriented gift and book shop, featuring an excellent selection of children's educational books and unique gift and craft items.

JUPITER INLET LIGHTHOUSE

Jupiter - 500 Captain Armour's Way, Lighthouse Park (I-95 to Indiantown Rd. east, turn left/north at US 1. Turn right at Beach Rd.) 33477. Phone: (561) 747-8380. **www.lrhs.org** *Hours: Saturday-Wednesday 10:00am-4:00pm. Admission: $6.00 each. Minimum height is 48" tall. No flip-flops or heels allowed.*

Climb the 105 steps of this newly restored historical treasure on the National Register of Historic Places. From steamships to railroads to the Civil War (lied silent in hopes of preserving it from harm) to modern uses. The first order Fresnel lens is magical to look at.

BISCAYNE NATURE CENTER / MARJORY STONEMAN DOUGLAS

Key Biscayne - Crandon Park, 6767 Crandon Blvd. (take I-95 or US 1 to the Key Biscayne Exit) 33149. Phone: (305) 361-6767. **www.biscaynenaturecenter.org**

The center offers hands-on marine exploration, coastal hammock hikes, fossil-rock reef walks, bike trips, local history lectures and beach walks to aquatic tourists. The display room has aquariums teeming with aquatic wildlife, sea turtle demonstrations, and stories about the Tequesta Indians while you can observe artifacts from archeological digs. Three walking paths and a bikeway meander through exotic flora leading to a north beach area where low tides expose a fossilized rock reef, offering a view seen on only one other location in the world. On Seagrass tours, a guide will brief you about the abundant sea life, then lead you waist-deep into the warm, salty water to see for yourselves. You'll run a net through the thick seagrass and be amazed at what critters you'll find. Sea urchins, sea cucumbers, pipefish, spotted slugs, blowfish, spider crabs and tiny fish just might fill the nets. Even tiny octopus or exotic puffer fish (the ones that bloat when they're stressed) may be seen. The critters, of course, are not harmed. They are returned to the sea grass. For $10.00, this is one of the best values in town. Your kids may not want to leave.

CAPE FLORIDA LIGHTHOUSE / BILL BAGGS CAPE FLORIDA STATE PARK

Key Biscayne - 1200 S. Crandon Park Blvd (I-95 to the Rickenbacker Causeway, all the way to the end) 33149. Phone: (305) 361-5811. **www.floridastateparks.org/capeflorida** *Hours: Park open 8:00am to sundown. Admission: $5.00 per vehicle.*

This historic lighthouse, built in 1884, is located on a very scenic beach at the southern tip of Key Biscayne. Be ready to ascend the 109 steps to the lighthouse watchroom and enjoy the view of the beach, Miami and Biscayne Bay from the top, view a short movie, and then tour the Keeper's Quarters. Walking and bicycle trails wind through native vegetation.

HISTORICAL MUSEUM OF SOUTHERN FLORIDA

Miami - 101 W. Flagler Street (I-95 take the NW 2nd St. exit, turn right. Turn right again on NW 2nd Ave. for one block. The Cultural Center is on left) 33130. Phone: (305) 375-1492. **www.historical-museum.org** *Hours: Monday-Saturday 10:00am-5:00pm, Sunday Noon-5:00pm. Admission: $5.00 adult, $4.00 senior & student w/ID, $2.00 child (6-12).*

They have activities for kids in their permanent collection spanning thousands of years of Southern Florida and Caribbean history. First, some 10,000 years ago the original humans in this area arrived - prehistoric Indian tribes. Much later, the geographic location of South Florida, guardian of the trade routes, determined its destiny for over 300 years following Ponce de Leon's visit in 1513. It was a period of interaction between people and nations, of red men interacting with white, of white with black and of black with red. In the very southern end of the peninsula came the blossoming of the island town of Key West as the center for the "wrecking industry." When that died, pioneers were encouraged to settle the land and drive the Seminole Indian out. The Seminole resisted. The 19th century brought more settlement, the Flagler railroad, and agriculture. Real estate and tourism booms began to appear. Geography and cultural diversity have made it the gateway between the United States and the Caribbean and Latin America in the last 50 years.

MIAMI ART MUSEUM

Miami - 101 W. Flagler Street 33130. Phone: (305) 375-3000. **www.miamiartmuseum.org** *Hours: Tuesday-Saturday 10:00am-5:00pm, Sunday Noon-5:00pm. Admission: $5.00 adult, $2.50 senior, FREE for children.*

The museum's permanent collection and exhibition features art from the 1940s to the present. The Second Saturdays are Free for Families program is the second Saturday of every month from 1:00-4:00pm The program features hands-on activities for children and adults and includes live music, storytelling, guided tours, gallery games and dance performances.

ISLAND QUEEN & BAYSIDE BLASTER

Miami - Bayside Marketplace, waterside (I-95 south to I-395 east. Exit at NE 2nd Ave/ Biscayne, continue straight. Make right on Biscayne, then left on Port Blvd. (NE 5th St.), stay on right) 33132. Phone: (305) 379-5119 or (800) 910-5119. www.islandqueencruises.com Admission: $17.00 adult, $8.00 child (4-12).(Island Queen) or $14.00 adult, $7.00 child (Bayside Blaster).

ISLAND QUEEN: Sit back and relax as you go on a bilingual narrated sightseeing cruise along scenic Biscayne Bay. See Miami's spectacular coastal sites; including the beautiful downtown Miami skyline, the Port of Miami, Brickell Key, Fisher Island and the celebrity filled islands of Miami Beach known as "Millionaire's Row."

BAYSIDE BLASTER: Thrill seekers, hold onto your hats and come experience an exciting speedboat ride aboard the Bayside Blaster! Race through beautiful Biscayne Bay to the celebrity-filled islands of Miami Beach known as "Millionaire's Row." It's the adventurous way to see Miami's spectacular coastal sites.

PARROT JUNGLE ISLAND

Miami - 1111 Parrot Jungle Trail (take I-395 east/MacArthur Causeway to first exit after the bridge-Parrot Jungle Trail, follow signs) 33132. Phone: (305) 2 - JUNGLE. www.parrotjungle.com Hours: Daily 10:00am-6:00pm. Admission: $27.95 adult, $25.95 senior, military & student w/ID, $22.95 child (3-10). Parking is $7.00 per vehicle.

Open since July 2003 on Watson Island (close to resorts and cruise ship terminals), the theme park is home to more than 3,000 exotic animals and 500 species of plants. Here visitors enjoy animal stage shows, one-of-a-kind interactive aviaries, plant nurseries, jungle trails, ape and monkey exhibits, a petting farm, as well as world-famous parrot shows, a new Serpentarium and Jungle Theater, an Everglades Habitat and more. All of the shows featured un-caged animals performing. Parrot Jungle Island offers memorable opportunities to: feed birds, fish and flamingos; interact with roaming trainers and animals; and, take photo-ops with some rare animals and exotic birds.

MICCOSUKEE INDIAN VILLAGE

Miami - MM 70, US 41 Tamiami Trail (25 miles west of the Florida Turnpike exit 25 in Miami on US Hwy. 41 (aka Tamiami Trail & SW 8th Street) 33144. Phone: (305) 223-8380. Hours: Daily 9:00am-5:00pm. Admission. Miscellaneous: A Miccosukee craft gift shop and Indian Restaurant are on the premises. The Miccosukee Restaurant features such delights as Miccosukee fry bread, pumpkin bread, Everglades frog legs, 'gator and catfish as well as standard American cuisine.

Guided tours take you through the past, present and future of the tribe through crafting (ex. Sewing patchwork, wood crafts, doll making, basket weaving) demonstrations, Native Island & Air Boat Tours through the River of Grass (By airboat discover a typical hammock village where a Miccosukee family lives), Cook Chickee (Cooking House), and Alligator Wrestling (Be amazed as tribesman risk their lives in a pit full of live alligators). The Miccosukee Museum provides a rare look into this people's past. Items from clothing to cooking utensils to games are displayed, and a small portion of a family village is re-created.

MONKEY JUNGLE

Miami - 14805 SW 216th Street (836 West to the Florida Turnpike south. Take exit 11 labeled Cutler Ridge Boulevard and Southwest 216 Street) 33170. Phone: (305) 235-1611. ***www.monkeyjungle.com*** *Hours: Daily 9:30am-5:00pm. Admission: $19.95 adult, $16.95 senior (65+), $13.95 child (3-9). Discount coupon on website.*

In the 1960s and 70s, if you visited this attraction, your car bumper was likely

adorned with the familiar orange-and-black decal promoting this site. Monkey Jungle is home to 400 primates, most running free on a 30-acre reserve.   Little steel bowls hang from long chains to allow humans to place food in the bowl and then the monkeys outside pull up the chain and pick out the snack (mostly peanuts and seeds). Shows allow the trainers to answer questions and share amusing facts. They start the show by ringing the giant dinner bell so all who want snacks come over. Monkeys, like humans, love to make friends. Witness crab-eating monkeys wade into the pool for "treats" and, if you are lucky, see them skin dive! Delve in the lush, tropical Amazonian rainforest for a look at exotics. What is monkeys' favorite fruit - just like us - whatever is in season. Or gander at a huge fossil deposit

Monkey says, "I wonder why THEY are in a cage?"

or rare Amazon parrots, the Cameroon Jungle and the Mandrill Baboons. Its gimmick, people, not animals, are caged! This place is so adorable!

GOLD COAST RAILROAD MUSEUM

Miami - 12450 SW 152nd Street (MetroZoo entrance) (Florida Turnpike south to exit 16 (SW 152 St.). Make a right (west) on SW 152 Street and continue for one mile) 33177. Phone: (305) 253-0063. www.goldcoast-railroad.org Hours: Daily 10:00 or 11:00am-4:00pm. Admission: $5.00 general, $3.00 child (under 12).

The kids will love to play with wooden model train sets including the beloved Thomas, while everyone will want to climb on board displays of historic railroad equipment. Such treasures as the Pullman car, Ferdinand Magellan, Franklin D. Roosevelt's private railroad car was also used by Truman, Eisenhower and Reagan. Another feature includes a model trail set.

TRAIN RIDES are offered on weekends for an additional fee. Train rides on the "Edwin Link Children's Railroad", or Link train, are regularly offered on weekends at 1:00pm and 3:00pm. The rides are suitable for both children and adults and consist of a 20 minute ride on 2-foot gauge track. The cost is $2.25 per person, all ages. Standard Gauge train rides using Diesel Equipment with the air-conditioned "Belle Glade" passenger coach are offered each Saturday and Sunday. The cost is $5.50 per person, all ages, for a 20 minute ride. Train departs once each operating day at 2:00pm. Kids can ride in the cab for $11.00 each.

MIAMI METROZOO

Miami - 12400 SW 152nd Street 33177. Phone: (305) 373-5437. www.miamimetrozoo.com Hours: Daily 9:30am-5:30pm. Admission: $11.50 adult, $6.75 child (3-12), $10.50 senior (65 and older). Miscellaneous: The Wild Earth Jeep Simulator takes you on a safari simulator (extra $5.00 fee).

One of the world's great zoos - the only one in the continental United States located in a subtropical climate. This 300-acre cageless zoo showcases more than 1,300 animals. They recently opened the long-anticipated Aviary Wings of Asia exhibit. This is home to more than 300 birds representing 70 species of exotic, rare and endangered Asian Birds in a large free flight area that feels like an Asian Jungle, the aviary air is alive with beautiful birdsongs, trickling brooks and a waterfall. It also features Dr. Wilde's World, a Children's Zoo, Wildlife Carousel, Guided Tram Tours, and Zookeeper Talks. In the Lakeside Water Play area everyone is invited to get wet with a water shooting frog, a pink flamingo and other fun zoo spouts. Cool Zoo™ Seahorse Water Play is another waterplay area to cool off. Misters are throughout the zoo complex and several shows are in air-conditioned indoors.

COOPERTOWN AIRBOAT RIDES AND RESTAURANT

Miami - 22700 SW 8th Street (11 miles west of the Florida Turnpike on US 41/Tamiami Trail) 33194. Phone: (305) 226-6048. www.coopertownairboats.com

Started in 1945, this is the Original Airboat rides. There is an abundance of Everglades wildlife to see: alligators, birds, otters, fish and turtles. Exotic plants and flowers abound as well. Then there is just the pure thrill of the airboat ride across the wide open prairie of sawgrass (our favorite part - feel like you're in a high-action movie)! The airboat ride takes 35 to 45 minutes and is an eight mile round trip over and through the sawgrass. The return trip brings the airboat on a tricky maneuver among the hardwood hammocks (islands of solid ground spotting the "River of Grass"), where all sorts of wildlife are seen. Before or after your tour, take the opportunity to hold a baby alligator (for real). Ever tried frog legs? Well, it's the specialty at the Coopertown Restaurant (as well as fried gator tails) and we dare you to try them. Tastes like chicken-fish.

WINGS OVER MIAMI MUSEUM

Miami - 14710 SW 128th Street (Kendall-Tamiami Executive Airport) 33196. Phone: (305) 233-5197. www.wingsovermiami.com Hours: Thursday-Sunday 10:00am-5:30pm. Admission: $9.95 adult, $5.95 senior (60+) and child (under 12).

Visitors can explore the fascinating history of aviation, reliving the events of World War II from a pilot's perspective while viewing a historic display of aircraft and aviation artifacts. Flying warbirds are the favorite in the indoor/outdoor display hangers.

MIAMI MUSEUM OF SCIENCE & PLANETARIUM

Miami (Coconut Grove) - 3280 S. Miami Avenue (I-95 to Exit #1A/SW 25 Road, stay in the right hand lane and follow the signs) 33129. Phone: (305) 646-4200. www.miamisci.org Hours: Daily 10:00am-6:00pm. Closed Thanksgiving and Christmas. Admission: $10.00 adult, $8.00 senior (62+), $6.00 child (3-12). Ticket price includes entrance to all museum galleries, planetarium shows, and the wildlife center. Ticket prices can vary during special exhibits.

Traveling and permanent exhibits are largely geared toward children exploring subject matter from dinosaurs to the properties of physics. Live science demonstrations and theater shows daily. (laser shows every first Friday of the month) Daily planetarium shows point out the stars of the season, while the Wildlife Center houses rare birds of prey and reptiles.

BARNACLE HISTORIC STATE PARK

Miami (Coconut Grove) - 3485 Main Hwy. 33133. www.floridastateparks.org/thebarnacle
Phone: (305) 446-9445. Hours: The Barnacle is open to the public 9:00am-4:00pm
Friday through Monday with guided tours at 10:00am, 11:30am, 1:00pm and 2:30pm. The
park is open Tuesday through Thursday for group tours with advance reservations. The
park is closed New Year's, Thanksgiving and Christmas days. Admission: $1.00 (age 6+).

This beautiful house with a whimsical name dates to a quieter time. The Barnacle, built in 1891, offers a glimpse of Old Florida during The Era of the Bay. Situated on the shore of Biscayne Bay, this was the home of Ralph Middleton Munroe, one of Coconut Grove's most charming and influential pioneers. Munroe's principal passion was designing yachts. In his lifetime, he drew plans for 56 different boats. A walk through a tropical hardwood hammock leads to the house. Regularly scheduled tours provide a glimpse of what life was like in the wilds of Florida.

CORAL GABLES' VENETIAN POOL

Miami (Coral Gables) - 2701 De Soto Blvd. 33134. www.venetianpool.com Phone: (305)
460-5357. Hours: Generally Tuesday-Sunday 10:00am-4:30pm or 11:00am-5:30pm year-
round. Open Mondays in the summer. Admission: $9.50 adult, $5.25 child (3-12). Reduced rates
November-March and for city residents. Children under 3 are NOT admitted to the facility.

These historic Venetian Pools were formed from a coral rock quarry in 1923 and fed 820,000 gallons of spring water daily. Considered one of the world's most unique and breathtaking municipal swimming pools, the non-chemical water provides a nice break from the chlorine and salt water, and the beautiful coral rock keeps the water nice and cool even in the summer sun. There are two waterfalls, coral caves and grottos. Hailed as one of the best destinations for families by locals, the Venetian Pool is a great alternative to the beach for family fun in the sun.

FAIRCHILD TROPICAL BOTANIC GARDEN

Miami (Coral Gables) - 10901 Old Cutler Road (US 1 to SW 42nd Ave/LeJeune Rd. Turn
left and drive south to roundabout. Take 2nd right onto Old Cutler Rd. for 2 miles) 33156.
Phone: (305) 667-1651. www.fairchildgarden.org Hours: Daily 9:30am-4:30pm except
Christmas. Admission: $20.00 adult, $15.00 senior (65+), $10.00 child (6-17). Fairchild
admission includes a narrated tram tour, offered hourly, plus admission to the Conservatory
and Whitman Tropical Fruit Pavilion at no additional charge. Miscellaneous: Garden café
and gift shop. Right next door to Fairchild is Matheson Hammock Park, which features a
toddler-friendly lagoon style beach, perfect for a late afternoon dip.

The 83-acre botanical garden boasts extensive collections of rare tropical plants including palms, cicadas, flowering trees and vines. Children can enjoy a naturalist treasure hunt, identifying various plants, insects and animals as they wander the lush, expansive grounds. Take a narrated tram tour past tropical fruit, sunken gardens, lily ponds and an outdoor rainforest. Or, go at your own leisure on winding paths and overlooks.

EVERGLADES ALLIGATOR FARM

Miami (Everglades) - 40351 SW 192nd Avenue 33034. www.everglades.com Phone: (305) 247-2628.

In 1985 the State of Florida permitted commercial farming of alligators and this family opened the first such farm in Dade County. In the 60's, the American alligator had almost become extinct and was placed on the endangered species list by the Federal Government. Commercial farming was correctly seen as a way to insure the preservation of this reptile, which traces its existence back to the time of the dinosaurs.This family-owned attractions invites visitors to enjoy an exhilaration airboat tour into the surrounding Everglades and a stroll around the farm to see the alligators, crocodiles, and wildlife that reside there, as well as a great display of local and exotic snakes. The Everglades Alligator Farm is currently home to about 2,000 alligators of all sizes!

FLORIDA YOUTH ORCHESTRA

Miami (Hollywood) - 1706 N. 40th Avenue 33021. www.floridayouthorchestra.org/ Phone: (954) 962-5666. The orchestra provides quality classical music education for talented musicians ages 6-19. Look for the orchesta to perform for concerts and local and regional TV.

BISCAYNE NATIONAL PARK

Miami (Homestead) - 9700 SW 328th Street (off US 1 between Miami and Key Largo) 33033. Phone: (305) 230-1100. www.nps.gov/bisc Hours: The water portion of Biscayne National Park is open 24 hours a day. Convoy Point is open daily from 7:00am to 5:30pm. The Dante Fascell Visitor Center is open daily from 9:00am to 5:00pm. Admission: FREE. Fees for boat rentals and tours.

A rarity among national parks, Biscayne is primarily aquatic. Of its 173,000 acres, 95% are under water. It's a moody place. Some days, the Bay's shallow waters are glassy smooth. Other times, the wind whistles and whips, creating white waves that bite like teeth at an angry sky (advice: monitor the weather before your visit). Teeming with sea life and plants, the park encompasses the turquoise waters of Biscayne Bay, the longest stretch of mangrove forest left on Florida's coast, living coral reefs and 40 of the northernmost Florida Keys. At the waterfront Dante Fascell Visitor Center, it is possible to join glass bottom boat tours, snorkeling and dive trips and island excursions or rent canoes and kayaks. Fishing is excellent. Patch reefs provide a snorkeler's paradise in shallow waters less than 10 feet deep. Living coral is home to a variety of sea life including tropical fish, sponges and spiny lobster. Manatees, dolphins and five species of sea turtles call the waters home, as do moray eels, stingrays, squid, starfish and hundreds of varieties of fish. Camping and shower facilities available with reservations.

CORAL CASTLE

Miami (Homestead) - 28655 S. Dixie Hwy (Take turnpike extension to Homestead, take exit # 5 (288th St.), go right for 2 miles to SW 157th Ave., turn right) 33033. Phone: (305) 245-6345. **www.coralcastle.com** *Hours: Daily 9:00am-8:00pm or 9:00pm. Admission: $9.75 adult, $6.50 senior (62+), $5.00 child (7-12).*

This place probably wins the designation for "most offbeat" tourist attraction; kids will love the quirky construction, built over the course of twenty years with homemade tools by one man in an odd, yet brilliant obsession. Giant pieces of coral rock were carved into a variety of objects by Edward Leedskalnin in the 1920s, as a tribute to a lost love. Today, you can leisurely tour Coral Castle via the 30 minute audio tour. Look for the carved Rocking Chair, the "living" Heart Table, the bath tub, and the Pressure Cooker (able to cook 2 dozen hot dogs at one time). Did you know coral rock is a great

How did he do it...amazing!

insulator? No one can determine how the creator found the perfect center of gravity enabling the 9-ton front gate to be opened by the simple push of a hand. Can you figure out how he did it? Even experts argue how it could be done - and, by one man only 5 feet tall and barely weighing 100 pounds.

MIAMI SEAQUARIUM

Miami (Key Biscayne) - 4400 Rickenbacker Causeway (I-95 to Key Biscayne exit, then take Rickenbacker Cswy. From south, take US 1 to Rickenbacker) 33149. Phone: (305) 361-5705. **www.miamiseaquarium.com** *Hours: Daily 9:30am-6:00pm. Admission: $31.95 general, $24.95 child (3-9). Parking $6.00. Rickenbacker Causeway toll $1.25. Miscellaneous: Food outlets and gift shops are available throughout the park. Also offers popular swim with the dolphins program and feeding sessions with sharks and manatees.*

The two-hour program lets visitors slip into a wet suit and enter the world-famous Flipper Lagoon for an up-close encounter with dolphins.

This place gained notoriety as the location for filming of 1960s hit TV show Flipper. Indeed, "Flipper" still has his own daily show at the Seaquarium, as does

Lolita, the killer whale. Laugh with the island adventures of Salty, the Sea Lion. It's the place where moray eels lurk in coral reef caverns, where shiny schools of exotic fish dance through underwater seascapes, and it's the only place where you will see the graceful beauty of four Pacific white sided dolphins combined with the awesome power of a three ton killer whale! Another popular

See Dolphins & Killer Whales in the water at the same time...

show, the Flipper Dolphin Show, takes place at the Flipper Lagoon, film location for much of the popular 1960s television show of the same name. Brave the "Splash Zone" if you dare. At the Manatee exhibit, guests come face-to-face with Florida's state marine mammal through poolside and underwater viewing areas. The manatees featured are part of the rescue and rehabilitation program at Miami Seaquarium. See Nile Crocodiles fed at Discovery Bay, and the new Salty's Pirate Playground, too. The shows are close together so you can watch them all without running from show to show. At this magical park, dolphins "fly" and whales can "walk"!

PINECREST GARDENS

Miami (Pinecrest) - 11000 Red Road 33156. www.pinecrestgardens.com Phone: (305) 669-6942. Hours: Daily 8:00am-6:00pm.

This 22-acre site sits on property once owned by Parrot Jungle. The Gardens include winding paths past a botanical garden, petting zoo (open several times daily), miniature donkeys and alpaca, a butterfly exhibit, a Cypress Slough, Sausage Trees, Turtle Island and the delightful Splash-N-Play Water Squirt Playground.

MIAMI CHILDREN'S MUSEUM

Miami Beach - 980 *MacArthur Causeway 33132.* **www.miamichildrensmuseum.org**
Phone: (305) 373-5437.   Hours: Daily 10:00am-6:00pm.   Admission: $10.00 general,
Miscellaneous: Subway restaurant on premises.   Rock climbing wall, extra fee.

This space includes 12 different galleries and many bilingual displays. The
Museum features interactive exhibits including a miniature supermarket,
television news studio, cruise ship and a giant sandcastle slide. Permanant
interactive exhibits include The Castle of Dreams, Bank, Health & Wellness
Center, Pet Central, Safety Zone, Supermarket, Television Studio, Meet Miami,
the Sea and Me (especially for children under five), Ocean Odyssey, Everglades
Park, Ports of Call: Brazil, Port of Miami, Cruise Ship, All About Art and the
World Music Studio. Something very fun to do is the simulated firetruck ride
and fire. Kids use virtual and hands-on equipment to maneuver through crowded
streets to a big fire where they have to safely put it out! MCM is one of the ten
largest children's museums in the country.

MIAMI DUCK TOURS

Miami Beach - 1665 *Washington Avenue (departing from South Beach - located between
Lincoln Road and 17th Street) 33132.* **www.ducktoursmiami.com** *Phone: (786) 276-8300.
(877) DUCK-TIX.   Admission: $32.00 adult, $26.00 senior (65+), $18.00 child (3-12).*

A 90-minute Land & Sea Adventure aboard
amphibious vehicles touring famous Miami
landmarks before a dramatic "SPLASH
DOWN" into beautiful Biscayne Bay for a
close up look at the many homes of the "Rich &
Famous" on Star Island (Shaq, Gloria Estefan,
the cat house, or Miami Vice). This is the unique
way to explore Miami by land and sea aboard
a vehicle equipped to do both. The "vesicles"
(part vessel, part vehicle) look like ducks on
wheels. Yell hello to J-Lo or Shaq, or sneak a
peek at the many famous art deco or cruise-
ship shaped buildings. As you glide through
downtown Miami and South Beach, your guide
quacks on about landmarks and encourages
you to interact with the locals…Next thing you

Captain Jenny helps the
boat get out of the water

know, YOU are quacking along. For the kids (and extroverted adults) this is sure
to be a highlight of your stay!

OLETA RIVER STATE PARK

Miami, North - 3400 NE 163rd Street   33160.   www.floridastateparks.org/oletariver/
Phone: (305) 919-1846.   Hours: Daily 8:00am-sunset.

An oasis of nature in the Miami metro area offering a wide range of recreation activities.

ROB'S REDLAND RIOT

Miami-Dade County - Phone: (305) 443-7973. www.redlandriot.com

Take a leisurely tour through rural South Miami-Dade County to learn about the pioneer era and stock up on fresh produce, orchids, exotic fruits and home-made delicacies during the winter and spring seasons. This is a FREE, self-guided tour that you can do anytime in your own car with friends. Get a copy online of the tour booklet, map and directions and off you go. Or, join a large planned group tour. As rural, family-based agricultural enterprises have faded, if you take a close look, there are still reminders of the pioneer era and the abundance of places to sample the bounty.

JOHN D. MACARTHUR BEACH STATE PARK

North Palm Beach - 10900 SR 703 (A1A) (2.8 miles south of the intersection of U.S. 1 and PGA Boulevard on A1A) 33408. www.floridastateparks.org/macarthurbeach/default.cfm Phone: (561) 624-6950. Hours: Daily 8:00am-sunset. The Nature Center is open daily from 9:00am-5:00pm. Miscellaneous: If you are interested in keeping up with the turtle nesting count, or if you would like to volunteer to help with the turtle program, please contact the staff at the Nature Center and let them know your interest.

The park is a sanctuary in the center of a major metropolitan area. A unique mixture of coastal and tropical hammock and mangrove forest, this barrier island provides a haven for several rare or endangered native tropical and coastal plant species. The park`s nature center shows visitors why the park is a biological treasure. Visitors may also view a 15-minute video on the park. Visitors can swim, picnic, and surf at the beach; scuba diving and snorkeling are also popular activities. Birdwatchers can see herons, brown pelicans, terns, sandpipers, and gulls. Anglers can fish in the lagoon by wading, kayaking, or canoeing-they can also fish from non-swimming areas of the beach. Whether you prefer kayaking, beach-walking or simply enjoying the quiet tranquility of our undeveloped beach, there is something for everyone. Each spring, comes the arrival of their sea turtle nesting season. Large numbers of loggerhead, green and leatherback turtles nest from early May through late August. Morning beach patrols will check and record the nesting activity of the various species of turtles that return to the undeveloped beach each year.

SEABRANCH PRESERVE STATE PARK

Stuart - 4810 SE Cove Road (about 10 miles south of Stuart. Access to the park is from SR A1A near the VFW parking lot) 34997. www.floridastateparks.org/seabranch/default.cfm Phone: (772) 219-1880. Hours: Daily 8:00am-sunset. Admission: FREE

Take a leisurely walk through the sand pine scrub, a unique habitat considered "globally imperiled," and most of all, enjoy "the Real Florida." In less than one mile, visitors can see rare sand pine scrub, scrubby flatwoods, a baygall community, and a mangrove swamp. Hikers can explore these natural communities over four miles of trails. New trail markers are in place. Informative, directional signs have been installed on the hiking trails in the park. These trail markers provide mileage remaining to reach the starting point as well as general directions.

JONATHAN DICKINSON STATE PARK

Stuart (Hobe Sound) - 16450 S.E. Federal Highway (12 miles south of Stuart on US 1. I-95 exit 96 east to US1) 33455. www.floridastateparks.org/jonathandickinson/default.cfm Phone: (772) 546-2771. Hours: WILDERNESS GUIDED BOAT TOURS - Departs dock daily at 9:00am and 11:00am, 1:00 and 3:00pm. Park open 8:00am-sunset. Admission: $9.50-$14.50 fee for boat tours (age 6+). Boat and cabin rentals vary in price. See website.

This park teams with wildlife in 13 natural communities, including sand pine scrub, pine flatwoods, mangroves, and river swamps. The Loxahatchee River, Florida's first "Wild and Scenic River", runs through the park. The 44-passenger LOXAHATCHEE QUEEN II takes visitors up the Loxahatchee River to the pioneer homesite of TRAPPER NELSON (2 hour tour focused on natural history sightings). The Loxahatchee Queen II docks at the Trapper Nelson site where passengers are met by a Park Ranger who guides them through the cabins and grounds once belonging to the "Wildman of the Loxahatchee." Trapper Nelson came to the area in the 1930s and lived off the land by trapping and selling furs.

Visitors can enjoy paved and off-road biking, equestrian, and hiking trails. Boating, canoeing, and kayaking along the river are also great ways to see the park. Anglers can catch freshwater fish along the riverbank or from a boat. The park offers two full-facility campgrounds and a youth/group primitive campground. ATLANTIC RIDGE wet prairie provides a critical habitat for endangered species of plants and animals.

PALM BEACH ZOO AT DREHER PARK

West Palm Beach - *1301 Summit Blvd. (I-95 exit 68 Southern Blvd. E to Parker Avenue. Turn right on Parker, right on Summit for one block) 33405. Phone: (561) 547-WILD. www.palmbeachzoo.org Hours: Daily except Christmas & Thanksgiving 9:00am-5:00pm. Admission: $8.95-$12.95 per person (age 3+).*

Over 23 acres of lush, tropical landscaped habitats that are home to over 900 animals from Florida, Central and South America, Asia and Australia. Enjoy the Florida Exhibit, Tiger Falls, Aviary, Children's Carousel, and the newly opened Tropics of the Americas – a multi-exhibit showcase of Mayan culture, animals and horticulture. Come see their stars, baby animals born here, including Caipora and Izel, the first jaguar cubs to be born on site at the Palm Beach Zoo. Bush dogs, Baird's tapirs, giant anteaters, the Caracol Observatory, Primate Island, suspension bridge and explorer's cave, Amazonian Market Place, and more! Bring your bathing suit and get wet in the Interactive Fountain (changing cabanas available), enjoy lunch at the waterfront air-conditioned Tropics Café, or shop for gifts of all types and prices at the Gift Store.

SOUTH FLORIDA SCIENCE MUSEUM

West Palm Beach - *4801 Dreher Trail North (I-95 exit Southern Blvd. Head east to Parker Ave. South on Parker, past Southern Blvd. to Summit Blvd. west to Drejer Trail) 33405. Phone: (561) 832-1988.   www.sfsm.org Hours: Monday-Friday 10:00am-5:00pm, Saturday 10:00am-6:00pm, Sunday Noon-6:00pm. Admission: $6.00-$9.00 per person. Additional $2.00-$4.00 for galaxy golf, laser or planetarium shows. Miscellaneous: Galaxy Golf - Putt your way around a universe of obstacles in this nine-hole miniature golf challenge! Each hole contains a science theme and facts...*

Interactive exhibits show you how to create clouds, generate electricity with a bike, marvel at optical illusions, and build and control your own robot! Natural history exhibits feature "Suzie," a 22,000 year-old mastodon found in Palm Beach County. Also, authentic and reproduction skeletons of whales, sharks and dinosaurs bring history to life. Native and exotic sea life from warm waters around the world populate the museum's aquariums (include Touch Tanks). Enjoy a walk around a winding trail of interactive exhibits. This outdoor trail features parabolic whisper dishes, a fossil dig with authentic Florida fossils, dinosaur tracks which tell a story and even an all original turtle-hop game! Exciting laser shows and star shows thrill young and old alike in the Aldrin Planetarium.

LION COUNTRY SAFARI

West Palm Beach (Loxahatchee) - *2003 Lion Country Safari Road (15.5 miles west of I-95 on Southern Boulevard (SR 80/98/441) 33470.* *www.lioncountrysafari.com* *Phone: (561) 793-1084.* *Hours: Daily 9:30am-5:30pm.* *No vehicles admitted after 4:30pm.* *Admission: $16.95-$20.95 (ages 3+).* *Coupon on website.* *Miscellaneous: Vehicles may be rented at the front office.* *Cars and minivans seating up to 8 people are just $10 and 15 passenger vans are just $18 per 1 1/2 hours.*

Lion Country Safari was America's first drive-through cageless zoo. Your family travels through the park in your own car (although rentals are available) and are given a CD containing the voice of a tour guide who explains about the animals. Windows must be rolled up at all times for safety. Are Lions really king of the jungle? Watch them romp and chase one another to decide. Equally impressive are the gazelles, giraffes, rhinos, water buffaloes and others. Take your time - generally, most folks pace themselves at 1½ hours. Although you may have been to drive-thru safaris further north, this one is less messy. Because you don't feed the animals, parents aren't constantly trying to disinfect their kids slobbered on hands and you don't have the extra expense of food pellets. It's less scary to do this tour for younger ones, too. After your tour, stop by Safari World. Begin with a boat ride on the Safari Queen, where you will learn about the siamangs and spider monkeys that inhabit the islands of Lake Shanalee. Or, if you prefer, do your own navigating on the paddleboats. Enjoy our newest attraction, Safari Splash, with 23 interactive water functions, play a round of miniature golf, tease your brain with a trip through their maze, or take a ride on the carousel, the El Paso Train, the flying elephant ride, or the Ferris Wheel. You can also enjoy the opportunity to interact with our Lories at the Lory feeding aviary, Giraffe at the their special feeding area, and Sheep or Goats at the Petting Zoo. All of these fun activities are included in your admission price, so be sure to plan extra time to stay for awhile.

SUGGESTED LODGING AND DINING

PELICAN BEACH RESORT - **Fort Lauderdale**, 2000 North Ocean Boulevard (US-1 North, which becomes Federal Highway. Turn right on SE 17th Street (FL-A1A). Continue on FL-A1A North for about 4 miles). (800) 525-OCEAN or (954) 568-9431 or **www.pelicanbeach.com**. Guest rooms and Hotel suite accommodations are oceanfront and include private balconies perfect for enjoying the gorgeous beach sunrise or moon glow. Each room is 100% nonsmoking and decorated with a relaxed elegance reminiscent of Florida's grand resorts, yet features modern amenities for a comfortable stay (microwave and mini-frig). Take a ride along the Lazy River or splash in one of two heated pools. Enjoy beachfront dining at North Ocean Grill (kids menu with several selections under $5.00) or bask in the warm Florida sun on the large veranda. Grab a scoop at "The Emporium" – old-fashioned ice cream parlor or sign up for Funky Fish children's activities. Funky Fish days are full of entry level snorkeling, shelling, nature and pizza parties. Or, maybe take a glass-bottom boat tour or boogie boarding day (daily age 4-17, from 10:00am-3:00pm with reservations). Underground valet parking and guests can check out board games. A Best Western affiliate so the pricing is reasonable but the décor is upscale, yet comfortable. A great place for a family reunion.

PACIFIC TIME RESTAURANT. www.pacifictimerestaurant.com (305) 534-5979. 915 Lincoln Road, I-395 east to north on Alton Road to 17th Street. Right on Michigan, begin to look for parking (the restaurant lies within the pedestrian only section, parking in Miami Beach is cheap, comparatively but you'll spend your money on food). Lunch served weekdays, dinner daily. Every guest can use utensils or chopsticks - the kids have fun learning to work food with them! The interactive kids menu begins with ordering, then appetizers (kiddie canapes is what our waiter called them - freshly sliced tomatoes and soda fried potato chips, then make dessert! What? If you can't eat dessert first, you might as well actually make it before your meal. The Little Extra Dough dessert ($8.00) was designed by the owner/chef Jonathan Eismann with his kids in mind (his oldest even does the artwork for the back of the menu). They bring your child cookie dough and decorations for them to prepare their own personalized cookie at the table. By the time the entrée arrives, the cookie is decorated and ready to be put in the oven. After you finish your entrée (kids menu includes smaller, mildly seasoned choices such as halibut, salmon, breaded chicken and penne pasta - drinks and dessert included, kids meals run $13.00-$18.00 for lunch), the waiter brings out your finished, baked cookie warm from the oven. And for adults? They feature Pan-Asian foods, mostly fresh seafood in exotic sauces and the menu changes daily. We'd suggest dining outdoors so you can people-watch the fashions that "style" by.

Chapter 8
South East - KEYS
(SE-KEYS)
Area

Key Largo

Islamorada

Big
Pine Key   Grassy Key

Marathon

Key West

Our Favorites...

* Dolphin Research Center - Grassy Key

* Theatre of The Sea - Islamorada

* John Pennecamp Coral Reef State Park - Key Largo

* Catamaran Boat Tours, Ft. Jefferson - Key West

* Going to Sunset on Mallory Square - Key West

* Hemmingway House - Key West

* Key West Shipwreck Historeum - Key West

* Mel Fisher Shipwreck Museum - Key West

* Old Town Trolley - Key West

FLORIDA KEYS ODDS-N-ENDS

Florida Keys - www.fla-keys.com Phone: (800) FLA-KEYS.

A sunken Spanish galleon of 1733 is the focus of the SAN PEDRO UNDERWATER ARCHAEOLOGICAL PRESERVE off Islamorada. Little remains of the underwater wreck after 250 years, but it continues to be a favorite of snorkelers and divers, and curators of the site have added authentic touches, including seven concrete cannon replicas and an 18th-century ship's anchor. A unique cemetery can be found on the beach at Cheeca Lodge (MM 82 oceanside) in Islamorada. Known as the PIONEER CEMETERY, this site contains the statue of an angel - one of the few structures that survived the hurricane of 1935. The ashes of that storm's many victims rest below the tiled mosaic of Islamorada at the base of the HURRICANE MONUMENT, where the Old Highway meets the new at MM 81.7. Also in Islamorada is ROBBIE'S MARINA (MM 77.5) where you can feed the hungry, jumping tarpon. Travelers cannot miss the larger-than-life dolphin statue at the DOLPHIN RESEARCH CENTER at MM 59 bayside on Grassy Key, but few realize that one of the first "Flippers" of television fame is buried beneath it. The OLD SEVEN MILE BRIDGE, MM 47 bayside in Marathon, is a historic and scenic spot for walking, jogging, cycling, rollerblading and sunset viewing. At the same MM 47 is PIGEON KEY (www.pigeonkey.org). Dotted with quaint cottages, historic Pigeon Key formerly served as a camp for laborers erecting the Seven Mile Bridge. This island now showcases a museum and offers opportunities to picnic and snorkel. Lower Keys visitors can visit the former Overseas Railway borrow pit now known as the BLUE HOLE. Located

just off Big Pine's Key Deer Boulevard at MM 30.5 bayside, the Blue Hole features a layer of fresh water floating over salt water, and attracts Key deer and provides a home to alligators, turtles, birds and fish. An observation platform allows for viewing. In Key West, NANCY'S SECRET GARDEN (305-294-0015), created by Nancy Forrester, has been described as a living work of art. Finding this place is tricky - the entrance is on Free School Lane, off the 500 block of Simonton Street between Fleming and Southard streets. Some plants are rare and endangered; others are extinct in their original habitats. A group of exotic birds reside among the lush foliage. And, finally, the SOUTHERNMOST POINT in Key West at

Whitehead and South Streets. A larger-than-life buoy marks the southernmost spot in the continental United States - only 90 miles from Cuba. It's the setting for a photo-op for virtually every visitor to Key West.

BAHIA HONDA STATE PARK

Bahia Honda Key - MM 37 Oceanside, 33010. ***www.bahiahondapark.com*** *Phone: (305) 872-3210. Hours: Park open from 8:00am-sundown. Concessions open 8:00am-5:00pm. Admission: All visitors are required to pay an entrance fee: one person $2.50, two people $5.00, $0.50 for each additional person pedestrians and bicyclist $1.50 per person. Once inside the park, visitors have access to all park buildings, beaches, etc. Your receipt is good for re-entry into the park during the same day.*

Home to the Florida Key's finest beach, this state park also features picnic and camping facilities, a marina, rental cabins, a watersports shop and a convenience store.

NATIONAL KEY DEER REFUGE AND WATSON NATURE TRAIL

Big Pine Key - Key Deer Blvd. At MM 30.5 bayside 33043. Phone: (305) 872-2239. ***www.nationalkeydeer.fws.gov/***

Tiny deer no larger than a mid-size dog roam freely here. A nature trail winds through protected pinelands. The visitors center, located in the Winn-Dixie Shopping Center (701 Key Deer Blvd.) is open from 8:00am-5:00pm weekdays.

DOLPHIN RESEARCH CENTER

Grassy Key - MM 59 Bayside 33050. Phone: (305) 289-1121. ***www.dolphins.org*** *Hours: Daily 9:00am-5:00pm. Last narrated session begins at 4:30pm. Closed on major holidays. Admission: $19.50 adult, $16.50 senior (55+), $13.50 child (4-12).*

The Dolphin Research Center specializes in behavioral research. The Center recently released a study that shows that dolphins have the ability to understand and identify numbers. See the math experts in person, and schedule an in-water interaction. Spend an hour or the whole day learning all about their family of Atlantic bottlenose dolphins and California sea lions. Experience the different "dolphinalities" during narrated sessions every half-hour.

From high-flying athletics and Dolphin Fun Facts to medical behavior training and research-in-progress, no two sessions are alike. Join their fun and cheer their progress. They love an audience! (we watched Tanner learn math). The shows are so authentic - you'll feel as if you're part of the team on a Discovery Channel documentary. This is a wonderful, surreal experience!

Besides the sessions, they also offer special programs:

DOLPHIN ENCOUNTER - the center's swim program, $180.00 per person.

DOLPHINSPLASH - a wade-in program that offers the opportunity to get waist deep in the water with dolphins, $130.00 per person.

MEET THE DOLPHIN - not in water but dock, $40.00 per person.

PAINT WITH A DOLPHIN - Degas, Monet or Turner? Not quite, but a *Delphi*, *Merina* or *Tursi*-created DolphinArt T-shirt is still a classic! T-shirts painted by

their dolphins are among the most popular items among visitors, staff and members! Now, you can help while a dolphin paints a shirt just for you! You'll pick two colors from our paint choices, then accompany the trainers to the dock area for an exciting behavior session. After the session, you'll get an up close introduction to the dolphins, then kneel and hold the T-shirt over the water while the dolphins paint! They'll take a commemorative photograph. The cost to Paint with a Dolphin is only $55.00 in addition to your admission price and the shirt is yours forever to wear or display. The program is open to ages 3 and up.

I can't believe the dolphin IS really painting!

INDIAN KEY STATE HISTORIC SITE

Islamorada - MM 78.5 Oceanside 33036. www.floridastateparks.org/indiankey/default.cfm
Phone: (305) 664-2540. Hours: Daily 8:00am-sundown.

In the early 1800s, this tiny island was the site of a lucrative business-salvaging cargo from shipwrecks in the Florida Keys. This island once housed the largest population between St. Augustine and Key West. In 1840, during the Second Seminole War, Indian warriors paddled to the island, killed most of the residents and burned the island structures to the ground. Accessible only by private boat or charter boat, visitors come here to swim, sunbathe, and hike. Canoeing, kayaking, boating, and fishing are also popular activities. The perimeter of the island provides one of the few near-shore areas for snorkelers and scuba divers to see coral. Ranger-guided tours are offered twice daily, Thursday through Monday. Tour boat services, as well as boat and kayak rentals, are available from Robbie's Marina. For tour reservations call (305) 664-9814.

LIGNUMVITAE KEY BOTANICAL STATE PARK

Islamorada - MM 78.5 bayside 33036. www.floridastateparks.org/lignumvitaekey/default.cfm
Phone: (305) 664-2540.   Hours: Park is open Thursday-Monday 8:00am-5:00pm.

When Spanish explorers first landed in the Florida Keys during the 16th century, they found tropical hammocks filled with more than 200 species of trees, shrubs and plants. The resin of one such tree was believed to have medicinal qualities and was given the name lignumvitae - Latin meaning "wood of life." Along with its medicinal benefits, as a hardwood tree it was harvested for the shipping industry. Today, the lignumvitae tree, which thrived in the Middle and Upper Keys, has given way to modern-day development. The tree's last stronghold is on its namesake island. Only 50 people are allowed on the key at one time - 25 on the nature trail and 25 in the clearing. You must reserve a spot in advance of a boating visit. Walking shoes and mosquito repellent are recommended.

THEATRE OF THE SEA

Islamorada - 84721 Overseas Highway, MM 84.5 Oceanside, 33036. Phone: (305) 664-2431. www.theatreofthesea.com Hours: Opens at 9:30am-4:00pm every day. Admission: $23.95 adult, $15.95 child (3-12). Miscellaneous: General admission includes dolphin, sea lion, and parrot shows, a guided tour of marine life exhibits, lagoon-side beach, and the bottomless boat ride. One of the shows is always taking place; guests join the one that is in progress when they arrive. It takes about two to two and a half hours to see all of the shows.

What began as a park in 1946 in a lagoon that was originally a rock quarry, everything here is entertaining and intimate. Kids don't have to wait in a long line to get a hug from a sea lion or pet a shark. Theater of the Sea is an educational and entertaining marine animal park where shows are up close and personal and the animals live in natural saltwater lagoons. The lagoons and

Go Classey! Hang on for the ride!

lush, tropical gardens at the facility are home to Atlantic bottlenose dolphins, California sea lions, sea turtles, tropical and game fish, sharks, stingrays, crocodiles, alligators, marine invertebrates, parrots, and birds-of-prey. All of the shows are adorable: dolphin like to dance and sea lions like to sing and be silly. The included bottom-less boat tour is very different. You sit around the sides of the boat, watching the dolphin play underneath. Watch closely as the mammals may want to show off and do some tricks - right through the boat! They also offer dolphin, sea lion and stingray swim programs, along with snorkel trips.

SWIM PROGRAMS: Imagine yourself eye to eye with the majestic dolphin or silly sea lion! A variety of trained behaviors, including kisses and dorsal tows, allow you to touch and interact with a mammal in a natural ocean water environment. You will also have an opportunity to snorkel, at the surface and below, allowing you to interact with the animal who will accompany you. Swim programs take place in a 10 to 15 feet deep natural salt-water lagoon. ($125.00-$155.00 per person - includes park admission to shows, ride). Our kids highly recommend the sea lion swim - their favorite in all of Florida!

WADE PROGRAMS: The Wade with the Dolphin is an exciting experience for non-swimmers and swimmers alike, allowing you to meet a dolphin up close and in the water, without swimming. Guests stand in 3 to 4 feet of water on a sandy beach and a dolphin joins them for swim by pets, cradles, and other behaviors. ($155.00 per person inclusive)

MEET DOLPHINS / SEA LION are $50.00 with touches but no swims.

ADVENTURE & SNORKEL CRUISE run $40.00 child, $65.00 adult and are offered twice daily (morning, afternoon) running 4 hours. Visit **Lignumvitae Key Botanical State Park.** Take a step back into the past and tour the Matheson House built in 1919. This once private island has changed little over the years. (closed Tuesday and Wednesday). Or, explore **Indian Key Historic State Park.** Learn about its colorful history of Indians, Spanish Explorers, wreckers, and pirates. Snorkel the coral reef. You can rent an AquaFM snorkel to listen to a narrative about local fish species you may encounter, along with any updates from your captain. Feed the tarpon fish at Robbie's Marina. Tarpon food can be purchased at Robbies. The Captain will teach you about the history and ecology of the area as well as identify marine life and answer your questions. A short stop will be made for soda, snacks, and rest rooms.

WINDLEY KEY FOSSIL REEF GEOLOGICAL STATE PARK

Islamorada - MM 85 bayside 33036. www.floridastateparks.org/windleykey/default.cfm Phone: (305) 664-2540. Hours: Park is open 8:00am-sunset. Education Center open Thursday-Monday 8:00am-5:00pm.

Instead of below the water, this site is an above ground coral reef. Formed of Key Largo limestone, fossilized coral, this land was sold to the Florida East Coast Railroad, which used the stone to build Henry Flagler's Overseas Railroad in the early 1900s. After the railroad was built, the quarry was used until the 1960s to produce pieces of decorative stone called Keystone. Today, visitors can walk along eight-foot-high quarry walls to see cross sections of the ancient coral and learn about the quarry and its operation- an important part of Florida's 20th century history. Samples of the quarry machinery are on display. Visitors can enjoy the natural attributes of this island while strolling five short, self-guided trails. Picnic tables are available.

DOLPHIN COVE CENTER

Key Largo - MM 102 bayside 33037. Phone: (877) 365-2683. www.dolphinscove.com Hours: Daily 8:00am-5:00pm. Miscellaneous: Additional activities available at the Center include kayak and eco-tours in the Everglades National Park.

Structured Dolphin Swims begin with a 30-45 minute educational briefing aboard one of their Everglades tour boats. During this time you will be able to observe the unique beauty of the backcountry while learning about dolphin natural history, intelligence, anatomy, and important information about your upcoming dolphin encounter. Dolphin swims take place in the natural lagoon. Swimmers will take turns entering the water and interacting hands-on with dolphins. All interaction is guided by a dolphin trainer, and one on one contact is guaranteed. $165.00 each.

NATURAL DOLPHIN SWIMS: Swimmers will be able to observe the dolphins around them, but not to reach out and touch them. Any contact that occurs must be initiated by the dolphins. In-water time is 30 minutes. Snorkel gear is provided. $125.00 each.

JUNIOR DOLPHIN ENCOUNTER: allows children who are too young to participate in the swim programs a chance to interact with dolphins from a floating platform. $70.00 each.

DOLPHIN WORLD

Key Largo - 33037. Phone: (954) 525-4441 or (800) 760-6949. www.dolphinworld.org
Hours: Daily 9:00am-5:00pm. Admission: Programs start at $70.00 up to hundreds of
dollars.

Enjoy the swim with dolphins programs in sunny and beautiful Florida, Key Largo / Key West Area, and Miami / Fort Lauderdale area. You will love swimming with dolphins, it's an incredible experience. The dolphin cove or salt water lagoon is a great place to meet your new friends the bottlenose dolphins. Incredible Dolphin Encounters in the Wild with easy reservations, Online or 800 number. Simple requirements, 5 years old and up, with guaranteed contact during Dolphin Swim. The Florida Marine Mammal programs includes the 1 Day Dolphin Animal Workshop, perfect for beginners with an adventurous spirit. The 2 Day Marine Animal Workshop, is for the person who enjoys and appreciates all of God's animals, trained Dolphins & Sea Lion encounters, Tropical Fish, Birds, and yes, even swimming with Sting Rays. Finally, the 3 and 4 Day Marine Science Workshop is the way to see and experience the difference between dolphins in a trained environment and dolphins in the open ocean environment, the ultimate swim with dolphin experience. The 1 Day Basic Marine Animal Encounter - Key Largo Area Includes: Dolphin Boat Ride, Dolphin Show, Sea Lion Show, Marine Park Tour, and Guided Instructional John Pennekamp Ocean Reef Snorkel Trip. (Does not include a Dolphin Swim or Sea Lion Swim Program)

DOLPHINS PLUS

Key Largo - MM 100 Oceanside, 31 Corrine Place 33037. Phone: (305) 451-1993.
www.dolphinsplus.com Hours: Daily from 8:00am-5:00pm. All of their classes are
reserved in advance with set times during each day.

At Dolphins Plus, visitors can enjoy natural (snorkel near them, play - $125.00 per swimmer) or structured (swims that are one-on-one interactive and behavior games $165.00 per swimmer). A Sea Lion Swim ($100.00) is very similar to the dolphin swim. Each program begins with a 20-30 minute (sea lion) or one hour (dolphin) educational briefing where you will learn about the animal's habitat, feeding habits, predation, behavior and discuss the human impact on this majestic coastal species. Kids must be at least 7 or 8 years old to participate and fairly good swimmers in deep water. Observers pay only $10.00 to watch near the water.

JOHN PENNECAMP CORAL REEF STATE PARK

Key Largo - MM 102.5 33037. Phone: (305) 451-1202 park or (305) 451-6300 boat tours. www.pennekamppark.com Hours: Visitor Center is open daily 8:00am-5:00pm. Park is open 8:00am-sunset. Admission: All visitors are required to pay an entrance fee. One person -- $3.50, two people -- $6.00, and $0.50 for each additional person, pedestrians and bicyclists -- $1.50 per person. Once inside the park, visitors have access to all park buildings, beaches, etc. Your receipt is good for re-entry into the park during the same day.

Miscellaneous: For visitors who are not interested in the park's underwater attractions, the park also offers two manmade beaches, canoe, kayak and boat rentals and nature trails. The park has 47 campsites. You'll find a 30,000 gallon salt water aquarium and displays on natural history in the Visitor Center. Guided Nature hikes on Thursday and Sunday at 10:00am by park rangers.

Divers, snorkelers and Keys visitors can thank the late Miami Herald editor John Pennekamp for helping to create the first undersea park in the United States. Established in 1961, it protects the miracle of America's only living coral reef! Pennekamp lies adjacent to the Florida Keys National Marine Sanctuary. The two preserves cover almost 3,000 square nautical miles of coral reefs, seagrass beds and mangrove swamps. The indigenous population here is composed of more than 600 species of fish and 55 varieties of coral, along with 27 species of gorgonians, or flexible corals. The coral provides shelter for crabs, sea urchins, snails, lobsters, shrimp, moray eels, worms, mollusks, starfish, sea cucumbers, sand dollars, barnacles and sponges. One of the park's most popular dive sites is the nine-foot bronze statue of Jesus Christ that rests in 20 feet of water - CHRIST OF THE DEEP. SPIEGEL GROVE, a retired US Navy Landing Ship Dock, is the largest ship ever intentionally sunk to create an artificial reef. To experience many underwater attractions, one needs to sign up for a guided underwater tour - which we highly recommend!

GLASS-BOTTOMED BOAT - The Spirit of Pennekamp tours passengers through the park's reefs where they can view a wide variety of coral, fish and other marine residents. Clean boats and lots of discussion about finds once over the reef. The kids' eyes are wonderful for finding sea life amongst the coral. What do sea fans look like? How many colors of fish and coral can you find? The neon Blue Tang (like Dory, the fish) were  the prettiest fish we saw. What a colorful and fun trip! Three tours offered daily: 9:15am, 12:15pm and 3:00pm. 2.5 hours. $15.00-$22.00.

John Pennecamp Coral Reef State Park (cont.)

SNORKELING - Dive boats take snorkelers three times daily on 2.5 hour reef trips which allow about 1.5 hours of actual time in the water. Weather permitting, the tour will take you to snorkel to Christ of the Deep. Trips are daily at 9:00am, Noon and 3:00pm. $23.95-$28.95 plus a small extra fee for equipment.

SAILING - Half-day sailing and snorkeling tours can be booked on board the Salsa, a 38-foot catamaran. Trips depart daily at 9:00am and 1:30pm. $30.00-$35.00 plus a small extra fee for equipment.

DISCOVERY GLASSBOTTOM BOAT

Key West - 251 Margaret Street (corner of Caroline & Margaret Streets, Historic Seaport) 33040. Phone: (305) 293-0099 or (800) 262-0099. www.discoveryunderseatours.com. Admission: $35.00 adult, $16.00 child.

This company features Key West's Only Underwater Viewing Room. See colorful coral, exotic tropical fish, and hundreds of varieties of marine life, without getting wet. The whole family can enjoy this fascinating and educational adventure. The upper deck provides seating in sun or shade. On the lower deck they offer seating outside or in the air-conditioned main salon. After a safety briefing, your narrator will conduct a waterside tour of the Historic Key West Seaport. This unique tour of the harbor presents numerous photo opportunities as you pass by places of interest (and, ideas for landlubber spots to hit). Then, the best part. As Discovery arrives at the reef, the passengers are invited below to a unique viewing room. There are 20 large windows set in the sides of the hull of the Discovery at a 45 degree angle. Guests enjoy a panoramic view out and over the reef as well as directly below. The tour is fully narrated by a knowledgeable crew.

GOING TO SUNSET ON MALLORY SQUARE

Key West - 33040. Phone: (800) ASK-KEYS. www.fla-keys.com Miscellaneous: Getting around the island is easiest by parking in one spot and then walking and biking around. There are plenty of bike racks to lock up bikes while shopping, site-seeing or eating.

For more than 20 years, "Going to Sunset" has been a tradition for residents and visitors alike. People of all ages flock to Mallory Square, the historic pier overlooking Key

West Harbor and the Gulf of Mexico, to enjoy the carnival-like atmosphere as the sun sinks beneath the waves with red-orange splendor. The Mallory Square performers offer a spectacle as some are sword swallowers sliding blades down their gullet; fire-eaters with asbestos insides; strongmen balancing a motor scooter on their chin or mimes costumed as a living statue. Jugglers, musicians and comics share their talents with the crowds. Most evenings, an Uncle Sam look-alike strolls along the pier giving away $22 bills. A kilted bagpiper paces in a mournful melody. And, no one can overlook the tightrope walker who can be seen balanced high above his audience, silhouetted against the sunset. The Market is full of shops - one where your kids may want to sample some "Pretty Good Popcorn." To enjoy the celebration to its fullest, it's best to arrive at Mallory Square at least 30 minutes before the sun actually sets and stay until it slips below the horizon. All the entertainment on the pier is free to watch, although entertainers pass the hat following their performances.

HARRY S. TRUMAN LITTLE WHITE HOUSE

Key West - 111 Front Street on Truman Annex 33040. www.trumanlittlewhitehouse.com Phone: (305) 294-9911.   Hours: Daily 9:00am-5:00pm. Admission: $11.00 adult, $5.00 child.

Truman, who visited Key West 10 times during his presidency, liked the island so much that he once wrote his wife, "I've a notion to move the capital to Key West and just stay." The Navy base's commandant's quarters, a 10-room West Indian structure, became his Little White House. Today, docents guide visitors through the meticulously restored residence, which looks much as it did in Truman's day. Items on display include the original piano and poker table - both used frequently by the former president. Learn "common man" stories about the former President and why he was called Truman the Human. The house has also hosted former presidents Dwight Eisenhower, John Kennedy and Jimmy Carter.

HEMINGWAY HOUSE

Key West - 907 Whitehead Street 33040. Phone: (305) 294-1136. www.hemingwayhome.com Hours: Daily 9:00am-5:00pm. Admission: $11.00 adult, $6.00 child. Miscellaneous: Visitors also can view the author's writing studio and enjoy the gardens. Many spend time making friends with the multitude of six-toed cats that roam the grounds - descended, so the story goes, from a feline given to Hemingway by a sea captain.

The house and gardens here are still "home" to one of the country's most renowned writers - the late Ernest Hemingway. Winner of both the Nobel and Pulitzer prizes, the author lived on the property with his second wife Pauline and their two children from 1931 to 1940. Hemingway wrote many of his best-

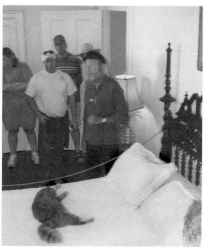

The resident cats really have the good life...

known works in the second-story writing studio adjoining the house. Among them were "For Whom the Bell Tolls," "The Snows of Kilimanjaro," and "To Have and Have Not," which is set in Depression-era Key West. Following his death, the unpublished manuscript that was to become "Islands in the Stream" was found in a vault in the property's garage. Today, the home's furnishings and atmosphere evoke the Hemingway era, as if the author were about to return from a fishing trip. Behind the house is the first swimming pool in Key West. Pauline had it built as a surprise for her husband, who was away covering the Spanish Civil War. When he learned that the pool cost $20,000, Hemingway took a penny from his pocket and angrily tossed it to the ground, saying she had spent his last cent. Pauline had the penny imbedded in the cement of the pool, where you can look for it on your tour. The storyteller guides and the adorable, napping Hemingway cats (they have 6 toes instead of five!) are the stars of this amusing tour!

KEY WEST AQUARIUM

Key West - One Whitehead Street 33040. wwwkeywestaquarium.com Phone: (305) 296-2051. Hours: Daily 10:00am-6:00pm. Guided tours are offered at 11:00am, 1:00pm, 3:00pm and 4:30pm. Admission: $10.00 adult, $5.00 child (4-12).

This was the first tourist attraction in the Keys. Open since 1934, the historic facility adjacent to Mallory Square was one of the first open-air aquariums in

the United States. Indoors, its very old-fashioned and that makes it kinda quaint. Among its residents are moray eels, sharks, sea turtles, barracuda, tropical fish, tarpon, parrotfish and grouper. The aquarium's "Atlantic Shores" exhibit features a 50,000-gallon tank displaying a cross-section of a near-shore mangrove habitat. The tank's inhabitants include tropical and game fish, sea turtles and birds. The aquarium also has a touch tank for hands-on interaction between sea creatures and visitors. During daily tours of the facility, visitors can observe feedings of resident sharks, rays and turtles while guides explain their habits and habitats. Participants in the guided tours have an opportunity to pet a live shark.

KEY WEST BUTTERFLY & NATURE CONSERVATORY

Key West - 1316 Duval Street 33040. Phone: (305) 296-2988. www.keywestbutterfly.com Hours: Daily 9:00am-5:00pm. Admission: $10.00 adult, $8.50 senior & military, $7.50 child (4-12).

One of only three major butterfly facilities in Florida, the conservatory features a 5,000 square foot glass-domed tropical butterfly habitat. Visitors can observe between 750 to over 1,000 butterflies from 30 to 50 species here, as well as learn about butterflies' role in the natural world and watching them hatch in special metamorphosis chambers. Everybody goes on and on about how beautiful this is.

KEY WEST LIGHTHOUSE MUSEUM & KEEPER'S QUARTERS

Key West - 938 Whitehead Street 33040. Phone: (305) 294-0012.   www.kwahs.com Hours: Daily 9:30am-5:00pm. Closed Christmas. Admission: $10.00 adult, $9.00 senior (62+), $5.00 child (6+).

Completed in 1847, the lighthouse guided mariners through the treacherous Key West waters until it was decommissioned in 1969. Today both the light and the Keeper's Quarters have been completely restored to show visitors what life was like for a lighthouse keeper in the days before electricity and automation. Visitors can climb an 88-step spiral staircase to the historic light's watchroom for a panoramic view of Key West. Step INSIDE a 12-foot "first order" lens circa 1858 (like stepping in a giant drinking glass) or learn the stories of two courageous female lighthouse keepers and observe historic artifacts, photos and journals. The landing/observation area on top is easy to step out onto for a great view of the harbor and town.

KEY WEST SHIPWRECK HISTOREUM

Key West - 1 Whitehead Street 33040. www.shipwreckhistoreum.com Phone: (305) 292-8990. Hours: Daily 9:45am-4:45pm. Admission: $10.00 adult, $5.00 child.

The museum combines actors, films, laser technology and actual artifacts from the shipwrecked "Isaac Allerton," which sank in Keys waters in 1856. Historeum visitors meet Asa Tift in his 1856 wreckers' warehouse, surrounded by the booty

The view from the top...wow!

from the reefs. Enjoy a fascinating video on the wrecking industry and hear tales from the families who made their fortunes in wrecking. Those who climb to the top of the 65-foot observatory can even scan the reefs for wrecks just as Key West's 19th-century captains did. Ring the bell if you see a capsized ship! This may be the best part of the Historium.

MEL FISHER SHIPWRECK MUSEUM

Key West - 200 Greene Street (corner of Greene & Whitehead Sts) 33040. Phone: (305) 294-2633. www.melfisher.org Hours: Daily 9:30am-5:00pm. Admission: $11.00 adult, $9.50 student, $6.00 child. Miscellaneous: Throughout the museum, interactive modules and innovative audio and video components make it an intriguing, engaging spot. Kids can create their own pirate flag or make a rubbing of a real silver bar.

Treacherous waters and navigational hazards surrounding the island chain have created a treasure trove of shipwrecks, making Key West the headquarters of shipwreck salvagers throughout the 1800s. The Museum holds the richest single collection of 17th-century maritime and shipwreck antiquities in the Western Hemisphere. Fisher, a longtime Key West resident, discovered the $400 million treasure of the shipwrecked Spanish galleon *Nuestra Senora de Atocha* in 1985

Touch a real $100,000+ gold bar!

after a 16-year search. In 1622, the Atocha was en route back to Spain laden with gold, silver and other cargoes from the New World when she was wrecked in a hurricane off the Florida Keys. Among the items on display are a fortune in gold, silver bars and coins destined for the coffers of Spain; a gold chain valued at more than a quarter of a million dollars (why is it called a money chain?); a horde of contraband emeralds; religious and secular jewelry; and a variety of rare navigational instruments and weapons. Kids (and parents) even get to hold in their hand a gold bar found on one of the wreck ships! Fisher and his team also recovered significant artifacts and treasure from the Atocha's sister ship, the Santa Margarita, and the English merchant slave vessel, Henrietta Marie. The Henrietta Marie sank in 1700 near the Marquesas Keys. From this wreck site, the society's archaeological teams excavated priceless English-made pewter ware, trade beads, ivory and cannons - as well as the iron shackles that are a chilling reminder of the slave trade's cruelty. What a sense of adventure this site inspires! As Mel says "Today is the Day!" …you find treasure.

PIRATE SOUL MUSEUM

Key West - 524 Front Street (one block off Duval) 33040. Phone: (305) 292-1117. www.piratesoul.com Hours: Daily 9:00am-7:00pm. Admission: $13.95 adult, $7.95 child.

Pirates have invaded Key West. The museum combines a unique collection of authentic pirate artifacts and state-of-the-art interactive technology to depict the pirate era from 1690 to 1730. Walk along Port Royal, Jamaica, circa 1690. Peep in the doors and find a treasure map. Load a flint lock pistol. Walk the dock and learn how pirates met their demise. Feel what it's like to be boarded by pirates as your ship is attacked. See a real Jolly Roger flag and an authentic Treasure Chest. Warning: Some exhibit spaces are designed on an adult level. Best for parents and teens with discretion.

RIPLEY'S BELIEVE IT OR NOT - KEY WEST

Key West - 108 Duval Street 33040. Phone: (305) 293-9939.   www.ripleyskeywest.com Hours: Open daily at 9:30am. Admission: $14.95 adult, $11.95 child (5-12).

Stories you can't imagine, People you won't believe…See amazing and bizarre displays of human and animal oddities, interactives, collections and more in 13 themed galleries and over 500 exhibits, including a shrunken torso once owned by Ernest Hemingway. Man battles shark or the 10,000 dimes car.

SUNNY DAYS CATAMARANS

Key West - (corner of Greene & Elizabeth Streets, Historic Seaport) 33040. Phone: (305) 296-6100 or (800) 236-7937.   www.sunnydayskeywest.com   Admission: $110.00 adult, $80.00 child (16 & under).   Miscellaneous: The company offers snorkel and dolphin trips too - half day - about half price.

"Fast Cat II" is a high speed power catamaran. The cool air conditioned cabin provides comfortable indoor seating. A rear sundeck is available for outdoor seating. The ride is a smoother, more pleasant ride. Dramatically fewer people experience motion sickness on catamarans. However, we must advise against rougher sea days (per weather channel) in winter as the waves easily reach 3-

5 feet or more and the way out can be very rocky. Either that, or pack motion sickness tablets and take them that morning.

Ready for snorkeling...on a very private beach

What to expect: 2 hours of travel time, each way. Continental breakfast upon boarding. 4 1/2 hours at Fort Jefferson. A tour of the Fort by one of their knowledgeable guides upon arrival (what famous people lived here? Why did toilets only flush during low tide?). Fresh, full Buffet lunch served in the picnic area of Fort Jefferson. Complimentary soft drinks, water & iced tea throughout the day. Snorkel gear is provided for endless time (well, at least a couple of hours) of easy snorkeling. Directly accessible from the beaches, the shallow waters (5-15 feet) make this area perfect for beginners and experts. You will see colorful corals, many varieties of tropical fish, starfish, queen conchs, and much more in this protected marine sanctuary. A Freshwater rinse is on board and snacks are served on the lazy way back. Be sure to bring your own swim wear, towels and sunscreen. A nice adventure away from the busy Old town Key west.

TRANSPORTATION TOURS OF KEY WEST

Key West - (departing from Old Town and New Town locations) 33040.

Take a mini-train or a trolley to get an overview of the attractions before you decide what you want to explore in-depth.

OLD TOWN TROLLEY - www.trolleytours.com or 305-296-6688. Trolleys run from 9:00am-4:30pm, daily. Tours depart from boarding locations (Bahama Village, Mallory Square, Welcome Center) approximately every 30 minutes. Reservations are not accepted and seating is on a first-come first-served basis. Parking is available at Mallory Square, Hilton Parking garage or at the Key West Welcome Center (N. Roosevelt Blvd.). Trolleys, styled after San Francisco cable cars, take 90 minutes for the entire tour, carrying passengers past more than 100 points of interest including the Hemingway Home, Seaport, the Aquarium and Mel Fisher Museum. Most of the old wealthy homes you'll pass are from fortunes in the sponge and cigar industries. Move farther out from Old Town past the west and south side of the island. Did you know Key West has to import sand? And, they are the only frost-free city in the USA. Get some great personal recommendations for eateries, too. A single fare allows passengers to disembark at any or all stops and reboard later. $25.00 adult, $12.00 child.

CONCH TOUR TRAIN - www.conchtourtrain.com or 305-294-5161. Since 1958, this mini-train has been conducting tours and chugging about Key West. Its small, open, canvas-canopied cars are pulled by propane-powered simulated steam engines with smokestacks, whistles and bells to delight railroad buffs of all ages. Passengers can board at Mallory Square or Flagler Station in the Historic Seaport district for 90-minute narrated tours that encompass Old Town, Duval Street, The Southernmost Point, and Historic Seaport. Operates daily 9:00am-4:30pm. $25.00 adult, $12.00 child. No on/off privileges.

TURTLE KRAALS MUSEUM

Key West - 200 Margaret Street (Historic Seaport district) 33040. Phone: (305) 294-0209. www.seaturtlemuseum.org Hours: Daily 11:00am-4:00pm. Admission: FREE

The museum sits on a former waterfront cannery next to the former turtle holding pens or kraals. Inside the museum you'll find photographs and a brief history of Key West's turtling industry, which was a booming business in the mid-1800s. Highlights include educational information about sea turtles and the modern-day-perils they face, as well as a display of turtle shells, skulls and sea turtle products. Museum organizers hope eventually to use the abandoned kraals as a home for turtles with disabilities who cannot survive in the wild.

FORT JEFFERSON / DRY TORTUGAS NATIONAL PARK

Key West - (access only by boat) 33041. Phone: (305) 242-7700. www.nps.gov/drto/ Hours: Ft. Jefferson on Garden Key is open during daylight hours; closed at dark. Loggerhead, East and Middle Keys are open year-round during daylight hours. Admission: $5.00 - 17 and older - 7 Days. Seaplanes of Key West, Sunny Days Catamarans, and Yankee Freedom are collecting the fee from their passengers. Miscellaneous: The Tortugas were first discovered by Ponce de Leon in 1513. Abundant sea turtles or "tortugas" provisioned his ships with fresh meat, but there was no fresh water-the tortugas were dry.

Almost 70 miles (112.9 km) west of Key West lies a cluster of seven islands, composed of coral reefs and sand, called the Dry Tortugas. The area is known for its famous bird and marine life, and its legends of pirates and sunken gold. Fort Jefferson, one of the largest coastal forts ever built, is a central feature. Fort Jefferson - the "Gilbraltar of the Gulf" - stands on Garden Key among a cluster of islands. Upon approach, you will find the view of the massive fort is overwhelming! Founded by the need to control navigation, construction on the gigantic fort, whose walls are eight feet thick and 50 feet high, continued for 30 years but was never completed. During the Civil War, Fort Jefferson served as a

Union military prison for captured deserters and housed four men convicted of complicity in Abraham Lincoln's assassination - including Dr. Samuel Mudd, the Maryland physician who unwittingly set the broken leg of assassin John Wilkes Booth. How did the yellow fever epidemic in the fort actually help Dr. Mudd leave? Today, visitors can journey

Entrance to Dr. Mudd's cell

to Fort Jefferson by seaplane, ferry or private vessel. Most take the complimentary guided tour of the fort, where they can step inside Dr. Mudd's cell and feel the prison chill, peer through the massive structure's gun casements and observe the amazing vista of sea, sky and sandy islands from the open third level.

FORT ZACHARY TAYLOR STATE HISTORIC SITE

Key West - (at the end of Southard Street on Truman Annex) 33041. Phone: (305) 292-6713. www.floridastateparks.org/forttaylor/default.cfm Hours: Florida state parks are open from 8:00am until sundown 365 days a year.

Fort Taylor, named for the country's 12th president, was built between 1845 and 1866. Controlled by the Union during the Civil War, the fort was the home base for a successful blockade of Confederate ships which some historians say shortened the conflict by a full year. The fort was used during the Spanish-American War, World War I and World War II. Once referred to as Fort Forgotten, the structure was rediscovered and excavated. Today the fort is believed to hold the largest collection of Civil War cannons in the nation. It is also the site of the popular annual Civil War Heritage Days event whose highlights include re-enactments of historic military maneuvers. The acreage surrounding the fort includes a shaded picnic area and a 1,000 foot beach on the Atlantic Ocean that features excellent offshore snorkeling and sunset views.

CRANE POINT

Marathon - MM 50.5 Bayside, 5550 Overseas Hwy. 33050. Phone: (305) 743-9100. www.cranepoint.org Hours: Monday-Saturday 9:00am-5:00pm, Sunday Noon-5:00pm. Admission: $7.50 adult, $6.00 senior, $4.00 student.

A one-of-a-kind, living record of Keys history, Crane Point is home to a Museum of Natural History, the Children's Museum and historic Adderley House (one of the oldest homes in the Keys built of tabby). Winding through endangered native foliage, unusual geologic features and colorful exotic vegetation, the rustic, quarter-mile trail leads visitors throught the site's mangrove, palm and hardwood hammocks. Once outside, look for Wild Willy the giant iguana - scanting along the railing, running free. On self-directed tours, visitors can walk through exposed ancient ocean fossils such as giant brain and star corals; native palms that visitors can touch; and red mangroves, known as "walking trees" for their long roots that give the tree a legged appearance. A wild Bird rehab center and flight habitat also are accessible via the trail. The property contains evidence of prehistoric Indian artifacts and a Bahamian village.

MUSEUM OF NATURAL HISTORY OF THE FLORIDA KEYS - Observe a 600 year-old dugout canoe, remnants of pirate ships and a simulated coral reef cave at the Museum of Natural History. Learn about the native Keys inhabitants, the early explorers, the pioneers and developers of the "Railroad that Died at Sea." See the Bellarmine jug (circa 1580), a shipwreck artifact that was found in 1980 in almost perfect condition in the Atlantic Ocean off the Florida Keys. Be introduced to the Key deer and other animals native to the Keys including turtles, snails, snakes and whales through the museum's displays.

CHILDREN'S MUSEUM OF THE FLORIDA KEYS - The small museum has various indoor/outdoor exhibits. Relive the swashbuckling adventures of Keys Pirates in the Children's Museum while climbing aboard a 17th century galleon, "Los Ninos de Los Cayos," an interactive vessel complete with pirate clothes and treasure. Enjoy learning about native shells of the Florida Keys through the museum shell collection and examine horseshoe crabs and other sea creatures in the touch tanks

SUGGESTED LODGING AND DINING

CHEECA LODGE - Florida Keys (**Islamorada**). MM 82 Overseas Hwy. (305) 664-4631 or (866) 591-ROCK or **www.cheeca.com**. "Barefoot elegance" is the trademark here and fishermen know it as the "Sport Fishing Capital of the World." The Lodge has over 200 beautiful guest rooms and suites or bungalows.

Accommodations (run $200.00-$400.00 per night for rooms, $300.00-$700.00 for villas) have a welcoming, deep textured, West Indies theme and each has a plasma screen entertainment system. A free-form freshwater pool and a saltwater lagoon are the centerpieces of the lodge's beachside and are flanked by stretches of long, white sandy beach with lounge chairs and thatch-roofed cabanas (some for spa treatments). The lagoon is stocked with indigenous fish and is a great place for kids to snorkel. A huge dock stretches towards the ocean and is the perfect spot for casting a fishing line or watching the sunrise. The Ocean Terrace Grill has a relaxed approach and offers a kid-friendly menu and casual indoor or poolside dining for breakfast, lunch and dinner. Maybe play tennis, golf or shop. The $39.00 Daily Resort Fee (per room) includes all inclusive tennis, golf, fishing, beach cabanas, kayaks and paddle boats plus other little perks. For an extra fee, family members can partake in parasailing, windsurfing, kayaking or Camp Cheeca for the kids (ages 4-12). Try painting a coconut or a scavenger hunt. Although daytime is full of fun by the pool or on the water, evening is beautifully lit with tiki torches all over the lagooned property - you'll feel you've escaped to the tropics and never want to leave! Probably the most family-comfortable elegant resort we visited in Florida.

ISLAND CITY HOUSE HOTEL - 411 William Street, **Key West**. **www.islandcityhouse.com**. (305) 294-5702 or (800) 634-8230. When you come to the Island City House, you will be greeted by special hosts - four little furry creatures that live amongst the inn (some cats are Hemingway cats with six toes). The cats are so famous, there is a book written about them. The Island City House Cats, written and illustrated by Janet D. Corneal, is a children's book that tells the tale of the "real" owners of the Hotel. All of their twenty-four suites have private baths, air conditioning, fully-equipped kitchens, ceiling fans, hardwood floors, televisions, and direct dial telephones. Rates run $125.00-$375.00 per night. They offer a large Pool (15 x 30) with a large sunning deck around pool. Complimentary continental breakfast is served daily in the lush tropical garden. Winding brick walkways meander past bromeliads in bloom, a babbling coral rock fountain and fish pond, and shaded secret garden seats. Maybe play available board games or rent a bike to stroll around the island. There are plenty of bike racks everywhere to lock up and explore museums and shopping within just 3 blocks. They even have cribs available. Can you tell why this guesthouse welcomes children?

FLORIDA KEYS CUISINE: Among the favorites are Key West pink shrimp, a delicacy generally considered sweeter than other crustaceans. The mollusk conch (pronounced konk) is impossible to pass up (although it's more bitter than sweet) in salads, chowder or fritters. Recipes vary from one restaurant to another. Stone crabs, renowned for their sweet and succulent meat, also are popular. Once the claws are removed, the crab is returned to the sea where, over the course of up to two years, the claws regenerate (a renewable resource). Stone crab claws are most commonly served warm with drawn butter or chilled with mustard sauce (seasonally mid-October to mid-May). Ropa vieja, a name that literally means "old clothes," tastes like heavenly shredded beef. Other favorite dishes are picadillo and roast pork or pork chunks. Cuban entrees are most often served with traditional black beans and yellow rice, sweet plantains and Cuban bread - and the most authentic place we recommend - EL MESON DE PEPE in Key West on Wall Street, right next to Mallory Square. A Cuban museum is here too. What is a Cuban Sandwich? Cuban bread, piled with Cuban-style ham and pork, salami, Emanthaler cheese, sliced dill pickle and spicy mustard. Warmed and flattened in a press and served hot and crispy. It is impossible to spend time in the Keys without sampling Key Lime pie. Our favorite - not too sweet, or too bitter is (www.blondgiraffe.com) BLOND GIRAFFE. Watch them thru the factory windows at 600 Front Street or 107 Simonton Street. There are no commercial Key lime groves in the Florida Keys today, but Key Largo boasted a large Key lime industry until about the mid-1930s. Key lime is great in homemade guacamole, too.

Chapter 9
South West (SW) Area

MANATEE
Ona 64
Bradenton
Sarasota
75
17
SARASOTA
DE SOTO
Venice
CHARLOTTE
GLADES
Port Charlotte
27
Boca Grande
Fort Myers
Sanibel Island
LEE
HENDRY
Ft. Myers Beach
Naples
75
Marco Island
COLLIER
Everglades City
41
MONROE

NW
NC
NE
CW
C
CE
SW
SE
Keys

Our Favorites...

* South Florida Museum / Parker Manatee Aquarium - Bradenton

* Mixon Fruit Farms - Bradenton

* De Soto National Memorial - Bradenton

* Wooten's Everglades Airboat & Swamp Buggy Tours - Everglades (Ochopee)

* Edison & Ford Winter Estates - Ft. Myers

* ECHO - North Fort Myers

* Naples Trolley Tour - Naples

* Solomon's Castle - Ona

* Ft. Myers Beach

* Bicycle Riding, Shell Museum - Sanibel Island

* Ringling Museum - Sarasota

BOCA GRANDE LIGHTHOUSE MUSEUM / GASPARILLA ISLAND STATE PARK

Boca Grande - 880 Belcher Road 33921. www.barrierislandparkssociety.org Phone: (941) 964-0060. Hours: Daily 10:00am-4:00pm (November-May) and Wednesday-Sunday only (June-October). Admission: $2.00 per vehicle. Tours are free but $1.00 donations are suggested.

The museum contains exhibits of the first Native Americans to arrive at Boca Grande as well as the Calusa Indians who appeared later. Exhibits explore the arrival of the Spanish to the area, the development of commercial fishing and the later appearance of the railroad. Stories of Boca Grande's two lighthouses are highlighted. Study the evolution of Boca Grande as a rich man's paradise that explains in part the community's status as "Tarpon Fishing Capital of the World." The museum is located within the grounds of (**www.floridastateparks.org/gasparillaisland/**) Gasparilla Island State Park.

STUMP PASS BEACH STATE PARK

Boca Grande - (south end of Manasota Key off I-75, exit 191) 33921. Phone: (941) 964-0375. www.floridastateparks.org/stumppass/default.cfm Hours: Daily 8:00am-sunset. Admission: $2.00 per vehicle.

At the southwest corner of Sarasota County there is a mile of beach where seashells and shark teeth wash up, and anglers fish the surf for prize catches. Visitors can enjoy an excellent view of the Gulf of Mexico, as well as a stretch of undeveloped Florida coastline. Visitors come to this secluded beach to enjoy the year-round swimming and sunbathing; shelling is best during the winter months. A hiking trail passes through five distinct natural communities that provide homes for many species of wildlife; covered picnic tables are located along the trail. While at the park, visitors might see West Indian manatees, gopher tortoises, snowy egrets, least terns, and magnificent frigatebirds. Ranger-led turtle walks and beach nature walks are available in the summer. Shelling is best in the winter.

EVERGLADES WONDER GARDENS

Bonita Springs - (old 41, 1 mile north of the Greyhound Track) 34135. Phone: (239) 992-2591. Hours: Daily, except Christmas, from 9:00am-5:00pm, with guided tours operating continuously until 4:15pm. Admission: $12.00 adult, $6.00 child (3-10).

The Gardens are one of Florida's earliest wildlife attractions. Botanists often refer to its lush tropical tree gardens as one of the finest in the world. Giant kapok, delightful akee, mysterious monkey puzzle, fascinating shaving brush and colossal Cuban laurel trees surround visitors as they learn of life in the vast and silent Everglades. (don't you love the names for some of these plants?) Watch guides feed giant gators. Playful otters perform shows on every tour and you may catch a close-up view of Florida panthers, black bear, American crocodiles and alligators, white tail deer, bobcats, hawks, owls, snakes and wild boars - oh my! Visitors exit the park through a unique natural history museum with artifacts and relics ranging from prehistoric through Calusa Indian eras.

SOUTH FLORIDA MUSEUM / PARKER MANATEE AQUARIUM

Bradenton - 201 10th Street West 34206. www.southfloridamuseum.org Phone: (941) 747-2556. Hours: Monday-Saturday 10:00am-5:00pm; Sunday Noon-5:00pm. Closed Mondays (May, June & August-December). Closed Thanksgiving Day, Christmas Day & New Year's Day. The Museum is closed for annual maintenance the first two weeks in September. Admission: $15.95 adult, $13.95 senior (60+), $11.95 child (4-12). Includes Museum, Aquarium and one Planetarium Show.

Discover Florida's story from the prehistoric to the present with life-sized casts of Ice Age mammals that roamed in Southwest Florida 12,000 years ago, realistic dioramas, and fossil exhibits that explain how Florida was formed. See materials which were collected from Florida archeological digs. Journey back to 16th century Spain in their Spanish Plaza with a replica of a 16th century chapel.

PARKER MANATEE AQUARIUM - is home to "Snooty", the oldest living manatee (over 58 years old!) born and nurtured in a man-made, protected environment. The pool holds approximately 60,000 gallons of water and includes both deep and shallow water to provide continuity for Snooty's feeding habits. Several aquarium shows occur each day. You must meet Snooty - he is so lovable and friendly with staff - he jumps right up on the dock to get treats! It's easy to see why Florida has fallen in love with this mammal.

Snooty comes up for a little treat

PLANETARIUM - A state-of-the-science, all digital full dome planetarium/theater. Features astronomy presentations, sound and light shows and wide-screen large format programming featured daily.

MIXON FRUIT FARMS

Bradenton - 2712 26th Avenue East (I-75 South to exit 220/SR 64 west for 5 miles. Just past the 2nd bridge turn left onto 27th St. East) 34208. Phone: (800) 608-2525. **www.mixon.com** *Admission: Adults: Lunch & Tour $10.00, Tour only $4.00. Children Lunch & Tour $4.00 (12 & under). Miscellaneous: Browse the 7,000 square foot gift shoppe for unique Florida gifts and gourmet foods.*

See GIANT lemons and try a "suprising" kumquat !

Come take a ride on the Orange Blossom Express! It's affordable family fun and you'll learn all the secrets of citrus while discovering a new world inside the live groves. Tours are packed full of educational tidbits and trivia. Learn Florida's history & cultural heritage, citrus origins, growth and industry – did you know citrus groves love bees and water vapor? Try a fresh kumquat right off the vine. Roll it and pop the whole thing in your mouth! Learn about the Good, the Bad and the Ugly. Witness Ponderosa lemons as big as grapefruit or oranges mixed with grapefruit in the shape of a bell. Take a peek in the packinghouse and juice processing facilities. Have a "ham" in the family? Take photos in the Grove's fun caricature photo stands. You'll also get to sample homemade fudge, fresh squeezed citrus juice and sliced oranges and grapefruit. Stay for one of Mixon's Famous "Orange Swirl" Ice Cream Cones (made from fresh squeezed orange juice) and sit out on Grandma Rosa's front porch. Add lunch and enjoy deli sandwiches, soups or salads. A bright, friendly and fun place to definitely put in your travel plans.

LAKE MANATEE STATE PARK

Bradenton - 20007 State Road 64 34212. **www.floridastateparks.org** *Phone: (941) 741-3028.* Located east of I-75, this 556-acre recreation area extends along the shores of Lake Manatee. Recreational activities include camping, swimming, picnicking and boating. Nature trails and fishing available.

DE SOTO NATIONAL MEMORIAL

Bradenton - PO Box 15390 (I-75 follow State Road 64 west (also Manatee Avenue), for approximately twelve miles to 75th Street West). Turn right (north) onto 75th Street West) 34280. Phone: (941) 322-1000. **www.nps.gov/deso/** *Hours: Daily 9:00am-5:00pm except major winter holidays. Admission: FREE*

The park commemorates the legacy of Spanish conquistador, Hernando de Soto, who in 1539 landed near Tampa Bay to begin a four year, four thousand mile trek through the Southeastern United States. Begin with a 22-minute movie as actors re-enact scenes from this expedition (shown every half hour). Go on the expedition via video and survive! Over one-half of the explorers didn't.

The presentation is necessary to orient your family to this time in early North American history. This expedition would never yield the gold and treasure these men so desperately sought and the Spanish began to re-think their desire to conquer it. Now, go outside and attend living history demonstrations (mid-December thru mid-April) in the replica Spanish Camp, try on pieces of armor (great photo ops), or walk the nature trail through a Florida coastal landscape similar to the one encountered by conquistadors almost five hundred years ago. We really learned a lot here and the interpreters and rangers are very helpful and interesting.

Try on a "steel" explorer hat!

MANATEE TROLLEY (MCAT)

Bradenton (Anna Maria Island) - 1108 26th Avenue E 34208. Phone: (941) 749-7116. **www.co.manatee.fl.us** *(click on transit) Admission: FREE*

On Anna Maria Island, from the Anna Maria Pier on the north to Coquina Beach on the south, the Manatee Trolley provides FREE transportation for shopping, dining, beach combing, and sightseeing. Trolleys are both air-conditioned as well as open-air seating. Connects with MCAT's nine routes serving the whole county. Trolleys offer wheelchair lifts and bike racks, too.

GAMBLE PLANTATION STATE HISTORIC SITE

Bradenton (Ellenton) - 3708 Patten Avenue (Exit 224 from I-75. Head west for 1 mile on US 301) 34222. Phone: (941) 723-4536. www.floridastateparks.org/gambleplantation Hours: Thursday-Monday 9:30am-4:00pm. Admission: FREE. Tours are charged.

This antebellum mansion was home to Major Robert Gamble and headquarters of an extensive sugar plantation. It is the only surviving plantation house in South Florida. It is believed that Confederate Secretary of State, Judah P. Benjamin, took refuge here after the fall of the Confederacy, until his safe passage to England could be secured. As you enter the mansion, it feels as though you stepped through a time portal that transported you back into the 1850s. The tour guide takes you into the first room, the parlor. There you see an extravagant piano, dating over 140 years old, that was purchased for only $25. You enter the next room and are introduced to picture molding.

SUN SPLASH FAMILY WATERPARK

Cape Coral - 400 Santa Barbara Blvd, 33991. www.sunsplashwaterpark.com Phone: (239) 574-0557. Hours: Wednesday-Sunday 11:00am-5:00pm (mid-March to mid-May); daily 10:00am-6:00pm, some 9:00pm (mid-May to mid-August); weekends only 11:00am-5:00pm (mid-August to September). Admission: $12.95 general 48 inches+, $10.95 guests less than 48 inches tall, $6.95 senior (55+), $2.95 infants (age 2 and under). Miscellaneous: Lounge chairs, life jackets, changing rooms and rental lockers are available.

Slide into a million gallons of fun at a waterpark that offers 12-acres of watery adventure. Enjoy giant waterslides, the popular Main Stream River inner tube ride, Lily Pads and a Tot Spot kiddie area featuring interactive squirt works, sand volleyball, a game arcade, and more.

CAPTIVA CRUISES

Captiva Island - South Seas Resort Yacht Harbour, Captiva Road 33924. Phone: (239) 472-5300. www.captivacruises.com Note: Reservations are essential as South Seas Resort is a private resort and guest passes are required for admission.

Captiva Cruises features several excursions to out-islands and shelling islands. Visit these four spectacular island destinations: Cabbage Key, Useppa Island, Cayo Costa and Boca Grande.

DOLPHIN WATCH & WILDLIFE ADVENTURE CRUISE: A 90 minute wildlife cruise on Pine Island Sound leaving at 4:00pm. $20.00 adult, $12.50 child.

BEACH AND SHELLING CRUISE: A three hour cruise to the secluded Cayo Costa State Park Islands. A naturalist on board guides nature lovers to the best shelling, bird-watching and hiking along pristine "old Florida" nature trails. CAYO COSTA STATE PARK (**www.floridastateparks.org/cayocosta/**), an island wilderness preserve, is a world-famous shelling destination. Boca Grande remains a charming seaside village. Morning cruise is from 9:00am-Noon. Afternoon cruise from 1:00-4:00pm. $35.00 adult, $20.00 child. Full day cruises available, too.

OUT-ISLAND CRUISES: A half day cruise to one of four exciting destinations, Cabbage Key, Useppa Island, Boca Grande, or Cayo Costa. Enjoy daily cruises aboard the Lady Chadwick. Located at Milemarker 60 on the Intracoastal Waterway, colorful Cabbage Key has a marina, historic inn, picturesque dining room, water tower view of Pine Island Sound and nature trails. Useppa Island, relives the glamour and history of a bygone era with pink pathways, lush tropical vegetation, the Collier Inn restaurant, as well as an island museum. Luncheon cruises run from 10:30am-3:30pm (purchased meals on Cabbage Key and Useppa Island are not included). $30.00 adult, $15.00 child.

SMALLWOOD STORE AND MUSEUM

*Chokoloskee - 360 Mamie Street 33925. **www.florida-everglades.com/chokol/smallw.htm** Phone: (239) 695-2989.   Hours: Daily 10:00am-4:00pm (December - May 1). Closed Wednesday and Thursday (rest of year).*

This old trading post, store and post office opened to serve the American Indians and pioneers whose livelihood came from hunting, fishing and farming in the Everglades and Ten Thousand Islands. Settlement brought a need for goods and mail and that need was met by the Smallwood Store. Established in 1906, this Trading Post served a remote area, buying hides, furs and farm produce and providing the goods required. It remained open and active until 1982. When the doors were shut, 90% of the original goods remained in the store. In the last few years Ted's granddaughter has reopened the store as a museum, and today it serves as a time capsule of Florida pioneer history. The center section of the building remains as Ted would have known it. The family's guest bedroom, kitchen and dining room are on display, along with exhibits relating to the area's history.

BIG CYPRESS NATIONAL PRESERVE

*Everglades (Ochopee) - 33100 Tamiami Trail East (I-75, state road 29, and U.S. 41 all travel through the preserve) 34141. Phone: (239) 695-1201.   **www.nps.gov/bicy** Hours: Daily 9:00am-4:30pm. Admission: FREE*

Big Cypress has a mixture of pines, hardwoods, prairies, mangrove forests, cypress strands and domes. White-tailed deer, bear and Florida panther can be found here along with the more tropical liguus tree snail, royal palm and cigar orchid. This meeting place of temperate and tropical species is a hotbed of biological diversity. Hydrologically, the Preserve serves as a supply of fresh, clean water for the vital estuaries of the ten thousand islands area near Everglades City. Visitors will find a recreational paradise with camping, canoeing, kayaking, hiking and birdwatching opportunities. Recently, the Preserve opened several new pedestrian boardwalks to enhance the visitor experience in the preserve. Travelers can pull off the Tamiami Trail Scenic Highway at the Kirby Storter Roadside Park and take a short walk into the quiet coolness of an ancient cypress forest, or watch for alligators at new viewing boardwalks at Turner River Road and at the park's Oasis Visitor Center. The visitor center offers a 15-minute movie about the preserve, a wildlife exhibit and book sales.

WOOTEN'S EVERGLADES AIRBOAT & SWAMP BUGGY TOURS

Everglades (Ochopee) - 32330 Tamiami Trail E (two miles east of the Everglades Welcome Center on the Tamiami Trail (US 41) 34141. www.wootenseverglades.com Phone: (800) 282-2781. Admission: $15.00-$18.00 per person (age 4 and up) for air boat or swamp buggy tours. Extra $6.00-$8.00 for Animal Exhibit. Combo discounts are recommended as every ride and attraction here is very well done. Prices vary by season.

Within Big Cypress Preserve, this company offers airboat and swamp buggy tours and has been for over 50 years.

SWAMP BUGGIES are like open flatbed monster trucks that safari slowly through the sawgrass into the cypress swamp. Travel through Halfway Creek,

filled with tropical flora and fauna native to the Everglades. Enjoy viewing native Strangler Fig Tree, beautiful orchids, airplants, deer, willows and more. Pass a recreated Chickee Hut Seminole village or learn about eating habits of the alligator family living here. On your final turn, you'll stop at the bank of freshwater springs where dozens of manatee live and raise their pups. Best manatee sightings in Florida!

High atop a GIANT Swamp Buggy

AIRBOAT TOURS offer native guides that will take you on an exciting five mile tour through old Native American Canoe Trails used during the Seminole wars. Weave through the maze of mangrove walking trees. It's a thrill ride when you skirt sideways over the grassy open areas.

Spend time before or after your tour at the Alligator & Animal Exhibit. Say a personal "hello" to over 200 live Florida Alligators and 27 of the endangered American Crocodiles. Catch a gator wrestling show or maybe an unrehearsed look at brave workers cleaning a crocodile cage - with the croc still in it! Also see the elusive endangered Florida Panthers and a rare black panther.

I'm a happy, smilin' crocodile...

Don't miss bobcats, raccoons, an otter and even a tiger. If you dare, have your photo taken while you're holding a live baby Florida Alligator (don't fear, its like holding a baby iguana).

EVERGLADES NATIONAL PARK

Everglades City - (Naples area, take U.S. 41 (Tamiami Trail) east to Shark Valley) 34139. Phone: Visitor Information (305) 242-7700. www.nps.gov/ever Admission: $10.00 per private vehicle for a 7 day pass.

Everglades National Park is the only subtropical preserve in North America and is part of the largest wetlands ecosystem in the United States. The western gateway to the Park is in Everglades City. Along the outskirts of the national park, numerous private tour operators provide airboat and swamp buggy excursions through the sawgrass plains, swamps and hardwood hammocks of this ecosystem. There is also a daily guided boat trip into the mangrove estuaries of the Ten Thousand Islands section of the Park. Look for wood storks and great blue herons wading, or watch for frequent encounters with dolphins and manatees.

VISITOR CENTER

Gulf Coast - Open All Year at 9:00am-4:30pm. Phone: (239) 695-3311. The Gulf Coast Visitor Center is located on the West Coast in Everglades City, in the northwest corner of the park. It is the gateway for exploring the Ten Thousand Islands, a maze of mangrove islands and waterways that extends south to Flamingo and Florida Bay. The visitor center has natural history exhibits, educational displays, and orientation films. The visitor center has park information, issues backcountry permits and park passes, and sells books and postcards. A gift shop is located downstairs. Restaurants, stores, lodging, and campgrounds are located nearby. Boat tours and canoe rentals are available at the marina, as well as nearby. These boat trips run daily, approximately every half hour. Canoes may be rented to explore Chokoloskee Bay and the Turner River. Backcountry permits are required for camping.

MUSEUM OF THE EVERGLADES

Everglades City - 105 Broadway Avenue West (south of the junction of CR 29 and US 41 (Tamiami Trail). Take CR29 south into the city to 105 West Broadway on the circle) 34139. Phone: (239) 695-0008. **www.colliermuseum.com** *Hours: Generally Tuesday-Saturday 10:00am-4:00pm. Admission: Donations welcome.*

The museum tells the story of a town deep in the Everglades and the building of the travel Tamiami Trail. Learn of the area's characters, pioneers and plume hunters. It begins with the earliest known settlers here, the Calusa Indians, whose civilization flourished in southwest Florida over 2,000 years ago.

EDISON & FORD WINTER ESTATES

Fort Myers - 2350 McGregor Blvd. (Interstate 75 (New Exit #136) travel West on Colonial boulevard (SR 884). Turn right onto McGregor Boulevard (SR 867) 33901. Phone: (239) 334-3614. **www.edison-ford-estate.com** *Hours: Monday-Saturday 9:00am-5:30pm, Sunday Noon-5:30pm. Closed Thanksgiving and Christmas. Admission: Combined ticket for both homes is $20.00 adult, $11.00 child (6-12). Lab & Museum only: $11.00 & $4.50. Florida resident and family discounts.*

In 1885, Thomas Edison first visited Florida and purchased property along the Caloosahatchee River where he built a vacation home. The 1886 "Seminole lodge"

His lab...as Edision left it...

served as a winter retreat and work place for the prolific inventor until his death in 1931. The inventor's charming "old-Florida" style home, laboratory and experimental gardens have been authentically maintained. Rare antique automobiles and Edison phonographs fill some spaces, the Laboratory where Edison turned goldenrod (a weed!) to rubber (yes!) another. Look for the pool made with Edison Portland Cement - and it has never leaked. The lab is a mouth-dropper - you can feel the genius' presence! Throughout the laboratory, all of his things are just as they were in his lifetime, including his "cat-nap" cot. Because of his deafness, Edison's sleep was undisturbed and relaxed him so much that 15-minute sleep to him was as good as is several hours to anyone else. Some might say he invented the "Power Nap"! Be sure the kids get to spend time in the Whiz Inventors Room of the Museum. Here they play a Charlie Brown Inventor video while the kids look over giant prototypes of Edison's inventions. There's even a worksheet to take home and make your own homemade light bulb! Did you know Edison invented the first Talking Dolls?

Edison's good friend Henry Ford followed close behind and purchased the neighboring property in 1915. "The Mangoes" was the winter getaway for the Fords. A 1914 Model T, 1919 Model T, 1917 Ford Truck and 1929 Model A are on display. Ford used General Electric appliances. Henry would ask guests to "take a seat" - it didn't mean sit - it meant take a chair and move it aside so they could clear the floor for square dancing - a Ford family passion. Edison and Ford spent many winters working, talking and even relaxing together in tropical southwest Florida. Can you imagine what those brilliant minds talked about?

Henry Ford's first V8 Engine

SOUTHWEST FLORIDA MUSEUM OF HISTORY

Fort Myers - *2300 Peck Street (I-75 south exit 138 west on MLK. One block south on Jackson) 33901. Phone: (239) 332-5955. www.cityftmyers.com/attractions/historical.htm Hours: Tuesday-Saturday 10:00am-5:00pm. Admission: $9.50 adult, $8.50 senior, $5.00 child (3-12).*

Housed in the restored Atlantic Coastline railroad depot, the museum features displays and exhibits of the history of southwest Florida from prehistory through the present. Displays include graphic depictions of ancient Florida: Paleo, Archaic, Calusa, and Seminole Indians; Spanish explorers; a Pullman rail car or an authentic replica pioneer "Cracker house." The first tourist to visit southwest Florida was Spanish explorer Ponce de Leon, who visited Pine Island in 1513 and was later mortally wounded in these same waters by a Calusa Indian arrow. One of the southernmost land battles of the American Civil War was fought in Fort Myers in early 1865 over cattle, with both sides claiming victory. Explore the

World War II airfield exhibit, which includes a recently excavated P-39 bomber that crashed into Estero Bay during the war and a restored AT-6 training plane. Students studying Florida History, Fort Myers History or American History will benefit greatly from a visit to this museum.

MANATEE PARK

Fort Myers - 10901 SR 80 (SR 80, 1.5 miles east of I-75 exit 141) 33905. Phone: (239) 694-3537 or (239) 461-7477. www.leeparks.org (click on Parks, then Regional Parks) Hours: Daily 8:00am-8:00pm (April-September), Daily 8:00am-5:00pm (October-March). Admission: Parking fee of $1.00 per hour or $5.00 daily maximum. No Pets. Observation area is FREE. Miscellaneous: Picnic areas & shelters, fishing cove & pier on the Orange River, canoe/kayak launch to the Orange River, program amphitheater and playground.

Baby & Momma Manatee in the wild...

Visitors can observe endangered West Indian manatees in their non-captive habitat from three observation areas during "Manatee Season." Manatee Park officially opens for "season" around mid-December as visitors are able to view several manatees daily in the Florida Power & Light (FPL) discharge canal. Please monitor gulf temperatures as best viewing occurs when it dips below 68 degrees. Best known for the Winter home for the Florida Manatee, this park is also the year round home for Florida native plants & butterflies. "All About Manatees" program daily at 11:00am and 2:00pm - November through March. Free guided walk through the native plants habitats at 9:00am every Saturday. Who will be the first in your group to spot the manatee's back or snout? It's a thrill to find them!

MANATEE WORLD

Fort Myers - 5605 Palm Beach Blvd (¼ mile East of I 75 at exit 141, SR 80. Coastal Marine Mart-orange & white striped bldg.) 33905. Phone: (239) 693-1434. www.manateeworld.com   Admission: $18.00 adult, $9.00 child (3-12). Miscellaneous: Largest offering of Manatee related books and gifts at the Manatee Magic gift shop.

Many people now know about manatees and their endangered plight. Most people don't know that Ft. Myers is home to one of the largest populations of wintering manatees in Florida. Take an educational and entertaining ecological boat safari into the natural habitat of the endangered West Indian Manatee. Observe manatees, along with alligators and a wide variety of bird life during the narrated tour on calm, protected waters. Although manatees are seen all year long in Lee County, hundreds of manatees congregate near Manatee World during the cooler winter months to feed and stay warm (best time to visit).

CALUSA NATURE CENTER AND PLANETARIUM

Fort Myers - 3450 Ortiz Avenue 33906. Phone: (239) 275-3435. www.calusanature.com Hours: Monday-Saturday 9:00am-5:00pm, Sunday 11:00am-5:00pm. Admission: $8.00 adult, $5.00 child (3-12) includes admission to the nature center, trails and all planetarium shows that day.

Outside, rustic boardwalks lead visitors on a tour of 105 acres of subtropical environment. Inside, permanent and changing exhibits of the natural history of southwest Florida are on display. There are more than 100 Florida native animals to see. Alligator and snake demonstrations hold visitors' interest twice daily. Naturalists guide walks and aviary tours several times a week. Changing planetarium starlit astronomy and laser light shows occur in the relaxing 90-seat theater.

BROADWAY PALM DINNER THEATRE

Fort Myers - 1380 Colonial Blvd. (Royal Palm Square) (I-75 N to exit 136 west, left on Sumnerlin) 33907. Phone: (239) 278-4422. www.broadwaypalm.com Admission: Broadway Dinner Shows $21.00 child, $45.00 adult. Children's Lunch Theatre $15.00 per person. Reservations recommended.

The Dinner Theatre advertises itself as southwest Florida's most entertaining destination. It features year-round professional musicals (like Cats and Oklahoma) and comedies for adults and children (like Little Mermaid or Jack in Beanstalk), and a lavish buffet (or kid-friendly buffet). Evening performances take the stage Tuesday-Sunday and matinee days vary. The staff and surroundings are very comfortable and part of the props are even in part of the serving floor. Occasionally, characters may come through the audience seating. And the food is so flavorful!

SIX MILE CYPRESS SLOUGH PRESERVE

Fort Myers - Six Mile Cypress Parkway (1.5 miles north of Daniels Pkwy, exit 131 off I-75) 33912. Phone: (239) 432-2004. www.leeparks.org/sixmile Hours: Spring/Summer 8:00am-8:00pm, Fall/Winter 8:00am-5:00pm. Admission: FREE. Parking costs 75 cents an hour. $3.00 daily maximum.

Visitors journey through this 2,200-acre wetland ecosystem on a mile-long boardwalk trail, where southwest Florida's diverse plant and wildlife are found.

See subtropical ferns and bromeliads. Watch for birds like herons, egrets, ibis and anhingas. Guided walks daily in the winter. Wednesdays only in the summer and fall.

SUN HARVEST CITRUS

Fort Myers - 14810 Metro Pkwy (southwest corner of Six Mile Cypress and Metro Parkway on the way to the airport) 33912. Phone: (239) 768-2686 or (800) 743-1480. *www.sunharvestcitrus.com Hours: Store open Monday-Saturday 8:00am-7:00pm, Sunday 10:00am-6:00pm. Admission: FREE Miscellaneous: They also have soft-serve ice cream, fruit smoothies, candies and baked goods for sale. Playground on premises.*

"Squeeze" in a stop to this huge packinghouse and retail store that offers in-season Indian River citrus fruit, five varieties of freshly squeezed juices year-round, and in-season gift fruit shipping. Watch as fresh juice is made while enjoying free samples of juices and fruit. Get a behind-the-scenes look at their state-of-the-art packinghouse operations. See for yourself how the hand-picked citrus is cleaned, graded and packed — all within hours after leaving the family's Indian River groves.

IMAGINARIUM HANDS-ON MUSEUM

Fort Myers - 2000 Cranford Avenue (historic downtown) (Interstate 75: Exit 138, west on Dr. Martin Luther King, Jr. Boulevard (State Road 82) for four miles and left on Cranford Avenue) 33916. www.cityftmyers.com/attractions/imaginarium.htm Phone: (239) 337-3332. Hours: Monday-Saturday 10:00am-5:00pm, Sunday Noon-5:00pm. Admission: $8.00 adult, $7.00 senior (55+), $5.00 child (3-12).

Interactive learning in the sciences. A giant Pipe-O-Saurus greets visitors at the entrance to the Florida wetlands zone. Once inside, one can stand in a Florida thunderstorm without getting wet, watch Eelvis, the live eel, slither through the coral in one of three 900-gallon aquariums, get blown away in the HurricanExperience, and broadcast the weather from a TV weather studio. Outside, visit the lagoon where fish, turtles, swans and alligators live beside a reptile retreat with iguanas, tortoises and more. Theater in the Tank video presentations and 3-D shows, too.

MOUND KEY ARCHAEOLOGICAL STATE PARK

Fort Myers (Estero) - (just east of Lovers Key in Estero Bay) 33928. Phone: (239) 992-0311. www.floridastateparks.org/moundkey Hours: Daily 8:00am-sunset. Admission: FREE Miscellaneous: The only access to the island is by boat; there are no facilities.

Framed in forests of mangrove trees, the shell mounds and ridges of Mound Key rise more than 30 feet above the waters of ESTERO BAY. Prehistoric Native Americans are credited with creating this island's complex of mounds with an accumulation of seashells, fish bones, and pottery. Mound Key is believed to have been the ceremonial center of the Calusa Indians when the Spaniards first attempted to colonize Southwest Florida. In 1566, the Spanish governor of Florida established a settlement on the island with a fort and the first Jesuit mission in the Spanish New World. The settlement was abandoned three years later after violent clashes with the Indians. Interpretive displays can be found along a trail that spans the width of the island. Located in Estero Bay, several miles by boat from Koreshan State Historic Site or Lovers Key State Park.

LOVERS KEY STATE PARK

Fort Myers Beach - Black Island, just south of Fort Myers Beach   33931. www.floridastateparks.org

A delightful tram transports visitors along a rustic boardwalk, crossing picturesque Oyster Bay and a scenario of mangrove isles, to one of the most private public beaches anywhere. Lovers Key claims a section of unspoiled beach where one can cast at surf line, picnic with raccoons, bird watch and search the shoreline for seashells.

SHELL FACTORY & NATURE PARK

Fort Myers, North - 2787 North Tamiami Trail (I-75: Take Exit 143 and turn left onto State Road 78 (Bayshore Road). Go 5 miles to US 41; turn right) 33903. Phone: (239) 995-2141 or (888) 4-SHELLS.   www.shellfactory.com   Hours: Shell Factory: Daily 9:00am until 8:00 or 9:00pm. Nature Park: Daily 10:00am-7:00pm. Waltzing Waters at sunset each night. Admission: Shell Factory: FREE.   Nature Park: $4.00-$8.00 per person (age 4+). All fun park activities carry a fee, also.   Miscellaneous: Dine at Southwest Florida's largest seafood restaurant—Capt'n Fishbones for a moderately priced lunch or dinner. With a full-service restaurant and outside dining venue serving breakfast, lunch and dinner, a Subway franchise, and Rosie's Gourmet Fudge with many delightful snack items, you'll never go hungry here.

The Shell Factory is billed as the "world's largest collection of rare shells, sponges, coral, fossils and sea life specimens" with more than 5 million shells. A gift shop visit is like a treasure hunt. Ever seen a shell priced at $2,300 or octopus coral? You can pick a pearl from an oyster or watch master glass blower and potter demonstrations.

FUN PARK & ARCADE: You can play arcade games, miniature golf, test the speed of your pitch at the pitching cage, bump into friends at the Bumper Boat lagoon, stop by The Patio for live entertainment from 7:00-10:00pm most evenings, or come for karaoke from 6:00-9:00pm Sundays.

The newly renovated NATURE PARK features a Petting Zoo, Environmental Education Center, and a Botanical Trail. Bobcats, raccoons, and llamas, oh my!

Watch playful prairie dogs as they greet each other by touching their teeth together, the "prairie dog kiss". You can even feed them a treat – remember bring quarters, as they always have a healthy appetite! Keep cool while you feed the turtles and fish that live in the misty ponds below the waterfalls. Next to the waterfalls, the Primate Pavilion currently houses ring-tailed lemurs. Come see Big Bertha, a 10-foot long female alligator, and her large friends at the Slough. (It's pronounced "sloo" or "slew" in case you were wondering.) On the weekends the alligators are fed. Feedings are usually around 2:30pm but call ahead as feeding times can vary. Resident Camel "Chico" gives camel walks.

Don't miss The Shell Factory's <u>WALTZING WATERS LIQUID FIREWORKS®</u> extravaganza of water, music and lights. The waters jump, twist, sway and swirl in a dance (sunset).

ECHO (EDUCATIONAL CONCERNS FOR HUNGER ORGANIZATION)

Fort Myers, North - 17391 Durrance Road (off of SR 78, one mile east of I-75 exit 143) 33917. Phone: (239) 543-3246. **www.echonet.org** *Hours: Nursery open mornings, daily except Sunday.*

Grinding plants to sprinkle on food for better nutrition...

Working to fight world hunger, ECHO (a non-profit Christian organization) invites you for a free tour of its working demonstration farm. They give HOPE - they teach poor how to grow food that adapts to even extreme conditions, and you may learn some new garden techniques yourself. ECHO's farm shows collections of tropical food plants in Florida, as well as herb gardens and animals in the Global Village. Tilapia - why are they easy and great to grow? Ever tasted Pummelo fruit - buy some at their store and try it. Bamboo really does "shoot" up fast. Visitors can see the useful plants and farming systems that interns are cultivating in urban rooftop plantings, rice fields, hillside farming systems (even some growing in car tire terraces), rain forest clearings, semi-arid tropics, hot humid lowlands and monsoon tropics. We discovered and bought seeds to plant a Moringa bush. This miracle plant is possibly the best source of nutrients in the world - it even contains protein! And, you can sample some - one salad a day of this stuff and you'll be able to keep the doctor away! What an amazing, heart-felt place to explore.

MARCO ISLAND SKI & WATERSPORTS TOURS

Marco Island - (depart from either the Marriott or Hilton, both on S. Collier) 34146. Phone: (239) 394-4344. www.marcoislandwatersports.com

This company offers exclusive guided waverunner tours through the mangrove forests of the Ten Thousand Islands, parasailing adventures, shelling and sunset cruises, and small watercraft rentals. The Ten Thousand Islands are like 10,000 puzzle pieces that you weave through - especially on their wave runner guided tours.

CALUSA SPIRIT ECO-SHELLING CRUISE: 2½ Hour Cruise offered 2-3 times per day. $49.00 Adults and $39.00 Children under 12 years of age. Shelling cruise transports guests directly from the shores of Marco Island to the private and serene beaches of Cape Romano. Scenic stops within the 10,000 Islands reveal close encounters with dolphin, manatee, and tropical birds. Once you arrive at Cape Romano, you'll receive shelling bags and sent quickly on your way to exploring the treasure filled beaches. Complimentary water and soda is provided, but we also suggest bringing a cooler or picnic lunch (being on the water somehow "wets" your appetite). Shelling has always been a popular attraction for Cape Romano and Marco Island, the two larger barrier islands that act as the entryway to the Ten Thousand Islands and the Everglades. Since Hurricane Wilma made landfall on Cape Romano, this area is experiencing an overwhelming abundance of unique and rare shells that have washed ashore. Lightning Whelk, Florida Fighting Conch, True Tulip, Florida Spiny Jewelbox, and Atlantic Figsnail are just a few of the plentiful and exotic shells which reside on Cape Romano's sandy shores. Happy shelling!

NAPLES AREA BOAT TOURS

COCOHATCHEE NATURE CENTER - 12345 Tamiami Trail North. (239) 592-1200 or **www.cocohatchee.org**. Five daily narrated boat tours through a pristine mangrove estuary featuring a variety of wildlife, including egrets, herons, dolphins and manatees. ($12.00-$24.00)

CONSERVANCY NATURE CENTER - 1450 Merrihue Drive. (239) 262-0304 or **www.conservancy.org**. the 14-acre Center has boat rides, trails, new exhibits and a wildlife hospital.

NAPLES PRINCESS - 550 Port-O-Call Way. **www.naplesprincesscruises.com** (888) 375-3230. Enjoy Naples Bay, see the homes of Port Royal, and cruise out into the Gulf aboard a 93 foot air-conditioned luxury yacht. The tours take 149 passengers on sightseeing, lunch, and sunset dinner cruises.

NAPLES TROLLEY TOURS

Naples - 1010 6th Avenue South 34102. www.naplestrolleytours.com Phone: (800) 592-0848. Hours: Eight full trips beginning at 8:30am until about 5:00pm.

See the best of Naples on board a vintage trolley and enjoy a fully narrated trolley tour covering more than 100 points of interest including historic Naples Pier and Tin City. Pass the oldest house, Millionaires Row, an old trading post, the Naples City Dock, the disguised parking garage, and many exclusive residences. The tours are hosted by knowledgeable guides who not only know the history of Marco Island but also have a pulse on current events and activities explorers can soak up after the tour. FREE reboarding - deboard the trolley at any convenient stop to shop, dine, or sightsee, then reboard the Trolley and it's on with the tour. Your pass allows you to get off as many times as you like to enjoy Naples. Tour at your own pace. Think Naples is for seniors? The average age is 25-41 - surprised?

NAPLES ZOO AT CARIBBEAN GARDENS

Naples - 1590 Goodlette-Frank Road 34102. Phone: (239) 262-5409. www.napleszoo.com Hours: Daily 9:30am-5:30pm. Last ticket sold at 4:30pm. Admission: $15.95 adult, $14.95 senior (65+), $9.95 child (3-12). Deep discounts for Florida residents.

Discover a world of wildlife just outside of downtown. Explore a day of fun shows, a cruise or two, plus get close to animals from alligators to zebras. The Zoo offers guests the opportunity to learn about the unusual flora and fauna of Madagascar at the new Primate Pavilion. Interpretive information overlooks a nearby island that is home to several species of lemur, native to Madagascar. Another eye-catching area is in Reptiles featuring a multimedia show on Serpents: Fangs & Fiction. Animals in residence at the zoo include Australia's Parma wallables and eastern gray kangaroos to Africa's moustached monkeys and Asia's reticulated python. Our favorite part was gliding past Islands of Monkeys, Lemurs, and Apes off the shores of Lake Victoria on a Primate Expedition Cruise. As the catamarans float next to the islands, the expedition guide narrates the interesting details about these fascinating animals. The majority of these species are now classified as endangered in their native lands. The opportunity for photography is exceptional. You can also take the tour more than once as the cruise is included in your admission. (each cruise is about 15-20 minutes long)

NAPLES BOTANICAL GARDEN

Naples - 4820 Bayshore Drive 34112. Phone: (239) 643-7275. **www.naplesgarden.org**
Hours: Wednesday-Saturday 10:00am-4:00pm. Open on Sundays Noon-4:00pm (winter thru early spring). Admission: $7.00 adult, $4.00 child (6-12).

They want people and plants to connect and plan for new lakes and lands to be developed over time. For now, "The Florida Gardens" is open featuring many familiar colors and shapes that you might see around the state. The new Pollination Pavilion has a butterfly aviary, a gecko habitat and nectar feeding stations for lorikeets (do they love to feed on sweets or what?).

COLLIER-SEMINOLE STATE PARK

Naples - 20200 E. Tamiami Trail (US 41, 17 miles south of Naples) 34114. Phone: (239) 394-3397. **www.floridastateparks.org/collier-seminole/default.cfm** *Hours: Daily 8:00am-sunset. Admission: $4.00 per vehicle. Boat tour, canoe rental and camping fees apply. Miscellaneous: The park concession has a snack shop and boat tours-call (239) 642-8898.*

This park features a wealth of vegetation and wildlife typical of the Everglades, plus a forest made up of tropical trees. Although rare elsewhere, the Florida royal palm is a common tree here. The park is also the site of a National Historic Mechanical Engineering Landmark, the Bay City Walking Dredge. Built in 1924, it was used to build the Tamiami Trail highway (U.S. 41) through the Everglades, linking Tampa to Miami. Hiking, bicycling, and canoeing trails offer opportunities for visitors to explore the park´s remarkable wilderness. The park has canoe rentals along with a boat ramp that provides access to the Blackwater River, where anglers can enjoy both freshwater and saltwater fishing. Campers can spend the night in a full-facility campground; youth/group and primitive campsites are also available. The picnic areas have pavilions and grills for use on a first-come-first-served basis.

FLORIDA PANTHER & TEN THOUSAND ISLANDS NATIONAL WILDLIFE REFUGE

Naples - 3860 Tollgate Boulevard, Suite 300 (refuge headquarters is in east Naples at Exit 15 of Interstate 75) 34114. Phone: (239) 353-8442. **http://floridapanther.fws.gov/**

The Refuge has recently opened two public hiking trails - the first public access to this important wildlife habitat refuge in its 16 years of existence. The Duncan Memorial Trail is .3 miles and is wheelchair accessible with a raised, shell-paved trail bed. An additional unimproved loop trail winds 1.3 miles through the refuge. Both trails open daily from sunup to sundown, closed after dark. Panthers are extremely rare and shy so sightings are unlikely, however, panther tracks may appear on the unimproved loop trail. Best chances to spot wildlife are early morning and late afternoon - watch for deer, bear, wild turkey and many species of birds. Another boardwalk should lead to a wetlands area, kiosks with interpretive information and more. Parking is available at the trail entrance on State Road 29 just north of I-75.

AVIARY & ZOO OF NAPLES

Naples - 9824 Immokalee Road (I-75 exit 111 east) 34120. Phone: (239) 353-2215. www.aviaryofnaples.com/park.htm   Hours: Saturday-Wednesday 10:00am-4:00pm. Admission: $8.00 adult, $4.00 child.

See hundreds of exotic birds, dozens of small exotic animals including a camel, alpacas, wallabies, soft bills and Galapagos tortoises.

CORKSCREW SWAMP SANCTUARY

Naples - 375 Sanctuary Road West (north of Immokalee Road (County Road 846), approximately 15 miles east of Exit 111 on I-75) 34120. www.corkscrew.audubon.org Phone: (239) 348-9151. Hours: Daily 7:00am-sundown. Admission: $10.00 adult, $4.00 child (6-18). Discounts for Audubon members.

A 2.25-mile raised boardwalk takes visitors through several distinct habitats found within the 11,000-acre Corkscrew Swamp Sanctuary, including the largest remaining virgin bald cypress forest in North America. The raised boardwalk takes visitors through environments: a pine upland, a wet prairie, a cypress forest, and a marsh. Interpretive signs along the boardwalk and a field guide and Children's Activity Book available at the admissions desk in the Blair Center allow each visitor to take the self-guided tour. Benches and rain shelters are along the trail. For those who do not wish to walk the full 2.25 miles, an optional trail shortens the walk to one mile. Volunteer naturalists are usually on the boardwalk to answer questions.

DELNOR-WIGGINS PASS STATE PARK

Naples - (I-75 Exit 111 west 6 miles) 34120. . www.floridastateparks.org

This small barrier island on the Gulf of Mexico is a real unspoiled Florida beach with coastal hammock for shade and picnicking. Many go shelling, swimming, fishing and boating. A concession is located in the parking lot. One of the best beaches in the nation, the mile long park is a popular seashore destination in Naples for canoeing and snorkeling, too.

SOLOMON'S CASTLE & BOAT ON THE MOAT RESTAURANT

*Ona - 4533 Solomon Road (SR 64 east about 30 miles from Bradenton, turn south at CR 665 and go nine miles) 33865. Phone: (863) 494-6077 or **www.solomonscastle.com**. Admission: $10.00 adult, $4.00 child. Miscellaneous: Lunch, "fit for a King" is served from 11:00am to 4:00pm on "The Boat in The Moat", a replica of a 60 foot 16th century Spanish galleon. Sandwiches around $7-8.00. Kids Menu.*

Featured on CNN, Better Homes & Gardens, and Extreme Homes, this structure was built entirely by the hands of the artist, Howard S. Solomon, internationally known sculptor. The bright exterior is made of aluminum printing plates discarded by the local weekly newspaper. There are more than 80 interpretations of stained glass windows throughout the Castle. Essentially, the castle serves as an exhibition gallery for several

A castle made from junk !

hundred pieces of Solomon sculpture; "The ones that didn't sell," he explains. Solomon gives a scripted tour of his work.. A gun that shoots toilet plungers is used "for flushing out perpetrators." The "Car With a V-8 Engine", a writer's block - just a total play on words. You'll never look at junk the same way again. The fascinating tour leaves you speechless and full of wonder!

GATORAMA

*Palmdale - 610 US Hwy 27 (2 miles south of the intersection of US 27 and SR 29) 33944. Phone: (863) 675-0623. **www.gatorama.com** Hours: Monday-Saturday 8:30am-5:30pm, Sunday 10:00am-5:30pm. Admission: $11.95 adult, $5.95 Critters less than 56 inches.*

Claimed to be the largest collection of alligators and crocodiles anywhere. One of Gatorama's main attractions for visitors and professional photographers is the natural Florida scenery in which these prehistoric beasts sunbathe in the warm tropical climate. Giant oak trees and palm trees cover the fifteen acre attraction. Visitors will also find other animals along the covered 1000 foot walkway and wooden bridge, monkey's, bobcats, raccoons, peacocks, ducks and geese all call Gatorama home, as do six species of crocodiles including the American Crocodile. Gatorama is the largest captive breeder in North America of the Acutus Crocodile.

EMERSON POINT PRESERVE & MADIRA BICKEL MOUND STATE ARCHAEOLOGICAL SITE

Palmetto - 5801 17th Street W (Emerson is on Snead Island. Madira Mound on Terra Ceia Island) 34221. Phone: (941) 721-6885 or (941) 723-4536.

This 365 acre, state-owned preserve contains a variety of native Florida coastal ecosystems. There are miles of trails and boardwalks that allow visitors to explore different habitats, as well as the largest remaining prehistoric Indian shell mound in the Tampa Bay area. Find salt marshes, beaches, lagoons, grass flats, mangrove swamps and hardwood hammocks. Visitors can enjoy guided hikes, bird watching, hiking, bicycling, fishing and canoeing.

AROUND THE BEND NATURE TOURS: offers short walks to discover natural sites in the county. Active programs, games and storytelling are part of the package. (941) 794-8773 or **www.aroundbend.com**.

MADIRA BICKEL MOUND STATE ARCHAEOLOGICAL SITE: The site's primary feature is a flat-topped temple or ceremonial mound, composed of sand, shell and debris and measures 100 x 170 feet at the base and 20 feet in height.

FLORIDA GULF COAST RAILROAD MUSEUM

Parrish - 34219. Phone: (941) 776-0906. www.FGCRRM.org Admission: $10.00 adult, $6.00 child (3-11). Additional fees charged for specials like Train Robberies and The Little Engine.

Many visitors ask, "Where are the displays?" The answer includes the museum's rolling equipment, and the historical items found in these cars. Instead of just looking at items, the museum takes you for a 13 mile round trip ride aboard the exhibits. The 1.5 hour train ride in vintage passenger cars goes through rustic Manatee County.

BABCOCK WILDERNESS ADVENTURES

Punta Gorda - 8000 State Road 31 (I-75 new exit 143 East on Route 78 to State Road 31. Go North 9 miles) 33982. Phone: (800) 500-5583. www.babcockwilderness.com Admission: $17.95 adult, $10.95 child (3-12).

Enjoy a taste of real Florida - travel a 90 minute Swamp Buggy Tour through the Babcock Ranch and Telegraph Cypress Swamp with a trained naturalist on a voyage through beautiful woods and deep, slow-moving waters. Logging, railroading, cattle ranching, vegetable and sod farming all have co-existed at one time or another on the ranch. Experienced guides offer in-depth descriptions of birds, animals, plants, and the cattle and horses that are raised on the ranch. Visitors will see panthers, bison, alligators, and many other animals living in

Southwest Florida. A museum featuring Florida history, Babcock operations, and natural history artifacts and exhibits is housed in a movie set used by Warner Brothers to film the Sean Connery movie entitled "Just Cause". Items available for purchase relevant to the ranch, the Wilderness Tour, and Florida are featured in the country store.

ADVENTURES IN PARADISE

Sanibel - 1159 Causeway Road (Port Sanibel Marina) 33957. Phone: (239) 472-8443.
www.adventureinparadiseinc.com

Boating excursions teach the eco-heritage of the Fort Myers/ Sanibel area. Trips include sealife encounters, tropical lunches, and shelling and snorkeling the outer islands. Times of departure and trip length vary.

SHELLING & SNORKELING THE OUTER ISLANDS ABOARD THE DOLPHIN WATERS. Board DOLPHIN WATERS (complete with restroom on board), to the outer islands & Cayo Costa. Watch Dolphins play, shell along pristine beaches 'til your heart's content, snorkel with the fishey's. Beach chairs, umbrellas and snorkel equipment on board. Lunch at "Barnacle Phil's". Swimsuits, beach shoes & shelling bag recommended. Departs 9:00am. Returns: 3:00pm. Adults - $55.00, Children - $35.00 (3 & under free).

MISS PARADISE SEALIFE ENCOUNTER EXCURSION: Cruise with a marine biologist and naturalist on this Sealife Encounter. You will cruise the bay while watching the dolphins at play and stop at a deserted island for netting - so wear your beach shoes. This cruise includes a natural history narration, sampling of marine animals and on-board aquariums for viewing the catch. Departs 12:30 PM Returns: 3:00pm. Adults - $35.00, Children - $25.00 (3 & under free).

CABBAGE KEY LUNCH: 10:00am-2:00pm, Tuesday, Wednesday, Thursday & Saturday! A boaters delight lunching at famous Cabbage Key, where dollar bills hang from the ceiling & walls, a custom started by fisherman inspiring Jimmy Buffet to write "Cheeseburger in Paradise". A must for beautiful cruising with the Dolphins. Walking Nature trails, climbing the water tower, and lunches that are "sea" inspired. Adults $45.00, Children $25.00 (3 & under free).

ECO-NATURE CANOE TOURS: Join a naturalist led tour by canoe or kayak while paddling thru a mangrove forest where natural beauty abounds. Enjoy discovering & learning about the back bay ecosystem unique to Southwest Florida. Trails will lead you around Connie Mack Island, out by Larry's Lagoon, through Gator Creek, to Stingray Bay and Sharks Bay. Going through Engine Trail and Ibis Isle, you will be on the look out for the Eagles nest and skinny through Snake Creek shielded by dense mangrove trees. Be on the look out for sightings of Egrets, herons, roseate spoonbills, pelicans, manatee, dolphin, river otters, gators, mangrove crabs, & jumping mullet. Paddle on your own or reserve a spot in the guides 4 passenger canoe & leave the paddling to him. Call ahead for reservations. Free trolley pick up at your hotel & condo on Sanibel. 9:00am-11:00am Monday thru Friday $30.00 adults / $15.00 children.

SANIBEL HISTORICAL VILLAGE AND MUSEUM

Sanibel - 950 Dunlop 33957. Phone: (239) 472-4648. Hours: Wednesday-Saturday 10:00am -4:00pm (November-mid-August), although summer and November hours close at 1:00pm. Admission: Donations of $5.00 per adult are welcomed. School children and younger are FREE.

Dedicated to the pioneer families of Sanibel and Captiva, the Village includes "Uncle Clarence Rutland's Home, Bailey's General Store ("If we don't have it, you don't need it"), Morning Glories (a Sears/Roebuck catalog home), Miss Charlotta's Tea Room (sit a spell), the 1926 Post Office and the Burnap Cottage. The Rutland House, built in 1913, typifies the Florida "cracker" style, designed for comfort in a very warm climate. Visitors discover pre-electric amusements, at least four ways to combat mosquitoes and a country kitchen with gadgets to confound. All the buildings are furnished with items from the early 1900s. A boardwalk and shell paths take visitors past a pioneer garden, antique Model T truck, surrey (fringe included), and a replica of a packinghouse with farm equipment.

BAILEY-MATTHEWS SHELL MUSEUM

Sanibel Island - 3075 Sanibel-Captiva Road 33957. Phone: (239) 395-2233 or (888) 679-6450. www.shellmuseum.org Hours: Daily from 10:00am-4:00pm year-round. Admission: $7.00 adult, $4.00 youth (5-16).

More than 30 colorful exhibits display shells from around the world, with special focus on shells of Sanibel & Captiva Islands and southwest Florida. Mollusks in

Action, a video showing live mollusks (what lives in those sea shells?), is shown five times daily. The Children's Learning Lab has hands-on displays and a live tank. Plan to go here midway during your stay on Sanibel if you are interested in shelling. It helps you identify what you are finding and which ones are rare, and then inspires you to find more. Lee County area beaches are ranked some of the best in the nation for shelling, with more varieties found here than anywhere else in North America.

For updates & travel games visit: **www.KidsLoveTravel.com**

The shelling posture is so common, it's given a name - the Sanibel Stoop and the Captiva Crouch! We found 6 varieties and counting.

J.N. "DING" DARLING NATIONAL WILDLIFE REFUGE

Sanibel Island - *1 Wildlife Drive (off Sanibel-Captiva Road) 33957. Phone: (239) 472-1100. http://dingdarling.fws.gov Hours: Daily 9:00am-5:00pm (November-April) and 9:00am-4:00pm (May-October). Admission: $5.00 to drive, $1.00 to bicycle or walk.*

This 6,000 acre wildlife refuge, named for Pulitzer Prize-winning cartoonist and pioneer environmentalist Jay Norwood Darling, is home to native bird, raccoon, otter, alligator and other wildlife. The refuge features wonderful birdwatching spots, delightful footpaths, winding canoe trails and a 4-mile scenic drive. Low tide, when birds feed, is the ideal time to visit.

TARPON BAY EXPLORERS: Learn more about the Refuge aboard an open-air tram or pontoon boat, as a naturalist guide explains the history and nature living here. You'll observe an amazing bird rookery and the egrets, herons, ibis, cormorants, and pelicans that call them home. Learn about the mangrove estuary, the Ding Darling refuge, and amazing wildlife. Dolphins and manatees are often spotted. All boat cruises also include the touch tank presentation (maybe get lucky and be able to touch a real sea horse found in these waters!). (~ 1 ½ hours). $7.00-$10.00 tram tours. $12.00-$25.00 boat cruises. (239) 472-8900 or **www.tarponbayexplorers.com**.

SANIBEL-CAPTIVA CONSERVATION FOUNDATION

Sanibel Island - *3333 Sanibel-Captiva Road 33957. Phone: (239) 472-2329. www.sccf.org Hours: Weekdays 8:30am-4:00pm (October-May); weekdays 8:30am-3: 00pm (June-September). Saturdays from 10:00am-3:00pm (December-April only). Admission: $3.00 adult (18 and older).*

The Foundation's Nature Center encompasses 260 of the 1,800 acres owned and managed by the preserve for wildlife on and around the area. They conduct estuarine research here and maintain a Visitors Center where folks can walk 4.5 miles of trails, climb an observation tower, experience a butterfly house, and enjoy a live marine touch tank. Guided trail tours, shoreline discovery walks and other programs vary throughout the year.

There are shells everywhere!

SARASOTA JUNGLE GARDENS

Sarasota - 3701 Bayshore Road (I-75 exit 213 University Parkway West. 2 miles south of airport off US 41) 34234. www.SarasotaJungleGardens.com Phone: (941) 355-5305 or (877) 861-6547. Hours: Daily 9:00am-5:00pm. Closed Christmas Day. Admission: $12.00 adult, $11.00 senior (62+), $8.00 child (3-12).

The area's only Zoological Gardens combines lush gardens and colorful macaws, pointy-tooth alligators and gentle flamingos that eat out of your hands (of course, the flamingos eat out of your hand, not the alligators). Traverse along 10 acres of cool, jungle trails and take in a show on this self-guided tour. Shows include subjects like Birds of Prey, Critters and Reptiles (hold a python if you dare). Also enjoy the Kiddie Jungle, Reptile World, Flamingo Café and gift shop.

G. WIZ - THE HANDS-ON SCIENCE MUSEUM

Sarasota - 1001 Blvd of the Arts (at the Bilvas Science & Technology Center) 34236. Phone: (941) 309-4949.   www.gwiz.org Hours: Monday-Thursday 10:00am-5:00pm, Friday 10:00am-8:00pm, Weekends 10:00am-5:00pm. Admission: $9.00 adult, $6.00 child (6-21), $2.00 preschooler (3-5).

Experience an array of interactive, hands-on exhibits and experiments. Not everything is labeled so kids walk into exhibits with no rules or clear directions - that's why it's called ExploraZone. Meet live snakes and sharks, or work on a giant Spirograph, Freeze Shadow, make a lightning bolt, construct your own Ball Machine or create an animation. Try a laser harp or guitar or see your heart beat.

Spyro Spinner Fun

GOLDEN APPLE DINNER THEATRE

Sarasota - 25 N. Pineapple Avenue (-75 Exit 210 (Fruitville Rd.), W. for 8 mi., make left on Cocoanut, proceed straight for 1 block and make a left onto Pineapple Ave) 34236. Phone: (941) 366-5454 or (800) 652-0920. www.thegoldenapple.com Hours: Evenings at 6:00pm buffet/ curtain at 8:00pm. Twilight at 4:00pm buffet/ curtain at 6:00pm. Matinees at Noon buffet/curtain at 1:30pm. Admission: $33.00-$45.00 per person.

Music…Comedy…Drama…all off Broadway actors and an in-house prepared buffet before each show. Examples of kid-friendly shows include "BIG" or "Beauty and the Beast".

MOTE AQUARIUM

Sarasota - 1600 Ken Thompson Parkway (exit 210 off I-75 west to US 41, turn left. Right at Gulfstream Ave. across Causeway to St Armands Circle. Exit circle at Blvd. of Presidents) 34236. Phone: (941) 388-2451. **www.mote.org** *Hours: Daily 10:00am-5:00pm. Lab Hours: 8:00am-5:00pm weekdays. Admission: $15.00 adult, $14.00 senior (65+), $10.00 child (4-12). Website coupon. General admission includes access to Mote Aquarium, the Marine Mammal Center and Mote's new Immersion Cinema.*

From the original focus on sharks, Mote research has expanded to include seven major areas of concentration, organized into seven research centers. Mote scientists are committed to that process of discovery: Advancing our understanding of the sea and what is needed to sustain it. Sometimes, they research hazards to the water, study shark behavior or maybe try to bring a species back to its native waters. In the aquarium, you can't miss the giant squid, octopus or the real seahorses (collected from nearby Bays). Think it's cool to see a shark? Find out what it feels like to BE the shark in the exciting 12-minute movie shown in Shark Attack Theater. Learn how sharks use their senses to catch their prey. There is also a 135,000-gallon shark habitat, stingray touch pool, and manatee and turtle exhibits.

PELICAN MAN'S BIRD SANCTUARY

Sarasota - 1708 Ken Thompson Parkway (1 mile north of St. Armands Circle, next to Mote Aquarium. 789N to first exit on right at St. Armands) 34236. Phone: (941) 388-4444. **www.pelicanman.org** *Hours: Daily 10:00am-5:00pm. Except Christmas and Thanksgiving. Admission: $6.00 adult, $4.00 youth (12-17), $2.00 child (4-11).*

A must-see for bird lovers - especially lovers of big birds. Nearly 70 species of permanently injured birds live in the safety of the Sanctuary's comfortable tropical setting. See pelicans, storks (yes, really), herons, egrets, cranes, hawks, owls, osprey and more.

MYAKKA RIVER STATE PARK

Sarasota - 13207 State Road 72 34241. Phone: (941) 361-6511. **www.floridastateparks.org** *Hours: Daily 8:00am-sunset. Admission: Entrance fee - $5.00 per vehicle. Separate fees for tours, camping.*

This is one of Florida's oldest and largest state parks. The Myakka River flows through tens of miles of wetlands, prairies and woodlands. Myakka is popular for hiking, fishing, camping, bicycling, and wildlife observation. Explore the treetops on the canopy walkway, and climb the 70-foot tower for an awesome view. MYAKKA WILDLIFE TOURS: (941) 365-0100. Call for schedules and rates.

Enjoy Safaris traveling on one of the world's largest airboats or on the land tram. During these informative tours, you will learn about Florida's natural wonders and animals. See alligators in the wild.

RINGLING MUSEUM OF ART

Sarasota - 5401 Bayshore Road (I-75, Exit 213 West on University Parkway) 34243. Phone: (941) 351-1660.   www.ringling.org Hours: Daily 10:00am-5:30pm. Closed thanksgiving, Christmas and New Years. Admission: $15.00 adult, $13.00 senior (65+) & Military, $5.00 child (6-17) and teachers.

The John and Mable Ringling Museum of Art is home to several art attractions. **The Art Museum** features significant holdings in European, American and non-Western art. On your way over to the mansion, check out the Banyan trees where the roots grow down from the branches! **Ca d'Zan** is the Ringlings' magnificent, 32-room Venetian-Gothic mansion on the bay. **The Circus Museum** displays

A circus king's home...

art and artifacts from the Ringling Circus enterprise. You can begin in the InterActive Area where kids pretend to be in the circus or watching a circus. Art takes the form of a Woodcarvers Studio with carousel animals in stages of production and crafters actively working on a new project while you watch. Kids light up in the wildly colorfun Circus Wardrobe Room and the "warehouse" Wagon Room full of life-size circus

carts. "Ladies and Gentlemen . . . Step Right Up to the Largest Miniature Circus in the World – **the Howard Bros. Circus!**" is in the new Tibbals Learning Center. The mini-circus is an authentic replica of Ringling Bros. and Barnum & Bailey Circus during the height of the tented circus era (early 1900s). The ¾-inch-to-

the-foot model covers 3,800 sq. feet and boasts a 55-car train, 152 wagons, 1,500 circus artists and staff, a 200-animal menagerie and eight main tents. Our kids comments -"I wish I could play with this!" This is worth the admission price alone! What a wonderful, colorful museum complex - don't miss it!

OSCAR SCHERER STATE PARK

Sarasota (Osprey) - 1843 S. Tamiami Trail 34229. www.floridastateparks.org Phone: (941) 483-5956. Along with the wildlife easily observed at Oscar Scherer State Park, there are a number of recreational activities available. A small freshwater lake provides visitors with a perfect location for swimming. Fishing is enjoyed in South Creek with freshwater species found above the dam and saltwater species found below the dam. A Florida freshwater fishing license is required for all persons 16 years of age or older. A saltwater license may be required. See a park ranger for specific license requirements. Visitors with a sense of adventure will find South Creek ideal for canoeing. Canoes may be rented at the ranger station. You may want to join a park ranger for a guided canoe program and learn more about the park's history and plant and animal life.

JUST DUCKY AMPHIBIOUS TOURS

Venice (Nokomis) - 1011 S. Tamiami Trail (depart just south of Capt. Eddies Restaurant) 34275. Phone: (941) 485-6366. www.florida-secrets.com/Florida_Tours/Ducky.htm Admission: $23.50 adult, $21.50 senior and child.

It's fun, relaxing and informative aboard the Vietnam-era military surplus vehicle known as a Larc 5: Light Amphibious Resupply Craft. Your 90 minute tour begins on land then travels picturesque inland waterways of Venice and Casey Key. Often dolphins swim alongside and an occasional manatee is sighted. You'll see ospreys, other wildlife, and beautiful waterfront sights. Cross a sandbar and then the JD Dolphin enters the water at the old railroad station park in Venice, returning to shore at Higel Park boat launch on Venice island. You'll then travel by land down scenic Venice Avenue and over the bridge that you had earlier gone under by water. Those of you who know us well, know how much we love Ducky tours!

SUGGESTED LODGING AND DINING

HALEY'S MOTEL - **Anna Maria Island**, 8102 Gulf Drive, Holmes Beach. (I-75 exit 220 Beaches exit. Take Rte 64 west to end. Turn right on Gulf). 941-778-5405 or 800-367-7824 or **www.haleysmotel.com**. Haley's Motel is just steps from the Gulf of Mexico and the beach. The new owners started renovations to restore this motel to its 1953 island charm and have upgraded the conveniences for your comfort, but keeping the 50's decor. Relax on a hammock, play pool or swim in the heated pool. They offer accommodations for every family size (rates start near $100.00 to $200.00 per night). Some are more traditional 50s, some have more modern charm, and they can accommodate 2-8 people in various room styles. Some units have screened in porches. The best part, they provide free bike rental and there are trails all over the island. If you don't want to bike, hop on the trolley that stops just one block from the motel. Haley's Motel is pet-friendly (many rooms - be careful if you have strong allergies, though) and the furnishings are dated but it's laid back and comfortable.

SANDBAR RESTAURANT - **Anna Maria Island**. 100 Spring Avenue, beachfront. **www.groupersandwich.com**. (941) 778-0444. Housed in a near century old building, this dining establishment captures old Florida. Ever popular are deckside nightly entertainment and native fresh Florida seafood - especially the proclaimed best grouper sandwiches in town. Kids Meals have regular items plus fish planks.

PEACHES RESTAURANTS - **Bradenton, Anna Maria Island, Ellenton**, nine locations. Daily 6:00am-2:30pm. Breakfast and lunch menu with Mom's home cooking. A cozy, country home setting is the venue for fresh baked goods and homemade soups at this no-fuss diner. Hungry patrons favor the chicken salad platter served with fresh fruit. The real hit is the peaches and cream coffee cake.

PINK SHELL BEACH RESORT - **Fort Myers Beach**. 275 Estero Blvd. (Exit I-75 at Daniels Parkway (Exit 131). At Summerlin Road, turn left and follow signs to Fort Myers Beach. Directly after Sky Bridge, turn right and travel 0.75 of a mile), Fort Myers Beach, FL 33931. (239) 463-6181 or (888) 309-2913 or **www.pinkshell.com**. Pink Shell Beach Resort & Spa has been an American beach tradition for more than 50 years, catering to the needs of generations of families with children. One of the recently added amenities is the "Octopool" at the new luxury condos at White Sands Villas. It's a zero-entry and undersea fantasy, featuring waving sea grasses, colorful tropical fish, coral reefs, starfish, seahorses, sculpted sea sponges, a coral encrusted archway with waterfall, a life-size octopus with illuminated eyes and a large conch shell fountain. Jo-Jos café restaurant is right off the pool and has the most kid-friendly menu and atmosphere. KiddsKampp is an adult-supervised child's (4-11) program designed to offer kid-friendly activities, while providing parents with free time to enjoy the spa, watersports or fishing. The program provides a meal, craft and take-home prize ($20.00-$30.00, daily except Sunday from 9:00am-1:00pm). And get this, young adults 12 and over are invited to help and become a member of the Junior Recreational Attendant Program. Mascot "Sparky the Cat" greets youngsters with themed activities like: Pirates, Sealife, Spies, Starz Search, Splish Splash or Yucky Gooey Kampp. The Resort offers a family Sand Dollar Package full of extras for families (starts at $305.00 per night). Daily recreational activities for families (like ours) seeking to spend quality time TOGETHER range from creating shell picture frames, to design a t-shirt, to ice cream buffets, poolside bingo, conch shell blowing contests and sandcastles. The Recreation Center offers Junior fishing pole rentals (used at the resort's own fishing pier) and movie and board game rentals, too. Accommodations range from efficiencies, one-or two-bedroom suites and deluxe beach villas (every room has a fully equipped kitchen/kitchette). Enjoy quick access to the sandy shores, great balcony views and spacious, kid-friendly rooms. They have 3 nice, heated, waterfront pools, tennis courts and watersport rentals are available. And the rooms are so comfortable...our favorite southern Florida Gulf resort.

MARCO ISLAND MARRIOTT RESORT. 400 S. Collier Blvd., **Marco Island**. (239) 642-2794 or (800) 438-4373 or **www.marcoislandmarriott.com**. Located directly on the Gulf of Mexico along 3½ miles of pristine white sand beach, this is the perfect location for families. Spend the day in the sand and sun with a wide array of watersports (wave runners, kayaks and parasailing) and heated pools in a lush environment. Or, rent a bike and cruise the island. The kids will love the Tiki Tribe Kids Programs, the game room, and the Tiki Pool with slides and waterfalls. Families like the choice of eateries including a Pizzeria, Ice Cream Parlor, and several tropical American casual dining restaurants. Parents can enjoy an invigorating day at the spa or a round of golf on their 18-hole championship course. Room rates average $150.00-$300.00 per night and they have a nice Family Escape package. At Easter, Memorial Day and Christmastime, the following activities are complimentary to resort guests: Hotel Scavenger Hunts/ Easter Egg Hunts; Poolside Bingo; Coconut Painting; Beach Games; Holiday crafts and fee and non-fee socials. They have a beachside shell washing station that is helpful cause there's so many shells on the beach!

NAPLES BEACH HOTEL EVERGLADES ROOM RESTAURANT - 851 Gulf Shore Blvd North (beachfront), **Naples**. This resort property has been named Naples' Best Family Resort. As you enter the lobby notice the seawater aquarium. The Everglades Room is a traditional dining room offering an elaborate breakfast buffet, as well as a la carte selections. Enjoy old Florida elegance and tremendous Gulf views. In season, a traditional (and very freshly prepared) Sunday brunch is served. If you're staying overnight, the resort offers complimentary year-round "Beach Klub 4 Kids" programs entertaining children ages 2-12 daily with activities such as swimming, arts and crafts, beach walks, sandcastle construction and games. A "Kids Night Out" complete with dinner, a movie and games, is available on weekend evenings for a nominal charge. This is a great place to breakfast before boarding the trolley to tour town. They have a stop in front of the hotel.

Chapter 10

Seasonal & Special Events

JANUARY

BROOKSVILLE RAID FESTIVAL

CW – **Brooksville**, Hernando Historical Museum & Sand Hill Scout Reservation (Hwy 50). **www.hernandoheritagemuseum.com**. (352) 799-0129. This festival is a re-creation of a civil war battle that happened in Hernando County in July of 1864. Has become the largest civil war reenactment in Florida with over 3200 re-enactors and their families participating, 32 cannons and 80 horses. The public is invited to tour, at no additional charge, the authentic confederate and union camps and actually see how they lived and what it was like during the civil war. Around 60 sutlers (Vendors) are there so you can purchase any civil war items you might want. They also have kettle corn, old time root beer and you can't leave without having a Fry Bread. Admission (Children under 6 and Boy Scouts in uniform admitted free). (third weekend in January)

UNCLE DONALD'S FARM COUNTRY FUN DAYS

CW – **Lady Lake**, Uncle Donald's Farm, 2713 Griffin Avenue. (352) 753-2882. This farm, open year round is best to visit now. City Slickers wanted and Country Folks too. Sheep Shearing, Sheep Dog Herding. Spinning and Weaving, Food Booths. Admission includes an old fashioned hay ride through the back pasture to see llamas, ostriches, and feed the cows. Pony rides are also available. Uncle Donald's is also a Wildlife Rehabilitation Center with more than twenty species of native wildlife; including birds of prey, reptiles, and a Florida Panther. Admission. (last weekend in January)

GASPARILLA EXTRAVAGANZA

CW – **Tampa**. **www.gasparillaextravaganza.com**. This alcohol-free family event is held each year on the Saturday before the Gasparilla Pirate Fest Invasion and Parade. There's a children's parade, air-invasion, the Piratechnic Extravaganza is a sea battle over Hillsborough Bay between the City of Tampa and Ye Mystic Krewe of Gasparilla featuring one of the largest presentations in the country. (third Saturday in January)

GASPARILLA PIRATE FEST

CW – **Tampa**. Downtown Franklin Street. **www.gasparillapiratefest.com**. For 100 years, pirates have invaded Tampa Bay. In celebration of the spirit of adventure and antics of legendary pirate Jose Gaspar and his merry mates. 1,000 rowdy pirates sail into downtown Tampa (late morning Saturday) – with cannons booming and flags flying – on a fully rigged pirate ship flanked by hundreds of pleasure crafts (trying to defend their city before taking the SE - KEYS to the city). The pirates then invade the city displaying their treasures in a colorful parade. Pirate's Chest Arts & Crafts show, the Gasparilla Midway, and local and national entertainment acts performing live on stages throughout downtown. FREE. (last Saturday in January)

OUTBACK BOWL GAME

CW – **Tampa**, Raymond James Stadium. **www.outbackbowl.com**. Tampa kicks off the first bowl game on New Year's Day. The teams are matched from the Big Ten Conference and the Southeastern Conference, for post-season college football competition. Spectators can participate in a variety of special events and sports activities prior to the game. Admission. (New Years Day)

DE SOTO ARCHAEOLOGICAL HISTORIC RE-ENACTMENT

NC – **Tallahassee**. (850) 922-6007. Site of the 16th century encampment of Spanish expedition leader Hernando de Soto and location of the first Christmas celebrated in North America in 1539. Discovery of copper coins here is the oldest ever unearthed in the U.S. (January)

HOGGETOWNE MEDIEVAL FAIRE

NC – **Gainesville**. Alachua County Fairgrounds next to the Gainesville Regional Airport on SR 222. (352) 334-ARTS. Join the crowd and cheer for your favorite contender as mounted knights joust in full plate armor on the tournament field. Applaud street performers who dance, juggle and jest for your amusement. Listen to minstrels playing period music and enjoy continuous live entertainment on seven stages. Browse through the bustling medieval marketplace for that perfect gift or trinket. Watch and enjoy as warriors and magicians battle one another in a living chess match, or test your own skills in games of chance, strength and skill. Watch and learn as artisans demonstrate their skills in blacksmithing, weaving, leatherworking, woodcarving, pottery and much more. Indulge in a fare fit for a king in our food court, where you can find sweet potato fries, fresh-squeezed lemonade and famous giant turkey legs. The Faire is the perfect place to bring even the youngest members of the kingdom. Children delight in visiting the royal pavilion, where they will become lords and ladies of the court of Hoggetowne. Indulge not only your children, but also yourself with rides on a camel, pony or even an elephant. Human-powered push rides further add to the authentic medieval fun. Admission. (last weekend of January and first long weekend of February)

ORANGE BOWL & JUNIOR ORANGE BOWL PARADE

SE – Miami & Coral Gables. Dolphins Stadium. **www.orangebowl.org** or **www.jrorangebowl.com**. Top college teams compete. The parade through the streets of Coral Gables features floats and marching bands down Miracle Mile, downtown. Admission for game. (evening of Jan. 3rd – junior parade on December 30th)

January *(cont.)*

THREE KINGS DAY PARADE AND FESTIVAL

SE – **Miami**. SW 8th St. between 4th & 27th Avenue. **www.netmio.com**. This annual community event pays homage to Hispanic heritage and Three Kings Day, with decorated floats, food booths, children's performances, and Latin musical acts. (January 8th or the Sunday near it)

FEBRUARY

SPEEDWEEKS

CE – **Daytona Beach**, **www.daytonainternationalspeedway.com**. Daytona 500 Speedway. (386) 253-RACE. The action kicks off with the open-wheel Rolex 24 Hours at Daytona and features daily racing events leading up to the finale Daytona 500 race. Admission. (first half of February)

MONTREAL EXPOS SPRING TRAINING CAMP

CE – **Viera**, Space Coast Stadium. (321) 633-9200. (February –March). Their single-A affiliate – the Brevard Manatees – is swinging with batter's up from March-September at the 7,600 seat stadium. Admission. (February –March, then all summer for Manatees)

FIESTA DAY

CW – **Tampa**, Ybor City. **www.visittampabay.com**. Started to honor the oldest residents living in Ybor, the festival now honors the Cuban, German, Italian, African-Cuban, Jewish and Spanish immigrants who first settled the former "Cigar City" in 1886. The Festival fills 14 blocks, with fun and activities such as cultural exhibits, concerts and arts and crafts. The Columbia Restaurant serves free Spanish bean soup, paella, café con leche and Cuban bread. FREE (last Saturday in February)

FLORIDA STATE FAIR

CW – **Tampa**. Cracker Country, **www.floridastatefair.com**. Florida State Fairgrounds. Held at an 1870-1912 Rural Florida History & Folklife Museum, this old-fashioned fair is meant to encourage future generations to understand rural heritage. From the rustic cypress log corn crib to the grand old two-story house, Cracker Country features thirteen original buildings. These buildings were moved to their present location from throughout the state, then restored and furnished with antiques of the period. Cracker Country is located on the Florida State Fairgrounds and is open during the State Fair. Daily History Alive living history demos are presented. Watch settlers' chores like shearing sheep and making sugarcane. Other exhibits are typical of a state fair. Arts, crafts, livestock, entertainment and food. The largest major fair in the Southeast with one of the largest midways in the country, its 94 rides and shows are spread over 325-acres. Admission. (two weeks in mid-February)

SANT'YAGO ILLUMINATED NIGHT PARADE

CW – **Tampa**, Ybor City. **www.VisitTampaBay.com**. The streets of Channel District and Ybor City come ablaze when hundreds of floats masked with lights and loaded with bands and pirates fill the streets for the Sant'Yago Night Parade. It's the city's biggest night parade and named for the Krewe of the Knights of Sant'Yago, a 250-member group that has its roots in the ninth-century Spanish Brotherhood of the Royal Order of St. James. The krewe designed the parade as a way to enhance and perpetuate Tampa's strong Latin heritage. The parade route begins at the Florida Aquarium where there are fun family activities such as amusement rides and live music. (second Saturday in February)

TALLAHASSEE TRADE FAIRE

NC – **Tallahassee**, Bradley's Country Store. 10655 Centerville Road. (850) 893-1647 or **www.tallahasseetradefaire.com**. Nestled along a canopy road, the original 1927 tin store sells more than 70,000 pounds of link sausage per year with famous Grandma Mary's time-proven seasoning. This 18th Century Encampment reenactment gathers around Bradley's pond utilizing 18th Century way of life. Dressed in Period costumes. Feature clothing, foods, crafts, and demonstrations. (always held President's Day weekend)

OLUSTEE BATTLE RE-ENACTMENT

NE – **Lake City**. Olustee Battlefield Historic State Park. **www.olusteefestival.com**. The largest Civil War re-enactment in the Southeast. Walk amidst a living history encampment, visit a period shopping area, chat with women flouncing about in hoop skirts, and cheer as Confederate soldiers rout the Yankees. (third weekend in February)

FLORIDA RENAISSANCE FESTIVAL

SE – **Deerfield Beach**. Quiet Waters Park. **www.Ren-Fest.com**. Knights in full armor jousting, birds of prey, a royal feast, 14 performance venues with continuous entertainment, period trades and crafts, delicacies of the middle ages and hundreds of costumed performers. Admission. (weekends only mid-February thru mid-March)

February *(cont.)*

EVERGLADES SEAFOOD FESTIVAL

SE – Everglades City. **www.evergladesseafoodfestival.com**. Seafood lovers come from all over the world for the annual festival. Stone Crab claws, fresh Gulf shrimp, grouper and much more are served up picnic style along with music, arts and crafts, rides and family fun. FREE. (first full weekend in February)

GREEK FESTIVAL

SE – Fort Lauderdale, St. Demetrios Orthodox Church. **www.stdemetrios.org**. Greek delicacies, dancers, live music. (second weekend in February)

HERITAGE FESTIVAL

SE – KEYS – Key West. Fort Zachary Taylor. (305) 292-6850. Colorful Civil War re-enactments and tours of Key West's historic Civil War era fortification. (second weekend in February)

CORTEZ COMMERCIAL FISHING FESTIVAL

SW – Village of **Cortex**, west of Bradenton on County Road 684. (941) 794-1249. An annual celebration that takes place in the picturesque fishing village of Cortez. The festival features fresh seafood, environmental exhibits, entertainment, arts and crafts with a nautical theme, net mending demos and boat tours and rides. (February weekend)

SINGING RIVER RENDEZVOUS

SW – Bradenton. Camp Flying Eagle, 16009 Upper Manatee River road. (941) 731-0029. Visitors will travel back in time to the days of the Mountain Men and fur Traders. Merchants dealing in pre-1840 style goods will have their wares on display and for sale or trade. As during a fur Trade rendezvous of days of old, competitions in black powder shooting, knife and hawk throwing and games of skill are scheduled. Ladies may even participate in a skillet toss contest. (February weekend)

CIRCUS SARASOTA

SW – Sarasota, Big Top, Tuttle Avenue (exit 210 off I-75). (941) 355-9335 or **www.CircusSarasota.org**. Thrilling family entertainment, much more than just your average circus. 90-minute shows. Admission. (February, almost daily, early evening & weekend matinees)

MARCH

ATLANTA BRAVES

C – **Kissimmee**, Disney's Wide World of Sports. (407) 939-GAME or **www.dwws.Disney.go.com**. Major League baseball spring training. Admission. (late February thru March)

HOUSTON ASTROS

C – **Kissimmee**, Bill Beck Blvd. (321) 697-3200 or **www.astros.com**. Major League baseball spring training site. (late February thru March)

WINGS N WHEELS AIR & MILITARY VEHICLE SHOW

CE – **Fort Pierce**, St. Lucie County Int'l Airport, Curtis King Blvd. (800) 804-5445 or **www.slcwingsandwheels.org**. Two-day airshow celebrating the United States military with re-enactments, children's activities and dozens of displays. Admission. (late March)

NEW YORK METS SPRING TRAINING

CE – **Port St. Lucie**, Tradition Field. (772) 871-2115 or **www.traditionfield.com**. (month-long)

VALIENT AIR COMMAND WARBIRD AIRSHOW

CE – **Titusville**. **www.vacwarbirds.org**. Next to a shuttle launch, it is the biggest air spectacle in the area with warbirds from yesteryear and years beyond soaring through the sky, including vintage C-47s and sophisticated 400 MPH F-86 Saber Jets. Admission. (second weekend in March)

DODGERS BASEBALL TRAINING

CE – **Vero Beach**, Holman Stadium. (772) 569-4900 or **www.vbdodgers.com**. The LA Dodgers play during spring training season in March. The Vero Beach Dodgers is the Class A farm team playing 70 home games from April-September. Activities for kids. Admission. (begins in March thru September)

BAY AREA RENAISSANCE FESTIVAL

CW – **Tampa Bay**. MOSI. **www.visittampabay.com**. Discover an enchanted realm of wizards and warriors amongst gourmet treats and unforgettable entertainment. With themed weeks, a taste of every culture is experienced. Wander past eight lively stages and street theater featuring jugglers, magicians, fire eaters and specialty acts. Live armored-jousting contests three times daily, human chess matches, minstrels, maidens faire, peasants, fools and Royalty. Admission. (late February thru early April)

March *(cont.)*

FLORIDA STRAWBERRY FESTIVAL

CW – **Plant City**. www.flstrawberryfestival.com. Celebrate the fabric of America at the Winter Capital of Strawberries. Famous for its strawberry shortcake (and a shortcake eating contest) and tasty fair food. Contests, clogging, top-name entertainment, parades, midway rides, ag exhibits, livestock and crafts. (first Thursday thru second Sunday in March, eleven days)

GASPARILLA FESTIVAL OF THE ARTS

CW – **Tampa**, Franklin Street Mall area and Lykes Gaslight Square Park. www.visittampabay.com. Hundreds of artists from around the world display their work of many mediums, including oil painting, water color, drawing, graphics, paper, fiber, jewelry, ceramics, photography and sculpture. The festival also features local and regional entertainment and a Hands-on Arts & Crafts children's workshop. (first weekend in March)

ST. PATRICK'S DAY PARADE

CW – **Tampa**, Ybor City. www.visittampabay.com. The streets of Ybor City come alive with hundreds of floats masked with lights and loaded with leprechauns. Everybody's Irish for the Parade as the streets are filled with crowds dressed in green clovers. Many food and trinket vendors will be there to satisfy the flavor of the day. (St. Patrick's Day)

YANKEES SPRING TRAINING

CW – **Tampa**, Legends Field. www.legendsfieldtampa.com. (800) 96-YANKS or Major League Baseball spring training site and home to the Tampa Yankees Class "A" affiliate. Admission. (Spring training in March, Affiliate games spring thru summer).

NATURAL BRIDGE BATTLEFIELD RE-ENACTMENT

NC – **Tallahassee**, San Marcos de Apalache State Historic Site/Natural Bridge Battlefield State Historic Site. (850) 922-6007. Annual re-enactment of 1865 Natural Bridge Civil War battle, featuring soldiers garbed in authentic uniforms bearing antique weapons. Confederates force a retreat of Union soldiers to the St. Mark's Lighthouse. This site has the distinction of being the only Confederate Capitol east of the Mississippi not to be captured. (early March)

MISS AGGIE DAY

NE – **Jacksonville**, Mandarin Museum, Walter Jones Historical Park. 904-268-0784 or www.mandarinmuseum.net. Miss Aggie Day is held on the third Sunday of March each year during Women's History Month. The day honors

Agnes Jones who was proprietor and postmistress of the Mandarin Store and Post Office from 1928 until it closed in 1964. Timucuans and English and Spanish explorers came by canoe, on foot and by horseback. Civil War soldiers, farmers, citrus growers and their families traveled by boat and by steamship. There is an 1876 farm complex, boardwalks through stands of cypress, picnic areas, a citrus grove and kitchen gardens. (third Sunday of March)

NATIVE AMERICAN INDIAN FESTIVAL

NE – **St. Augustine**, Francis Field on Castillo Drive. (904) 829-9438. Sample buffalo stew, roasted corn and other Native American food at this annual outdoor event that features the food, music, art and craftsmanship of Native Americans. Friday is Kid's Day. Admission. (first weekend in March)

SACK OF ST. AUGUSTINE: CAPTAIN ROBERT SEARLE'S RAID OF 1668

NE – **St. Augustine**, Downtown Plaza in the Historic District. (407) 843-9967 or **www.searlesbuccaneers.org**. Relive a calamitous day in history as the Historic Florida Militia reenacts the Sack of St. Augustine in 1668, when Capt. Robert Searle and his privateers sailed from Jamaica to loot the silver ingots held in the royal coffers in town. From their encampment at Fountain of Youth Park, visitors can view, examine and photograph authentic 17th century arms, equipment and food, as the buccaneers proceed to attack Spanish soldiers and St. Augustine citizens at the downtown plaza. Townspeople and soldiers flee up St. George Street to the Redoubt at Orange and Cordova Streets. FREE. (first Saturday in March)

LIGHTHOUSE FESTIVAL

NE – **St. Augustine** Lighthouse and Museum. **www.staugustinelighthouse.com**. (904) 829) 0745. Bring your family and join the fun, when admission to the tower, grounds, and museum is offered for free from 11:00am-6:00pm. The historic Light Station will offer something for everyone, including living history activities, live entertainment, pony rides, children's games and crafts, a variety of refreshments, and even a baked goods contest. FREE. (third Saturday in March)

ORIOLES BASEBALL SPRING TRAINING

SE – **Fort Lauderdale** Stadium. (954) 775-1921 or **www.orioles.com**. Watch team practice at no charge (mid–to–late February) and games in March.

ASIAN CULTURE FESTIVAL

SE – **Miami** (Homestead). **www.fruitandspicepark.org**. Fruit and Spice Park. Features Asian crafts, food, arts, dance, and music. Children will receive an Asian Passport and can get it stamped as they visit exhibits across the Festival. When completed, the children receive a gift. Admission. (first weekend in March)

March *(cont.)*

DAY OUT WITH THOMAS™

SE – **Miami**, Gold Coast Railroad Museum. **www.goldcoast-railroad.org**. Thomas the Tank Engine, the classic storybook friend, rolls into Miami for a fun-filled family event offering a 20 minute ride with Thomas, storytelling, video viewing, and live music. Admission. (second weekend in March)

CONCH SHELL BLOWING CONTEST

SE – **KEYS** – **Key West**. **www.oirf.org**. An Old Island Days tradition, this unique contest features novel sounds produced by contestants in several age categories as they attempt to make "music" on fluted conch shells. (second Saturday in March)

PITTSBURGH PIRATES SPRING TRAINING

SW – **Bradenton**, McKechnie Field (9th Street W & 17th Avenue W). (941) 747-3031. Watch the Pittsburgh Pirates prepare for MLB regular season during Spring Training. Bring the whole family out to the ball game, and indulge in hot dogs and peanuts while enjoying a day of America's favorite pastime – Baseball. (Workouts are held at Pirate City from 10:00am-1:30pm during March & April)

GAMBLE PLANTATION'S ANNUAL OPEN HOUSE

SW – **Ellenton**, Gamble Plantation. (941) 723-4536. Come experience an authentic Civil War encampment. Free tours of the Mansion and Patten House. Live cannon and Civil War era weapons, period costumes, uniforms, and Civil War field equipment. Early craft demonstrations and period foods for sale. (March weekend)

BOSTON RED SOX SPRING TRAINING

SW – **Fort Myers**, City of Palms Park, 2201 Edison Avenue. (239) 334-4700 or **www.redsox.com**. Watch a Boston Red Sox baseball game in Florida at the City of Palms Park. Call for tickets. (late February – March)

MINNESOTA TWINS SPRING TRAINING

SW – **Fort Myers**, Lee County Sports Complex. 14400 Six Mile Cypress Pkwy. (239) 768-4210, (800) 33-TWINS, **www.twinsbaseball.com** or **www.miraclebaseball.com**. Call for ticket and schedule info. Spring training camp home for the Minnesota Twins. Following Twins baseball in March, stick around for Miracle Baseball in April. Average game is about 2½ hours. (March-April)

SWAMP BUGGY RACES

SW – **Naples**, Florida Sports Park. **www.swampbuggy.com**. If you like exciting displays of speed, unusual vehicles and mud, these unique events are for you. Held three times annually, the races feature everything from down home functional swamp buggies to high tech racing machines. The racetrack is a muddy mess that includes a huge puddle called the Sippy Hole – often the downfall of lesser buggies. Admission. (first weekend in March, last weekend in October, last weekend in January)

PALMETTO HERITAGE DAY

SW – Palmetto Historical Park. (941) 723-4991. Celebrating the town's past. The Heritage Station Post Office is open for business with special one day cancellations. A Historic Park Open House, live entertainment, yellow rice and chicken luncheon. (March weekend)

APRIL

RON JON EASTER SURFING FESTIVAL

CE – **Cocoa Beach**. **www.eastersurffest.com**. Nearly 250 surfers slip through totally tubular tunnels while beach lovers watch. The largest and longest-running beach event in Florida. (Easter weekend)

ST. LUCIE METS

CE – **Port St. Lucie**, Tradition Field. 525 NW Peacock Blvd. (772) 871-2115 or **www.traditionfield.com**. Admission. (home games April thru August)

CHILDREN'S ART FESTIVAL

CE – **Vero Beach**, Museum of Art. (772) 231-0707. A large arts facility on the Treasure Coast hosts guided gallery tours, videos, concerts, drama and workshops of/for budding young artists and appreciators of art. (April)

HIGHLAND GAMES

CW – **Dunedin**, north of Clearwater. **www.dunedinhighlandgames.com**. This small town celebrates its founding fathers Scottish heritage with competitions including piping, dancing, drumming, caber tossing, other athletic events and food. Scottish shops and historic Society. (April)

FLYING HIGH CIRCUS

NC – **Tallahassee**, Florida State University Big Top. (850) 644-4874. America's first and most prestigious collegiate circus celebrates more than 50 years of performances at FSU under the big top, showcasing aerial acrobatics, precision stunts and colorful clowns. (April)

April *(cont.)*

SPRING FARM DAYS & PIONEER BREAKFAST

NC – **Tallahassee**, Tallahassee Museum. (850) 575-8684. Springtime activities on an 1880s farm in the South – sheep shearing, wool spinning and "yarn" telling – by costumed pioneers. (April)

WORM GRUNTIN' FESTIVAL

NC – **Sopchoppy**. (850) 926-1848. The outdoor event has participants searching for worms with live entertainment as part of the fun. A Worm Monarch is crowned at the day's end. (April)

EGG HUNT AND SPRING FEST

NE – **Jacksonville**. MOSH. (904) 396-MOSH. Dust off your Easter baskets for a FREE egg hunt and then come to MOSH for a Spring Fest included with admission to the museum. (first Saturday in April)

EASTER EGG HUNT

NE – **Ponte Verde**. World Golf Village. (904) 940-4123 or **www.wgv.com**. The Easter Bunny will stuff thousands of eggs with treats and goodies for kids ages 1-8. Bring you own baskets to join in the fun. In addition to one of the area's largest egg hunts, the event will feature face painters, magicians and costumed characters to entertain children. FREE. (second Saturday in April)

GREAT METROZOO EGG SAFARI

SE – **Miami** Metrozoo. **www.miamimetrozoo.com**. For children 12 and under, there will be continuous egg safaris at the Picnic and Special Events fields; face painting, crafts, a bounce house, rock climbing, the Easter Bunny and more. (Easter Weekend)

UNDERWATER EASTER EGG HUNT

SE – KEYS – **Key Largo**. (305) 451-3020. Easter bunny hosts annual underwater egg hunt off Key Largo to benefit Kids In Special Situations. (Easter Weekend)

MAY

TOMATO AND HERITAGE FESTIVAL

CW – **Tampa Bay** (Ruskin), E.G. Simmons Park. **www.visittampabay.com**. The delicious Ruskin tomato is undoubtedly the star of the festival and highlights include "The Great Tomato Cook-off," the crowning of the Tomato Queen, and the all-you-can-eat sliced tomatoes. Live entertainment, a farmer's market, and a Cinco de Mayo celebration with spicy Mexican food also. (first full weekend in May)

WATERMELON FESTIVAL

NC – **Newberry.** www.newberrywatermelonfestival.com Canterbury Equestrian Showplace. Free watermelon slices, eating and seed spitting contests were all early favorites of the community. The main events of the festival were, and continue to be, the crowning of the Newberry Watermelon Festival Queen and the winner of the "Big Melon" contest. (second weekend in May)

HUMANATEE FESTIVAL

NC – **St. Marks.** San Marcos de Apalachee State Historic Site. (850) 925-6216. Welcome the Wakulla River manatee herd back to the area with live music, children's programs and guided tours of the historic site. (May)

FLORIDA FOLK FESTIVAL

NC – **White Springs.** www.floridastateparks.org/stephenfoster Stephen Foster Folk Culture State Park. The talents of participating singers, dancers, crafters and storytellers provide a glimpse into Florida's rich cultural past. 15 stages going during the day with performances starting at 10:00am. Headliner Saturday night. Don't miss the Folklife Area. This area offers a look at traditions related to food, occupations, music and dance. Here you'll enjoy learning about honey, wine making, organic farming and more. The Friday and Saturday dance parties are based on the lively social dances of Florida's many cultures. Take the kids to the children's tent for some fun, visit Cousin Thelma Boltin's Craft and Gift Shop and watch demonstrations at the Craft Square. Of course no festival is complete without the smell of tasty treats in the air. A real variety from Florida favorites such as seafood and southern food to ethnic specialties such as curries and seasoned lamb. Admission. (Memorial Day Weekend)

WORLD OF NATIONS CELEBRATION

NE – **Jacksonville.** Metropolitan Park. Join friends and neighbors on an exciting trip around the globe without leaving town. Celebrate rich cultural traditions and unique heritage of people from around the world as you travel through the World of Nations to experience the food, art and customs from lands near and far. Saturday night features fireworks choreographed to music. (first long weekend in May)

SAIL JACKSONVILLE

NE – **Jacksonville.** Downtown Riverfront. The riverfront comes alive with tall ships from around the world giving tours, in-the-water events such as the Parade of Sail and Pirate Battle, land-side demos like boat building, port operations, seamanship demos, live entertainment, children's activities and performance artists. (Memorial Day weekend)

May *(cont.)*

FIRST COAST BIRDING AND NATURE FESTIVAL

NE – St. Augustine Amphitheatre. (800) 653-2489 or **www.getaway4nature.com**. Celebrate and learn about Northeast Florida's outstanding bird life and the abundant natural habitats that sustain them. May is the peak of the spring migratory period and the festival features field trips, boat trips, and workshops. One of the highlights of the festival is the Greathouse Butterfly Farm Encounter where visitors have actual contact with butterflies as they hand feed them with tiny pieces of watermelon. FREE. (second long weekend in May)

JUNE

ANASTASIA STATE PARK'S BEACH BASH

NE – **Anastasia Island**, Anastasia State Park. (904) 461-2035 or (904) 814-2113. Enjoy a day of sand castle building, scavenger hunts, nature walks and other fun family activities. Sand castles must be all-natural in keeping with the park setting. Prizes awarded. Walk the nature trails that meander through the ancient dunes shaded by hammock. Admission per vehicle. (first Saturday in June)

DRAKE'S RAID

NE – **St. Augustine**, Fountain of Youth Park. (407) 843-9967. Relive history as the English corsair, Sir Francis Drake, and his raiders return to St. Augustine in an authentic re-creation of the 1586 sack of the city. Open to the public, the raiders' camp at the Fountain of Youth Park features displays of the arms and armor, craft skills, and lifestyles of the period explained by authentically-clad interpreters. In the late afternoon, Drake and his followers will descend on the city's historic district. Early evening will witness the English attack on the town, the Spanish residents' defense, with pike and musket skirmishes, and the simulated destruction of the town by the invaders. FREE. (first Saturday in June)

FATHER'S DAY AT THE WORLD GOLF VILLAGE

NE – **Ponte Vedra**, World Golf Hall of Fame. (904) 940-4123 or **www.wgv.org**. Give Dad something he can truly appreciate this Father's Day. Admission is complimentary. Guests can also try their hand at a special Challenge Hole competition. FREE. (Father's Day)

CHANGING OF THE GUARD, SPANISH MILITARY

NE – **St. Augustine**, Government House, Plaza de la Constitucion. (904) 825-1004. Witness twilight time in colonial St. Augustine as soldiers guarding the town are dismissed for the night, and their replacements arrive to take over guarding the Government House. The commander of the new watch puts the replacement soldiers through a rigorous drill before they take over their posts. The retiring soldiers are ordered to clear their weapons with the command of "Disparen!" the resounding blast of musket fire assures 18th century St. Augustine that the changing of the guard has taken place and the town is safe for the night. FREE. (every Saturday at 7:00pm late June thru Labor Day)

BILLY BOWLEGS FESTIVAL

NW – Destin/Ft. Walton Beach. (850) 244-8191. Ruffian pirates aboard 300 flag-flying fleets invade the harbor to "capture" the Emerald Coast in honor of local pirate legend Billy Bowlegs. The week-long buccaneer bash features the largest fireworks display in NW Florida, coastal treasure hunts and torchlight parades. (June)

TROPICAL FRUIT FIESTA

SE - KEYS – Islamorada. (305) 853-1685 or **http://monroe.ifas.ufl.edu/** A FREE family-friendly event for tropical fruit lovers of all ages. Presentations by tropical fruit experts, tropical fruit for sampling, children's area with activities, top-quality fruit trees for sale. (fourth Saturday in June)

JULY

JULY 4TH CELEBRATIONS

- ❑ **CE** – Daytona International Speedway. www.daytonainternationalspeedway.com (386) 253-RACE. Pepsi 400 NASCAR runs under the lights on Independence Day weekend.
- ❑ **CE** – Fort Pierce, Veterans Memorial Park. (722) 462-1935. Music, games, food and fireworks.
- ❑ **CE** – Port St. Lucie, Lyngate Park. (772) 871-7362. Parade, live music, arts and crafts, family activities and fireworks.
- ❑ **CW** – Tampa, Harbour Island Waterwalk. (813) 223-4141. fireworks, music, food and entertainment.
- ❑ **NC** – Celebrate America. Tallahassee, Tom Brown Park. (850) 891-3965. Largest fireworks display in the Big Bend, a spectacular flag presentation, sporting events and patriotic performances entertain nearly 50,000 flag-wavers.
- ❑ **NE** – Jacksonville. Metropolitan Park. (904) 630-3690 or www.coj.net. Happy Birthday, America celebration highlighted by a free concert featuring national recording artists and the Skyblast, the First Coast's most spectacular display of fireworks above the St. Johns River.
- ❑ **NW** – Destin. www.destin-fwb.com. Biathlon, Lincoln Park lakeside picnics, children's games and fireworks extravaganza over the Boggy Bayou.
- ❑ **SE - KEYS** – Islamorada. Village of Islands. www.islamorada.fl.us. Playground and rides, clowns and beach area for whole family at Founders Park. Community members bring food to share and fireworks at night.
- ❑ **SW** – Arcadia. Bull-A-Rama Extravaganza. Downtown & 124 Heard Street. (800) 749-7633 or www.arcadiarodeo.com. Top bull riders from the Southeastern Bullriding Series, Mutton Bustin' and Calf Scramble, Junior Bullriding and Steer riding. Arcadia Rodeo Shoot-out gang, Spirit of America Parade. Admission.

July *(cont.)*

HEMINGWAY DAYS

SE - KEYS – **Key West**. **www.hemingwaydays.com**. The anniversary of Ernest Hemingway's birthday is marked by a festival commemorating the Pulitzer Prize-winning author's decade-long residence in town. Among its highlights are the "Papa" Hemingway Look-Alike Contest, the Lorian Hemingway Short Story Contest directed by the author's granddaughter, a Caribbean street fair, an offbeat "Running of the Bulls," and a party at the Home and Museum. (near or on July 21st)

JULY / AUGUST

ANNA MARIA ISLAND TURTLE WATCH

SW – **Bradenton Beach**. (941) 778-1435 or **www.islandturtles.com**. A non-profit organization striving for a suitable habitat for sea turtles, people and the eco-system of the island and its surrounding waters. Wander thru the education center and then go out on a reserved Turtle Walk to observe their nestings. FREE. (scheduled evening walks in July & August)

SEPTEMBER

FAMILY SALSA DAY FESTIVAL

CE – **Melbourne**. (321) 253-0363. Guests enjoy the weekend celebration of Hispanic culture featuring Calypso and Latin Music, Caribbean food from Jamaican Jerk Chicken to Banana Fritters. Attendees elect the Queen of the Puerto Rican Day Pageant at the conclusion of the festival. (September)

PIONEER DAYS FESTIVAL

CW – **Dade City**, Pioneer Florida Museum & Village (One mile north of Dade City off Highway 301 North, east on Pioneer Museum Rd.). (352) 567-0262 or **www.pioneerfloridamuseum.org**. Music, Arts and Crafts Show, Outhouse Races, Civil War Re-enactments, traditional crafters, living history demos, children's activities, and antique car displays. Admission. (Labor Day weekend)

NATIVE AMERICAN HERITAGE FESTIVAL

NC – **Tallahassee**, Tallahassee Museum. (850) 575-8684. Canoe sculpting, roof thatching, native arts and crafts, and traditional Indian games give exposure to lifestyles and traditions of several area Indian tribes. (September)

OCTOBER

BIRDSONG NATURE CENTER JUBILEE

NC – **Thomasville**, Birdsong Nature Center. (229) 246-5388. Family-style day of fun with nature walks, hay rides, "Bird Window" viewing, story telling and pony rides ending at sunset with a bonfire and bamboo "firecrackers." (October)

FLORIDA FOREST FESTIVAL

NC – **Perry**. (850) 584-8733. The State's No. 2 commodity – timber – receives due recognition with forestry exhibits, live entertainment, a "parade of wood," plus the "World's Largest Free Fish Fry." (October)

GREEK FOOD FESTIVAL

NC – **Tallahassee**, Holy Mother of God Greek Orthodox Church. (850) 878-0747. Twenty-four hours of Greek food, fun and festivities (historically held every other year in October)

GEORGIA-FLORIDA WEEKEND

NE – **Jacksonville.** www.flga.org. Georgia-Florida Sports Complex. Bulldog and Gator fans combine to the RV City, the Championship Dreams Festival (the home of interactive games, autograph sessions with former Bulldog and Gator players and other sports celebrities), the Georgia-Florida Hall of Fame Ceremony and more. (last weekend in October)

SEAFOOD FESTIVAL

NW – **Destin**. (850) 837-6241. To kick off the world-renowned Fishing Rodeo, more than 50,000 seafood aficionados savor every deep water dish imaginable, from shark-kabobs and barbecued shrimp to fried alligator and crawfish cheese bread. Toe-tapping entertainment, crafts and curiosities fill the playful weekend. (October)

PUMPKIN FESTIVAL

SW – **Bradenton**. Hunsader Farms. (941) 322-2168 or **www.hunsaderfarms.com**. A little something for everyone. Come and enjoy crafts, country music, clogging, Civil War Battle Re-enactment, Pumpkin games, Pioneer trades, hayrides, pony rides, chainsaw sculpting, corn maze, scarecrows, petting zoo, barnyard playground, sweet corn, BBQ, pumpkin pie, and apple cider. Admission. (last two weekends in October)

OCTOBER / NOVEMBER

NORTH FLORIDA FAIR

NC – **Tallahassee**, North Florida Fairgrounds. (850) 878-3247. Largest event in north Florida and south Georgia with nearly 224,000 fun-lovers enjoying 11 days of thrills, chills and spills.

NOVEMBER

FALL COUNTRY JAMBOREE

CE – **Barberville**. Pioneer Settlement (just west of US 17 & SR 40). (386) 749-2959. Tens of thousands attend the two-day event which features folk arts, blacksmithing, folkways, entertainment, living history displays, farm animals, children's stage and hands-on area, and pioneer food. Admission. (first weekend in November)

SPACE COAST BIRDING AND WILDLIFE FESTIVAL

CE – **Titusville**, Brevard Community College. (321) 268-5224. Families flock to the destination, home of the largest collection of endangered wildlife in the country, for this festival. Considered one of the premier birding festivals in the U.S., the festival offers a unique opportunity to interact with the world's leading scientists or take a field trip or boat trip to go exploring. (week before Thanksgiving)

BIRTHPLACE OF SPEED CELEBRATION

CE – **Daytona**, Ormond Beach. **www.ormondchamber.com**. Commemorates the first timed automotive trials which took place on the sands of Ormond Beach in 1903. This nostalgic event features antique auto races on the beach. (November)

NAVY UDT-SEAL VETERAN'S DAY WEEKEND

CE – **Fort Pierce**, Navy Seal Museum. **www.navysealmuseum.com**. Navy Parachute Teams demo with several exciting freefall demos from high altitude and work in the sky maneuvering their parachutes in dynamic formations. The SEALS will surprise visitors with repelling from Helicopters. There will also be static displays of boats, weapons, communications equipment, Desert Patrol Vehicles. After visiting the museum, folks will learn how critical a role our Frogmen, who trained at Fort Pierce, played in successfully getting Marines and Army troops ashore at Normandy and the many Japanese held islands of the Pacific. Sunday morning memorial ceremony on the beach to pay tribute to the UDT & SEAL Teammates who have died. BBQ and entertainment. Admission to museum. (Veteran's Day weekend, mid-November)

BRADLEY'S HISTORIC COUNTRY STORE FUN DAY

NC – **Tallahassee**, Bradley's Country Store. (850) 893-1647. Country celebration with crafts, wagon, horse and buggy rides, can grinding, syrup making and of course, Bradley's famous homemade sausage. (November)

SCOTTISH HIGHLAND GAMES AND CELTIC FESTIVAL

NC – **Tallahassee**, Sunny Hill Farm. (850) 894-6270. Attracts more than 25,000 participants with internationally known entertainers performing traditional Scottish, Irish and Celtic music and song. Competitions include weight toss, stone toss, hammer throw and more. (November)

WINTER ON THE FARM

NC – **Tallahassee** Museum. (850) 575-8684. Weaving, candle making, cane grinding and blacksmith demonstrations highlight activities of yesteryear on an original 1880s farm. (November)

JACKSONVILLE LIGHT PARADE

NE – **Jacksonville**, Downtown Waterfront – Northbank and Southbank. **www.coj.net**. Kick off the holiday season with a light parade. The St. John's River is transformed into a sparkling cavalcade of holiday spirit as the finest area boats parade down river. The evening is topped off with a wonderful fireworks display over the river, featuring the signature bridge "waterfalls". FREE. (Thanksgiving weekend)

HARVEST FESTIVAL

SE – **Miami** (Sweetwater), Fair Expo Center. **www.fairexpo.com**. More than 300 craft artists display items ranging from wood crafts to toys, miniatures to quilts, and more. Also features folk arts, historical reenactments, food and entertainment. (weekend before Thanksgiving)

WINTERNATIONAL THANKSGIVING DAY PARADE

SE – **Miami**, NE 125th Street. Annual parade featuring more than 70 floats and marching bands takes place at 10:00am Thanksgiving morning. The festival runs thru the weekend and features carnival rides, dancing, singing, food and crafts. (Thanksgiving weekend)

AMERICAN SANDSCULPTING FESTIVAL

SW – **Fort Myers** Beach resorts. **www.sandfestival.com**. Join artists from around the continent as they create amazing works of art on the beach. (mid-November for 5 days)

NOVEMBER / DECEMBER

MAGICAL INDOOR SNOWFALLS AT THE GARDENS

SE – **Palm Beach**, The Gardens of the Palm Beaches. (561) 775-7750. Let it Snow, Let it Snow, Let It Snow. The forecast calls for fun and flurries all season long. Daily indoor snowfalls in the winter wonderland of Grand Court every half-hour. FREE. (Thanksgiving thru Christmas)

SANTA'S ENCHANTED FOREST

SE – **Miami**, Tropical Park. **www.santasenchantedforest.com/santas**. An enchanting holiday wonderland filled with rides, food and an impressive array of lighting displays. (Mid-November thru first full week of January)

PIRATES IN PARADISE

SE - KEYS – **Key West**. **www.piratesinparadise.com**. Key West's rich seafaring history is recognized each year when this event attracts a scurvy crew of pirates and wenches. Festival highlights include a sea battle fought by historic tall ships, pirate sailing excursions, living history encampments featuring arts and crafts, entertainment by pirate re-enactors, literary readings and lectures by authors and historians with a passion for the sea, and the authentic re-enactment of a pirate trial. (late November and early December)

A CHRISTMAS CAROL

SW – **Sarasota**, Osolo Theatre Festival, 5555 N. Tamiami Trail. **www.asolo.org**. Few holiday events are as eagerly anticipated or as warmly received. Discover the true spirit of Christmas along with Scrooge, Tiny Tim and a host of other wonderfully familiar characters, and share the joy of this special experience with a new generation. Admission. (Thanksgiving weekend thru end of December)

DECEMBER

KISSIMMEE-ST. CLOUD HOLIDAY SEASON OFFERINGS

C – **Kissimmee**. **www.floridakiss.com**.

KISSIMMEE HOLIDAY EXTRAVAGANZA holiday tradition featuring a living Nativity, high school marching bands and a mile of community floats all festooned with twinkling holiday lights. The parade route is along Lakeshore Drive through historic downtown. The second weekend in December nighttime celebration also features strolling performers, a fireworks display and 20 tons of snow. FREE (Admission charged for all theme park and dinner shows, see websites listed within the main text of the book).

ICE! Gaylord Palms Resort. Explore a wondrous world of ice carvings in this frigid Florida freezer, where 5,000 blocks of ice are transformed into holiday scenes such as frolicking polar bears, Santa's workshop, and an awe-inspiring Nativity. Also ICE! Castle, racing slides, winter forest scene with waterfall and a horse carriage that guests can hop on. (Daily just before Thanksgiving through January 2nd)

WALT DISNEY WORLD – all parks are decorated with ornaments. MGM Studios Spectacle of Lights (a million lights and angels magically appear overhead). EPCOT Candlelight Processional, which tells the story of the Christian holy birth and features celebrity guest readers and the Holidays Around the World showcase of seasonal decorations from around the globe. MAGIC KINGDOM has Mickey's Very Merry Christmas Party. (Thanksgiving thru Jan. 2nd)

UNIVERSAL ORLANDO – showcases one of America's favorite parades, the Macy's Holiday Parade. Authentic, larger-than-life balloons hover over the crowds along the parade route, while marching bands and Santa Claus ride along. ISLANDS OF ADVENTURE holds court with the Grinch at the WHOHolidays celebration at the Whoville Whobilation. (mid-December thru early January)

SEAWORLD ORLANDO Waterfront becomes a wonderland with a huge Christmas tree, holiday decorations. (Thanksgiving thru Jan. 2nd)

CHRISTMAS AT DIXIE STAMPEDE – holiday tradition features spectacular holiday music, ice-skating, a giant living carousel, majestic horses, snowfall and a visit from Santa. The lavish production also has a seasonal twist on the friendly rivalry between North and South Poles – still with audience participation. A highlight of the show is a living Nativity scene. (November thru Jan 2nd)

ARABIAN NIGHTS – Breathtaking displays of a variety of equestrian styles, skillfully orchestrated – the season comes to life when the Genie shows the lovely Princess how the holidays are celebrated around the world. Acrobatic elves, dancing reindeer, sugar plum fairies and a disbelieving Sultan. (late November thru early January)

CHRISTMAS IN THE GARDENS

CE – **Fort Pierce**, Heathcote Botanical Gardens. (722) 464-4672. Holiday lights, carols, arts and crafts and Santa. (mid-December)

RAID ON FORT PIERCE CIVIL WAR REENACTMENT

CE – **Fort Pierce**, Savannas Recreation Area (1400 East Midway Road). (772) 871-5358. Living history, demonstrations, authentic Civil War camps. (early December)

December *(cont.)*

SANTA FEST & HOLIDAY PARADE

CW – **Tampa.** **www.visittampabay.com.** Enjoy the city of Tampa's annual holiday celebration, featuring visits with Santa Claus, parade, and continuous entertainment on five stages. Visitors can enjoy 30 tons of snow, an outdoor ice skating rink, and hands-on activities for children of all ages. (first Saturday in December)

WINTER FESTIVAL

NC – Downtown **Tallahassee.** (850) 891-3866. Explosion of seasonal activities featuring an awe-inspiring Celebration of Lights with festive parade, Jingle Bell Run and numerous stages offering musical and dramatic performances. (December)

WINTER CELEBRATION

NE – **Jacksonville**, Mandarin Museum. **www.mandarinmuseum.net**. The day's events feature a hayride, old-fashioned children's crafts and games, musical entertainment, Civil War re-enactors, Santa Claus, refreshments, and a holiday gift shop. (first Saturday of December)

NIGHTS OF LIGHTS CELEBRATION

NE – **St. Augustine.** (800) 653-2489 or **www.getaway4florida.com**. This celebration adds a stunning element of holiday beauty to the historic city. The celebration gets underway at the Plaza de la Constitucion with entertainment by Showtime USA and continues with the All Star Orchestra and the lighting ceremony. Many events, tours and concerts fill this month: Christmas Parade, Grand Illumination, Christmas tour of homes, Regatta of Lights, Historic Inn Tour, Las Posadas Celebration, and the Twelfth Night Ball and concert. (December month-long)

MICCOSUKEE INDIAN ARTS FESTIVAL

SE – Miccosukee Indian Village, approx. 27 miles west of the Florida Turnpike. **www.miccosukeeresort.com/events.html**. Experience the color and pageantry of costumed Indians from all over America at the Village. Arts, crafts, native foods and more. (December 26 thru January 1st)

FLORIDA KEYS HOLIDAY FESTIVAL

SE – **KEYS** – **Islamorada.** Chamber members promise a 30-foot high community holiday tree with falling snow through its branches as carolers gather round to sing traditional holiday songs. The event also features a holiday parade with floats, bands and antique cars as well as an arts and crafts holiday bazaar. (first weekend in December)

GOOMBAY CELEBRATION

SE – KEYS – **Key West**, Bahama Village. Each year the festival attracts thousands of people who view and purchase African arts and crafts, sample foods and delicacies from a variety of cultures and countries, and enjoy live musical entertainment ranging from gospel to reggae. (first weekend in December)

THE NUTCRACKER

SE – Miami. Artistic Dance Theater. Gusman Center for the Performing Arts. (305) 374-2444 or **www.ticketmaster.com**. Admission. (first weekend in December)

SE – Miami City Ballet. Jackie Gleason Theater, Miami Beach. Art Deco District/South Beach. **www.miamicityballet.org**. George Balanchine's classic ballet, performed with beautiful sets, costumes, music and internationally known dancers. Admission. (third weekend in December)

SW – Bradenton Ballet Repertory. MCCs Neel Auditorium. (941) 359-1768. Celebrate the holiday season with a holiday tradition. Admission. (December)

GAMBLE PLANTATION HOLIDAY OPEN HOUSE

SW – Ellenton. Gamble Plantation. (941) 723-4536. Come experience an authentic Civil War encampment. FREE tours of the Mansion and Patten House. Live cannon and Civil War era weapons, period costumes, uniforms and field equipment. Early craft demos, food, music and learning for the family. FREE. (December weekends)

HOLIDAY HOUSE

SW – Fort Myers, Edison, Ford and the Estates. (239) 334-7419. Santa visits and other artists and authors stop by too. Admission. (month-long December)

CHRISTMAS BOAT PARADES

❑ **CE** – Cocoa Beach. (321) 783-1207. An endless stream of boats reflect holiday cheer gliding gracefully along the Banana River decked with up to 12,000 twinkling lights while carol singing and bell ringing ashore greet floaters with a special ho, ho, ho. (second Sunday in December)

❑ **NW** – Destin, Ft. Walton Beaches. www.destin-fwb.com. Starring the largest charter fleet in Florida, a sparkling procession of festively bedecked boats parade through Destin harbor as mesmerized celebrants observe merrily from beaches, harbors, bridges, decks and docks. (December)

❑ **SE** – Pompano Beach. www.pompanobeachchamber.com. Intracoastal holiday boat parade. FREE. (third Sunday in December)

❑ **SE – KEYS** – Key Largo. (305) 451-1592. Decorated boats will parade on Blackwater Sound. (second Sunday in December)

❑ **SW** – Cape Coral. (239) 772-9578. Holiday Boat Along. The celebration begins at the park, which features live holiday music, decorated trees, Christmas crafts and food for sale. The boat parade starts at night. FREE. (third weekend in December)

❑ **SW** – Naples Bay, Naples City Dock or bayfront restaurants. Bayside watch the annual parade of festively lighted and decorated boats. (first Sunday in December)

NEW YEARS EVE CELEBRATION

NE – Jacksonville, downtown. **www.coj.net**. Ring in the New Year in style with the town's biggest New Year's bash. Featuring food, live entertainment, Gator Bowl team pep rallies and fireworks.

Master
Index

Activity Index

PROUDLY

MADE IN THE USA

AMUSEMENTS

C - Lake Buena Vista, *Walt Disney World - Animal Kingdom*, 11

C - Lake Buena Vista, *Walt Disney World - Disneyquest Indoor Interactive Theme Park*, 12

C - Lake Buena Vista, *Walt Disney World – Epcot*, 12

C - Lake Buena Vista, *Walt Disney World – General*, 10

C - Lake Buena Vista, *Walt Disney World - Magic Kingdom*, 13

C - Lake Buena Vista, *Walt Disney World - MGM Studios*, 14

C - Lake Buena Vista, *Walt Disney World – Waterparks*, 15

C - Orlando, *Fun Spot Action Park*, 22

C - Orlando, *Universal Orlando*, 24

C - Orlando, *Wet'N Wild Orlando*, 26

C - Orlando, *Wonderworks*, 26

C - Winter Haven, *Cypress Gardens*, 33

CE - Daytona Beach, *Daytona USA & Daytona Int'l Speedway*, 42

CW- Plant City, *Dinosaur World*, 68

CW- Tampa, *Adventure Island*, 76

CW- Tampa, *Busch Gardens Tampa Bay*, 76

CW- Weeki Wachee, *Weeki Wachee Springs*, 79

NW- Destin, *Big Kahuna's Water & Adventure Park*, 132

NW- Panama City Beach, *Coconut Creek Family Fun Park*, 137

NW- Panama City Beach, *Shipwreck Island Waterpark*, 137

SE - Fort Lauderdale (Sunrise), *Wannado City*, 154

SE – KEYS - Florida Keys, *Florida Keys Odds N Ends*, 174

SE – KEYS – Islamorada, *Theatre Of The Sea,* 177

SW- Cape Coral, *Sun Splash Family Waterpark*, 200

SW- Fort Myers, North, *Shell Factory & Nature Park*, 209

ANIMALS & FARMS

C - Clermont, *Citrus Tower*, 3

C - Kissimmee, *Green Meadows Petting Farm*, 6

C - Lake Wales, *Florida's Natural Growers Grove House*, 15

C - Orlando, *Discovery Cove*, 27

C - Orlando, *Sea World Adventure Park*, 28

C - Orlando, *Gatorland*, 30

C - Sanford (Lake Monroe), *Central Florida Zoological Park*, 31

C - Silver Springs, *Silver Springs*, 32

CE - Christmas, *Jungle Adventures*, 40

CE - Fort Pierce, *Manatee Observation And Education Center*, 47

CE - Melbourne, *Brevard Zoo*, 50

CE - St. Cloud, *Forever Florida / Crescent J Ranch*, 55

CW- Apollo Beach, *TECO Manatee Viewing Center*, 64

CW- Clearwater, *Clearwater Marine Aquarium*, 64

CW- Homosassa, *Homosassa Springs Wildlife State Park*, 66

CW- Tampa, *Florida Aquarium*, 73

CW- Tampa, *Lowry Park Zoo*, 74

CW- Tampa, *Big Cat Rescue*, 77

NC - Gainesville, *Santa Fe Community College Teaching Zoo*, 85

NC - Gainesville (Alachua), *Mill Creek Farm*, 89

NE - Jacksonville, *Jacksonville Zoo And Gardens*, 110

NE - St. Augustine, *Marineland*, 117

NE - St. Augustine, *St. Augustine Alligator Farm Zoological Park*, 117

NW- Fort Walton Beach, *Gulfarium*, 134

NW- Panama City Beach, *Gulf World Marine Park*, 139

NW- Panama City Beach, *Zoo World Zoological & Botanical Park*, 137

SE - Fort Lauderdale (Coconut Creek), *Butterfly World*, 153

SE - Fort Lauderdale (Davie), *Flamingo Gardens*, 154

SE - Juno Beach, *Loggerhead Marinelife Center*, 156

SE - Miami, *Parrot Jungle Island*, 159

SE - Miami, *Monkey Jungle*, 160

SE - Miami, *Miami Metrozoo*, 161

SE - Miami (Everglades), *Everglades Alligator Farm*, 164

SE - Miami (Key Biscayne), *Miami Seaquarium*, 165

HISTORY (cont.)

NE - St. Augustine, *Old Jail*, 120

NE - St. Augustine, *Old St. Augustine Village*, 121

NE - St. Augustine, *Oldest House Museum Complex*, 122

NE - St. Augustine, *Oldest Wooden School House In The USA*, 122

NE - St. Augustine, *Ponce De Leon's Fountain Of Youth*, 122

NW- Apalachicola, *John Gorrie Museum State Park*, 130

NW- Apalachicola, *Orman House State Park*, 130

NW- Blountstown, *Panhandle Pioneer Settlement*, 131

NW- Fort Walton Beach, *Indian Temple Mound And Museum*, 134

NW- Pensacola *(N.A.S.), National Museum Of Naval Aviation*, 140

NW- Port St. Joe, *Constitution Convention Museum State Park*, 142

SE - Boynton Beach, *Schoolhouse Children's Museum*, 147

SE - Clewiston, *Ah-Tah-Thi-Ki Museum*, 148

SE - Fort Lauderdale, *Old Fort Lauderdale Museum Of History*, 151

SE - Jupiter, *Jupiter Inlet Lighthouse*, 157

SE - Miami, *Historical Museum Of Southern Florida*, 158

SE - Miami, *Wings Over Miami Museum*, 162

SE - Miami (Coconut Grove), *Barnacle Historic State Park*, 163

SE - Miami (Coral Gables), *Coral Gables' Venetian Pool*, 163

SE – KEYS – Islamorada, *Indian Key State Historic Site*, 176

SE – KEYS – Islamorada, *Windley Key Fossil Reef Geological State Park*, 179

SE – KEYS - Key West, *Fort Jefferson / Dry Tortugas National Park*, 189

SE – KEYS - Key West, *Fort Zachary Taylor State Historic Site*, 190

SE – KEYS - Key West, *Harry S Truman Little White House*, 183

SE – KEYS - Key West, *Key West Lighthouse Museum & Keeper's Quarters*, 185

SE – KEYS - Key West, *Key West Shipwreck Historeum*, 185

SE – KEYS - Key West, *Mel Fisher Shipwreck Museum*, 186

SW- Boca Grande, *Boca Grande Lighthouse Museum / Gasparilla Island State Park*, 196

SW- Bradenton, *De Soto National Memorial*, 199

SW- Bradenton, *South Florida Museum / Parker Manatee Aquarium*, 197

SW- Bradenton (Ellenton), *Gamble Plantation State Historic Site*, 200

SW- Chokoloskee, *Smallwood Store And Museum*, 201

SW- Everglades City, *Museum Of The Everglades*, 204

SW- Fort Myers, *Edison & Ford Winter Estates*, 204

SW- Fort Myers, *Southwest Florida Museum Of History*, 205

SW- Fort Myers (Estero), *Mound Key Archaeological State Park*, 208

SW- Sanibel, *Sanibel Historical Village And Museum*, 218

MUSEUMS

C - Lakeland, *Explorations V Children's Museum*, 16

C - Orlando, *Train Land International*, 22

C - Orlando, *Ripley's Believe It Or Not! Orlando Odditorium*, 23

C - Orlando, *Word Spring Discovery Center*, 30

C - Polk City, *Fantasy Of Flight*, 30

CE - Sebastian, *Mel Fisher's Treasure Museum*, 54

CE - Titusville, *American Police Hall Of Fame & Museum*, 56

CE - Vero Beach, *McLarty Treasure Museum*, 59

CW- St. Petersburg, *Florida International Museum*, 68

CW- St. Petersburg, *The Pier*, 69

CW- Tampa, *Kid City - The Children's Museum Of Tampa*, 74

NC - Tallahassee, *Tallahassee Automobile Museum*, 98

NE - St. Augustine, *Potter's Wax Museum*, 123

NE - St. Augustine, *Ripley's Believe It Or Not! Museum*, 124

NW- Panama City, *Junior Museum Of Bay County*, 136

For updates & travel games visit: **www.KidsLoveTravel.com**

<u>TOURS</u>

Travel Journal & Notes:

Travel Journal & Notes:

Travel Journal & Notes: